STEPPING UP

LEADING THE CHARGE TO IM[...]HOOLS

By L[...] [...]leen M. McKee

Published by:

Effective Schools Products, Ltd.
2199 Jolly Road, Ste. 160
Okemos, MI 48864
(517) 349-8841 • FAX: (517) 349-8852
http://www.effectiveschools.com

Stepping Up:
Leading the Charge to Improve Our Schools
Call for quantity discounts.

Copyright 2006 Lawrence W. Lezotte

Cover design by Millbrook Printing
Book design by Brandy Church

Manufactured and printed in the United States of America.

ISBN 1-883247-26-8

This book is dedicated to the memory of my parents,
Charles and Jean, who, when confronted with
my debilitating polio as a child, "stepped up."
With the highest expectations and heroic personal effort,
they changed my world. And that has made all the difference.

— *Lawrence W. Lezotte*

To my mother, Mary McKee,
the very first leader I ever knew,
who taught me the most important thing
a leader must do...
never give up.

— *Kathleen M. McKee*

TABLE OF CONTENTS

FOREWORD

 THE SCOUTMASTER'S DILEMMA

The scoutmaster of Woodchucks Troop 234 is about to take a group of 25 young scouts on an eight-mile hike to a lake for an overnight camping experience next Saturday. He's led this particular hike many times before, but this year the Woodchuck Council has made the event a competition. They have also changed the route to make it more difficult, one that involves hiking through a fairly dense woods and some rocky trail. Troop 234 is scheduled to leave at 10:00 a.m. and arrive at the lake no later than 3:00 p.m. If they don't make it by 3:00 p.m., their group will be disqualified from the competition. The scoutmaster is concerned about getting all the boys to the designated spot on time. Here are some of the facts that cause him concern:

1. *Some of the boys in the group naturally walk fast and others naturally slow.*

2. *Some of the boys are very excited by the idea of the hike and the overnight camping; others are only going because their parents are making them.*

3. *The scoutmaster is virtually certain that each boy is capable of completing the hike, but he is not sure that the young man who's leg is in a cast and is on crutches can get there by 3:00 p.m.*

4. *Some of the boys are more physically fit and will be able to cover greater distances without resting while others will need to rest more frequently.*

5. *While most of the boys are sure to be at the designated trailhead at or before 10:00 a.m., three or four of the boys are likely to be late (their parents are not as responsible as they should be). This means that the group will probably not have the full five hours to cover the eight miles.*

6. *If the scoutmaster places himself at the front of the line in order to set the proper pace, he may leave some of the slower walkers behind. If he sets a slow enough pace to keep all the scouts together, the faster walkers will become disgruntled, discouraged, turn on the slow walkers, and when they get home, probably complain to their parents that hiking is boring.*

7. *If the scoutmaster places himself at the rear of the line to be sure that no scout is left behind, the fast walkers may set too fast a pace, get way out ahead, wander off and get lost, but—technically—not left behind.*

8. *The scoutmaster is responsible for every scout; it really doesn't matter whether a scout is lost because he was left behind or because he wandered off in boredom and frustration. If any scout fails to reach the lake on time, the entire troop fails. If that happens, some parents may get angry and move their children to another troop. In addition, the Woodchuck Council could replace the scoutmaster or even disband the troop entirely.*

Faced with this dilemma, the scoutmaster begins to wonder if he's cut out to lead this troop. He's willing to work hard at the task, but is in a quandary about how to assure that all 25 scouts arrive at the lake by 3:00 p.m.

Our scoutmaster's dilemma is not unlike the challenges educational leaders are facing today. Suddenly, the educational landscape has transformed into something very different from what teachers and administrators have ever known. The element of competition has been injected into public schooling through schools of choice. The K-12 route has been made more difficult with higher standards. Educators must now be accountable for seeing that all children master these higher standards, regardless of the differences and disadvantages they bring to the schoolhouse door. And if one subgroup of students fails to meet adequate yearly progress, the entire school is labeled as "needing improvement"—a euphemism for "failing." Further failure results in ever-more-serious sanctions, with parents being able to move their students to other schools and the possible removal of the principal. Yes, the world has changed dramatically in terms of its needs and expectations for educating our youth. Unfortunately, public education has not. Why? The reason is simple:

Principle #1
The current system of public education is ideally suited
to produce the results it is now producing.

Make no mistake, the current system is as productive—maybe even more so—than it has ever been throughout its proud history. Since it's functioning so well, you might ask, then just what is everyone complaining about? The unfortunate fact is this...

Principle #2
The current results the public education system
is producing are *not* the ones this country needs or wants.

What is causing this obvious disconnect? This large and growing gap between current results and societal needs is driven by two macro changes in our society, both beyond the control of the schools. The first change is the increasing diversification of the children of our country; today we have more minorities, more English language learners, and more poor and disadvantaged students than ever before. The second change is the global technological revolution, which is redefining the very nature of work available to adults in the United States. This redefined work requires both different and higher skill levels.

Clearly, one does not have to be the proverbial rocket scientist to realize that the diversification of the public school customers is not going to stop or even slow down. If anything, it is going to increase for the foreseeable future. Likewise, it does not require a rocket scientist to conclude that the genie known as the global technological revolution is not going to crawl back into the bottle. Again, if anything, the global technological revolution is going to increase both in its speed and ambiguity.

These powerful new forces impact every sector of our society. Given the inevitability of these forces, and the demand for improved student learning from government, business, higher education, and parents alike, the options available to public education are limited.

Principle #3
The educational system _must_ change
in response to our changing society.

To ignore these forces and embrace the status quo is to accept the fate, not of an endangered species, but of an extinct species. It is probably fairly safe to assume that if you are reading this book you are not ready to go the way of the dinosaur. We must assume that you are willing to entertain the possibility that schools **can** change in response to the powerful forces acting upon them.

In considering how one might go about changing the school, two possible approaches come to mind. First, there is the "bottom-up" approach to change. In this case, the top of the system-in-place simply waits for those at lower levels in the system to demand that the schools change in response to the outside forces. The other approach we will refer to as the "top-down" approach. In this case, we would look to the leadership of the system-in-place to demand that the school change. Which course of action would seem to have the greater promise of success?

We know that the system-in-place known as the public school system was never designed to successfully teach a high-standards curriculum to the ever-more diverse students. Therefore, we know that changing the school response to successfully confront the new educational realities of the 21st century will require _systems change_. History tells us that systemic reforms of the type needed by education today rarely "bubble-up" from the bottom of the system. And yet the research on the top-down strategy of change has shown that mandated change, without participant buy-in, won't last. What, then, is the alternative?

Principle #4
Simply put, sustainable school reform and the very survival of public education requires effective leaders who can create and manage a process for change that inspires commitment and action from others.

Unfortunately, leaders who can manage such sweeping change are in short supply in public education. The purpose of this book and its activities is to help those individuals who are seeking to fill the void of leadership with the information and skills they need to be effective change agents in their schools. Specifically, this book seeks:

1. To provide current and aspiring educational leaders with the concepts and principles that will allow them to assess their own leadership abilities and skills;

2. To help current and aspiring leaders expand and enhance their leadership skills through increased knowledge, insight, and practical exercises; and

3. To create a context and structure within which leader knowledge and skills can be applied and tested using a continuous school improvement framework.

Few educators—or non-educators, for that matter—would challenge the notion that the stakes are very high for our country when it comes to school reform. The majority of those who have thought about the monumental task of improving public education so all children can be successful would agree that leadership is a critical component. Given what's at stake for our children and our nation, we approach this book with this question:
Can we find enough individuals who understand and are committed to meeting the challenge of changing public education, who are willing to "step up" to the role of leader?

Those who understand the need for systemic change and have a burning desire to make it happen have the first crucial requirements for becoming effective leaders. *Are you willing to "step up" to the role of leader?* If you are, this book will help you in your quest to become an *effective* leader who can initiate, manage, and monitor positive, successful, and sustainable change leading to improved student learning and achievement.

Principle #5
Our children and our schools deserve nothing less.

INTRODUCTION

"LEARNING FOR ALL" COMES OF AGE

- *All children can learn and come to school motivated to do so.*
- *Schools should be held accountable for measured student achievement;*
- *Schools should disaggregate measured student achievement to ensure that **all** students are learning.*
- *School reform efforts should be collaborative, research-based, and data-driven.*

Sound familiar? They should.

These are the basic principles upon which No Child Left Behind (NCLB) is based. They are also the basic tenets of the various regional accreditation agencies, including the North Central Association. But what you might not know or remember is that *these principles were first articulated as the core principles of the Effective Schools researchers—Ron Edmonds, Wilbur Brookover, Larry Lezotte, and others—more than 30 years ago.*

Although the Effective Schools research, its advocates, and its practitioners have supported and championed the learning-for-all-mission for decades, it has been largely an act of choice by the schools that adopted this approach. That meant that schools have been able to continue "business as usual" if they so desired, despite increasing evidence that the system-in-place was failing to meet the needs of a significant and growing number of students. Because the public school system was designed for compulsory attendance with learning being optional, and *not* compulsory learning, educators have been able to ignore the fact that too many children were being undereducated. The fact that the number of children falling between the cracks of the system-in-place tended to be disproportionately from among the poor and minority groups may have made it that much easier to ignore.

That is, until now.

FROM VOLUNTARY TO MANDATED

What was once simply a "nice idea" espoused by a small group of educational advocates and researchers, and a personal choice for courageous risk-taking educators, has now, with the passage of No Child Left Behind, been codified into the "law-of-the-land." NCLB represents a fundamental change in the moral purpose or mission of schools.

NCLB requires that schools not only improve, but *keep on improving year after year until 100% of the students are proficient or above.* The law describes this process of improving every year, year after year, as achieving **Adequate Yearly Progress (AYP)**. Every year, a school must improve student achievement by a specified level until all students meet specified learning standards. Although the label is new, the concept behind Adequate Yearly Progress is not. AYP is closely related to the Total Quality Management philosophy of W. Edwards Deming, which advocates continuous improvement and the tenets of the Effective Schools movement, which has long advocated continuous monitoring of student progress with appropriate adjustments to instruction to ensure all children master the curriculum.

Two things are clear. First, as the effects of failing to meet AYP have begun to be felt, more and more educators are recognizing that schools must find a way to respond to the mandate. When asked what problem or issue most concerns educational leaders today, a spokesperson for an organization that represents those leaders responded with an unqualified, "How to help low-performing schools." However, it is also clear that most educators don't know what changes are needed or how to bring about those changes in a way that is sensible and sustainable over the long term. As they struggle to find the "right" program, system, or initiative, educational leaders are coming face-to-face with two basic truths about the current system-in-place called K-12 education:

1. The current system was never designed, or for that matter, was never intended to successfully teach all students to a high-standards curriculum; and

2. The system-in-place has a tremendous amount of inertia to do again tomorrow what it did yesterday. As a result, it continually reinforces the status quo and, as history has shown, exhibits little tolerance for those few champions of change who have attempted to redirect the education system toward the democratic ideal of learning for all.

A NEW DESTINATION, AN OLD MAP

Many more educators than are given credit recognize that it is a form of insanity to believe that if we do again what we have been doing, we will get different results. They realize that the old map of educational strategies won't take them to their new destination of "learning for all." They understand that change is needed and are willing to do what is necessary to bring it about, even if their efforts place their careers at risk. However, most educators have never been given the opportunity to learn the knowledge and skills to identify what changes are needed, or how to go about creating a process for change. And while NCLB and the individual state accountability programs to which it is tied make it clear what student performance results the schools are expected to achieve, for the most part, they do not provide the schools and districts with much guidance as to *how* this new mission and these expected results could be successfully accomplished. As a result, educators are overwhelmed by the enormity of the task, frustrated with ineffective efforts, and stymied by the inertia of the system-in-place.

Absent either a clear vision of what to do or how to create the needed sustainable changes, many educators have tried one of the following strategies listed on the next page:

The Dysfunctional Change Strategies Rubric

Level 1. Prepare a memorandum (via e-mail, if the school is high-tech and internally networked) indicating that "they" want all students to achieve at a high level, so "please work harder."

Level 2. Prepare a memorandum indicating that "they" want all students to achieve at a high level so the principal will be around to visit all classrooms—*time permitting*—to determine that everyone is working hard. Teachers will receive written feedback from the principal indicating their instructional strengths and weaknesses in a timely fashion—*time permitting*.

Level 3. Order refreshments, schedule a room, and invite all staff to a mandatory meeting after school to discuss what is working in the classroom and who or what needs to change. The principal indicates that it would be unacceptable to say that the teachers are working hard, the students aren't, and "they" need to change (the coded message is that the powers-that-be don't want to hear the truth). The notes from the brainstorming will be written, edited, and distributed to all staff in a timely fashion—*time permitting*. These notes are intended to make it easier for everyone to have a clearer vision of what working hard is like.

Level 4. With great reluctance, the principal calls the central office, admits that s/he doesn't know how to get everyone to work any harder, and asks for assistance. Central office staff agrees to come to the school, meet with the staff, and reinforce the idea that the Board of Education and Superintendent, not just the principal, wants everybody to work harder—*time permitting*.

Level 5. Recognizing that everyone seems to be working hard, yet many of the same students who were not learning before are *still* not learning at a high level, the principal concludes that a new curricular program must be the answer. With the guidance of the central office, the principal appoints a committee to research and recommend a new program. Surely this is the solution to the school's learning problems! The teachers, who knew from the outset that a new program was the answer, gladly follow through and complete the task in a timely fashion.

The recommended program is purchased with a clear warning that teachers will need to be trained to successfully implement the program. The principal and the teachers, without hesitation or opposition, support the call for training and promise to follow through to assure a high-quality implementation—*time permitting*.

The Dysfunctional Change Strategies Rubric would be humorous except for the fact that it describes current reality in far too many schools and districts attempting to respond to the mandate that all students successfully master a high-standards curriculum. Be assured, educators who use one or more of the dysfunctional change strategies are not "evil people" who get up in the morning wondering how they can hurt students and disappoint society today. For the most part, these educators are making a good-faith effort to use the knowledge and skills they were taught en route to the classroom or principal's office. Unfortunately, that knowledge and those skills were appropriate for schools and classrooms before it was decided that all students should master a high-standards curriculum. The new moral imperative demands bringing *new knowledge* to bear through *new learning systems* and *new educator behaviors*. The challenge is made even more complex and challenging because educators are expected to change the system even while the system is moving down the "educational highway" at full speed. This approach to reforming schools while they are at full speed is like a man trying to change his trousers while on a dead run. Don't be surprised if the man and the school fall on their faces.

A Comprehensive Approach to Change

Is successful and sustainable school reform even possible? The answer to the question is "yes," *if the conditions are right*. The history of school reform clearly indicates that successful and sustainable school reform cannot be done piecemeal. The purchase of a new program alone will not likely make much change in student success. Likewise, staff development that takes the form of an "event" is not likely to make much difference either. Don't misunderstand, new programs, new strategies, and staff development may well contribute to sustainable school reform . . . but only if each is part of a comprehensive approach to change. Research has shown, time and again, that you cannot impose change from the top down. It may take hold for a while, but eventually, without the buy-in of those

Schools and districts must adopt a "big picture" approach to reform that is collaborative and inclusive, data-driven, research-based, and focused on both quality (high standards) and equity (for all students).

Within this context, effective leadership is central and essential.

who must implement and sustain the change, the system will return to the former processes and the organization will revert to "business as usual." On the other hand, the call for change rarely bubbles up from the bottom of a hierarchical organization. Even on those rare occasions when it does, it usually takes a long time and our current situation demands immediate change. Given this proverbial "rock" and a "hard place," it is the leader's responsibility to find the appropriate balance between the two approaches. The leader must create and communicate the vision of a preferred future in such a way as to inspire followers to buy-in to the change process. The leader must also be able to create a certain amount of pressure and a sense of urgency for change without causing a sense of panic, hopelessness, and despair. This is a challenge few educators have been trained to meet.

Given this challenge you, as a leader, need two things: 1) the knowledge, skills and behaviors required to initiate change and lead your faculty, staff, parents, and students in the march toward improved learning, and 2) a proven model of organizational change that is relevant to education.

Learning to Lead

Whatever the model of school improvement chosen, the degree to which a school or district is successful in implementing positive and sustainable change depends on a very important factor: **an effective leader**. Fortunately, leadership is *not* something that is innate and inborn. Nor is it a product of personality or charisma. Leadership arises from the effective use of a specific set of skills and behaviors that can be learned, practiced, and refined. However, effective leadership is always found in a specific context. That is to say, while there may be a common set of leadership skills that can be learned, they must be adapted to the organizational context within which the leader must operate. Because leadership is contextually contingent, this book is designed and written in such a way as to help you identify, learn, and practice the specific skills and behaviors you will need to effectively lead continuous and sustainable school improvement in your school or district.

THE MODEL FOR CHANGE

Ron Edmonds made a statement many years ago that is still as relevant today as it was then. He said, "We have found schools that had effective leadership that were not yet effective schools, but we have never found an effective school that did not have an effective leader." What he was saying is that, when it comes to school effectiveness, leadership is a necessary but not sufficient condition. But effective leadership combined with a proven "theory of action" or framework can accomplish the seemingly impossible.

One proven theory of action is the Effective Schools Continuous School Improvement Process. This framework will provide you with an excellent vehicle through which you can create the kind of continuous and sustainable improvement called for in today's educational environment. This model for change is inclusive and collaborative, and will help you as the leader inspire your stakeholders to commit to a vision of a preferred future. It is a multifaceted framework that integrates systems thinking, total quality management concepts, and over three decades of effective schools research that has focused on what works in schools. This model will provide the framework as we talk about leading the change effort.

In every book, there is an implied contract between the authors and the readers. Readers have a right to expect that the authors will bring them relevant and applicable information on the topic of interest; we have done our best to meet this aspect of the implied contract by providing you with the skills and knowledge you need to create and manage change focused on improved student learning. On the other hand, as authors we believe we have a right to expect you to consider the concepts, skills, and behaviors presented herein and make a good-faith effort to make them actionable in your setting.

HOW TO USE THIS BOOK

To help you gain a deeper understanding of the concepts presented within this book, we've included a variety of exercises and self-assessment tools. Some are checklists and worksheets designed to inform and guide you, while some are simply questions upon which we'd like you to reflect. We would suggest that you write down your reflections and look back at them periodically, both as you progress through this book and later, once you've had an opportunity to implement the suggestions offered within these pages.

Like the continuous improvement process itself, the effective leader never stops learning and growing and we hope you will reference this book frequently as you work to expand and hone your leadership skills. We hope this book will inspire, guide, and convince you that you can, indeed, "step up" and become an educational leader who can truly make a difference, who can create positive and inclusive learning communities where no child is left behind.

Our children and our public schools deserve nothing less.

1

THE CONTEXT FOR SUSTAINABLE SCHOOL REFORM

In their extensive review of research on how principals impact student learning, Kenneth Leithwood and his colleagues state that leadership always occurs within a context. What constitutes effective leadership in one situation would not necessarily represent effective leadership in another. For example, the leader behaviors called for in an emergency situation would be very different from the leader behaviors required to create a long-term commitment among employees to change their work pattern. The current context for educational reform represents a radical change for education and demands new and different ways of leading than was true in the past.

RAISING THE BAR

To understand the current context for educational leadership, one needs to go back to the early 1990s and the beginning of the accountability and standards movements. At that time, we came to the realization that the United States had entered a global skills "war," prompted by the worldwide technological revolution. This meant that our schools needed to raise the bar of expectations around curricular standards. We needed to modify the curriculum to make it more rigorous and more relevant for the modern world.

With this realization, we came face to face with two serious problems. First, far too many students were not mastering the current curricular standards. Second, even those who *were* meeting the existing standards were being taught an outdated curriculum that left them poorly prepared for the competition caused by the global technological revolution. To many of the advocates of change and the policymakers, the answer to this dilemma seemed obvious: *raise curricular standards*. A clear benchmark of this collective epiphany was reflected in a meeting of U.S. governors hosted by IBM in the mid-1990s. Virtually every governor in attendance pledged to raise curricular standards in their respective states. With few exceptions, the governors and the chief state school officers kept their promises; thus, the high standards movement was created and moved forward "full-speed ahead."

INCREASING ACCOUNTABILITY

The advocates of higher standards initially failed to recognize that raising the bar wouldn't, in and of itself, improve student learning and meet the demand for better-educated students. As student performance continued to lag, it became apparent that while raising standards was necessary, it was far from sufficient to assure that students who were not meeting the *existing* lower-standards curriculum, would master a higher-standards curriculum. What was needed, the reformists decided, was a system that would hold students and the schools they attended accountable for student learning. This prompted what has come to be called the accountability movement.

Like the standards movement that largely preceded it, different states approached the accountability challenge in different ways. Some states pretty much stayed with their current state assessment programs but insisted that the results be made public for all to see by issuing a school or district "report card." Other states radically changed their approach to assessing student learning. Of these, some states adopted controversial high-stakes tests that students had to pass to earn a high school diploma. The controversy regarding assessment-based accountability generally, and high-stakes testing specifically, is far from over. Nonetheless, these two major change forces—raising the standards bar and requiring all students to jump over it—redefined the context for educational leadership today.

In the broader context, the standards and accountability movement changed the essential vision for how schools should operate. To meet the challenges of increasing global competition, schools were now expected to not only *teach* students, but to ensure that students *learned* what was taught. As schools attempted to meet the state mandates, more and more educators came to the realization that the current public education system was never designed to successfully teach a high-standards curriculum to all students.

> *"When the music changes, so must the dance."*
>
> — *African Proverb*

THE ARRIVAL OF
NO CHILD LEFT BEHIND

The capstone of the standards and accountability movement came in 2002, when President George W. Bush signed the No Child Left Behind Act (NCLB) into federal law. As each state sought to individually address the challenges of higher standards and more rigorous accountability, NCLB changed the landscape in fundamental ways. While there were many changes, only the key provisions that represent the major contextual forces educational leaders must confront will be cited here.

1. **Sanctions:** NCLB made it clear that there would be severe consequences, financial and other, if schools, districts and even individual principals were unable to fulfill the intent of the legislation. Previously, the calls to demonstrate more success for disadvantaged and minority students were generally incorporated into the state's accountability process, but with few sanctions.

2. **Disaggregation of Student Achievement Data:** Prior to NCLB, many schools and districts and even some states engaged in disaggregating student performance data as a useful problem-finding strategy

for school reform. Many more, however, were content to measure student achievement in the aggregate. This allowed schools and districts with fewer poor and disadvantaged students to focus on overall average achievement. This painted a deceivingly positive picture of student achievement that ignored the academic struggles of various student subgroups. Enter NCLB. Not only does NCLB require schools and districts to disaggregate student performance data, it has tied sanctions to the results. Furthermore, NCLB included special-needs students as a separate category. This has come to be a major flashpoint for the criticism of NCLB.

3. **Adequate Yearly Progress:** NCLB mandated that every school make adequate yearly progress (AYP) with every identified subgroup toward the goal of 100 percent proficiency by 2012. The law further stipulated that if a school or district failed to meet its AYP target with even one of the identified subgroups, the school or district would be classified as failing.

4. **Increased Testing:** Many teachers have historically viewed testing for accountability purposes as an intrusion on and a diversion from student learning.

NCLB mandated a significant increase in student assessment, requiring testing every year from grades 3-8. Classroom teachers, and many others as well, see this as unnecessary and counterproductive to the learning mission itself.

NCLB is different than any public education legislation that came before in that it ties resources to school success and a loss of resources to lack of success; federal funding now hangs in the balance based on how schools and school districts perform. Individual schools and school districts cannot opt out of NCLB, even if they don't accept federal money themselves; once a state accepts federal funding for their schools, every district and school within that state becomes accountable to the law's requirements. However, a few states have started to question whether the cost of implementing NCLB requirements actually exceeds federal education funding. As a result, many of the provisions of NCLB, as well as the law itself, have or will be challenged in court and in the halls of state legislatures and Congress.

While it is impossible to know the final outcome of these legal challenges, it is pretty certain that the fundamental changes NCLB calls for relative to successfully teaching all children a high-standards curriculum are not going to disappear. NCLB has created a "perfect storm" around standards, accountability, and sanctions, the impact of which exemplifies U.S. Jurist Oliver Wendell Holmes' comment, "a mind once stretched by a new idea never regains its original dimension."

> "The dogmas of the quiet past are inadequate to the stormy present. The occasion is piled high with difficulty, and we must rise with the occasion. As our case is new, so we must think and act anew."
>
> — *Abraham Lincoln*
> *16th President of*
> *the United States*

NO CHILD LEFT BEHIND AND THE PERFECT STORM

The term "perfect storm," which you may recognize from the movie of the same name (2000) or the book upon which it is based (Junger, 1997), was coined by a meteorologist to describe the confluence of three severe weather systems that created a single storm of unheard force that devastated the east coast in October of 1991. The phrase has come to describe the confluence of three significant events, *usually events beyond one's control,* that creates a force of extraordinary and unstoppable impact.

NCLB, along with the standards and accountability movements that preceded it, have combined to create the "perfect storm" for public education. And while there may be procedural and policy adjustments over time, these three significant forces combined have fundamentally changed the core business of public education from *adult-centered teaching* to *student-centered learning*. This change is here to stay.

The "perfect storm" analogy is especially relevant to education in that the third event, the passage of NCLB, was an event beyond the control of educators that made school change no longer optional. This is a good news/bad news message. The "good news" is that the conversation is no longer around the question of whether we *should* change the schools, but about *how* we should change the schools. The "bad news" is that those who must implement the required changes have had no voice in the conversation. In the United States, free people often resist change, not because they disagree with the change per se, but because they were not given a choice or even a voice.

> *"We often refuse to accept an idea merely because the tone of voice in which it has been expressed is unsympathetic to us."*
>
> — *Friedrich Nietzsche*
> *German Scholar &*
> *Philosopher*

THE EFFECTS OF HIGHER STANDARDS AND INCREASED ACCOUNTABILITY ON THE EDUCATIONAL LEADER'S ROLE

This educational "perfect storm" and its mandate for change have profoundly affected the way that principals and administrators must lead their organizations. The effective leader must now be a "jack of all trades" and "master of all." But the specifics of what that means is less clear in relation to the expectations implied by NCLB and state mandates.

To examine the accountability challenges that leaders face, Kenneth Leithwood developed a four-fold classification of accountability approaches. Each approach originates from a very different theory about the problems of public education and the solutions to correct them, and each requires different leadership capacities. Each demands a different set of knowledge and skills, most of which today's leaders have not had the opportunity to learn. Here is a summary of Leithwood's four accountability approaches:

- **The Market Approach.** Also known as the "exit option," the purpose of this approach is to increase competition among schools for students. This approach embraces school-of-choice options like charter schools, magnet schools, voucher systems, and tuition tax credits. In the market approach to school reform, leaders focus on "helping their organizations respond quickly to changing demands of the educational marketplace." This means leaders must have, or gain, entrepreneurial and marketing skills like evaluating the competition and finding a niche for their schools.

- **The Decentralization Approach.** In decentralization approaches, school leaders become facilitators of the school team to ensure that all stakeholders have input into school decisions. Typically, they are also given more control over and responsibility for budget, physical plant, personnel, and curriculum. Creating and coordinating an inclusive and collaborative process requires a set of specific skills, and increases time demands on leaders, even as increased fiscal and logistical responsibility increases. In response, leaders must nurture and build the capacity for leadership in others, and delegate tasks and responsibilities as capacity grows.

- **The Professional Approach.** This is really a two-pronged approach, one site-based as teachers are given more involvement and control over decision-making and curriculum planning, and the other mandated by the professional standards movement. For professional approaches to school reform, school leaders must know about and be able to implement proven practices. They must set expectations for quality and equity and create the conditions in which teachers can gain the necessary skills to meet those expectations. It also requires that leaders monitor the progress of staff growth and learning, mobilize resources to support that learning, and inspire and encourage staff to embrace professional development.

- **The Managerial Approach.** In the managerial approach, school leaders become "strategic planners" who rely on data to make decisions. This requires that leaders become skilled at choosing, collecting, analyzing, and communicating data and its implications to all stakeholders. They must be able to develop strategic action plans to address the problems identified by the data analyses. Leaders must also become "strategic managers" who can monitor progress toward educational goals.

NCLB has incorporated elements of all four approaches, with its emphasis on offering parents alternatives to failing schools (market), involving parents in decision-making (decentralization), requiring teachers be certified in their content area (professional approach), and reporting disaggregated data on student achievement (managerial). According to Leithwood, this eclectic approach to accountability creates a job that's unmanageable, leaving the educational leader feeling pulled in a dozen different directions.

This is especially so since school and district leaders typically haven't been trained to initiate and manage such sweeping change. Clearly, the challenge to current and aspiring leaders is to identify and implement the elements of these approaches that make sense within the context of their school or district, and either obtain the skills or find the expertise needed to make it happen. To do this, they will need a "theory of action" or proven strategy that will allow them to successfully navigate the storm.

Leader Assignment:

Consider the questions below:

- *Which of Leithwood's approach or approaches to accountability provide the primary basis for your school or district's school improvement efforts?*

- *What skills reach across all approaches? Of these, at which ones do you feel proficient? On which ones do you think you need more training to feel confident?*

ADEQUATE YEARLY PROGRESS = CONTINUOUS SCHOOL IMPROVEMENT

As educational leaders have worked to meet Adequate Yearly Progress targets for all groups each year since 2001, they have found it difficult to sustain improvements from year to year. Many are seeing improvements in year one, just to see scores backslide the next. As educators look down the road at meeting AYP year after year for the next ten years or so, they are recognizing that a new program or initiative isn't enough. They are coming to the realization that they need a different approach to increasing and sustaining student achievement, one that will lead to continuous improvement.

In the current perfect storm of educational reform, each school and each school district of which it is a part needs a new system of continuous improvement that will lead to improved student learning, year after year, until every child can master specified standards.

Unfortunately, the culture of public education has not been one that supported the notion of continuous improvement. Schools have been traditionally evaluated on inputs (number of teachers with advanced degrees) and school processes (number of science courses). Only recently have some states and accreditation bodies required schools to embrace certain aspects of continuous improvement, like annual improvement plans or the analysis of student data. As a result, most school districts do not currently have the required systems and subsystems in place to initiate and manage continuous school improvement. Therefore, the journey ahead is long and demanding. It will require a level of leadership rarely seen in education, or any other public sector arena for that matter. Complicating things even further is the fact that most current and upcoming school leaders have not been taught the necessary knowledge and skills required to create and sustain a system of continuous school improvement.

Current and future leaders in education need two things if they are going to successfully navigate the "perfect storm" and successfully lead sustainable school reform: a proven and practical model of continuous improvement, and the knowledge, skills and behaviors needed to lead it.

A Proven and Practical Model for Continuous School Improvement

The Effective Schools Continuous Improvement Process represents a proven framework for sustainable change. It is grounded in the Effective Schools research and philosophy that has advocated "learning for all" as the primary mission of public education for more than 30 years. Throughout these years, many educational leaders have embraced this vision and used their leadership skills to create innovative systems and organizational cultures to advance it. Much of this model of leadership is based on the lessons learned from those courageous leaders who were willing to arrive at the future first. The Effective Schools Continuous Improvement Process, in the hands of a knowledgeable and skilled leader, has proven to be successful in the past and is still relevant and useful today as building and district administrators strive to meet the challenges that define the current context for educational leadership.

"The principle goal of education is to create men who are capable of doing <u>new</u> things, not simply repeating what other generations have done."

— Jean Piaget
Swiss Psychologist

Overview of the Model

Most people have an intuitive sense of what it means to be engaged in a continuous improvement process. For example, let's suppose that one day you put on your favorite pair of pants and they were too tight. You realize that you have gained weight over the winter and now you decide you must lose it so you can fit back into your summer clothes. This is your AIM or MISSION. Your weight-loss "mission" is supported by at least one CORE BELIEF (you can indeed lose the weight) and at least one CORE VALUE (maintaining the proper weight will enhance your overall health, and that is a good thing).

Given your mission, core beliefs, and values, your next step would be to gather and STUDY appropriate data. You would weigh yourself to determine how much you currently weigh and how much you need to lose. You might also "drill down" by collecting data about your current caloric intake by keeping a food journal. You may collect data about your current exercise routine. With these data in hand, you would determine how many pounds you need to lose (e.g., 10 pounds).

Using the data on caloric intake and exercise, you would REFLECT on what strategy you are going to use by considering various options for weight loss. You might investigate the different types of diets that are available (e.g., low fat, low carb, reduced calorie) and exercise options to determine which ones are best suited to you, given your food preferences and lifestyle. You would finally settle on the model or framework to guide your weight-loss actions.

The next logical step would be to make a specific PLAN for dieting by selecting the type and amounts of food you'll eat and the fluids you'll consume. In addition, you'll need to make a specific action plan for the amount, type, and schedule of exercises you'll be doing. You will need to determine what resources you need to implement your plan by creating a shopping list for appropriate food, athletic shoes, or exercise equipment, etc.

At this point, you have a weight-loss goal and specific action plans designed to achieve the goal. Only one final step remains on your weight-loss journey—as Nike™ says, "Just DO it!" To accomplish your goal, you must *execute* the action plans. As you implement your plan, intuitively you will frequently monitor your progress. You will look at outcome measures: you'll step on the scale and see if your weight has changed and try on your slacks to see if they fit. But you will also intuitively monitor the *process* to determine if it's working (e.g., grapefruit makes you sick, you're frequently missing your afternoon workouts, you don't mind the low-carb diet). As the action plans are implemented, the entire cycle begins again to determine whether the goal has been achieved, whether the diet or exercise action plans need to be adjusted—this is the heart and soul of the continuous improvement process. Let us hasten to add that you would intuitively engage in the continuous improvement cycle (STUDY-REFLECT-PLAN-DO) *if you were serious about the goal of losing weight!*

The steps in this intuitive continuous improvement cycle are similar to those described in the continuous improvement literature. The cycle is usually referred to as the Shewhart Cycle, named after the individual credited with its development. Ordinarily, the Shewhart Cycle is written as the Plan-Do-Check-Act cycle. We have adapted the original Shewhart Cycle to accommodate the fact that schools and school districts are existing systems somewhere on the journey to their MISSION, and to discourage educators from jumping right into the planning phase without laying the proper groundwork.

Our approach to continuous school improvement is outlined in the diagram below.

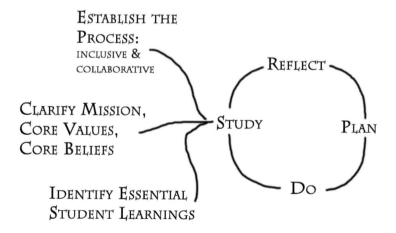

MODIFIED SHEWHART

ESTABLISH THE PROCESS:
INCLUSIVE &
COLLABORATIVE

CLARIFY MISSION,
CORE VALUES,
CORE BELIEFS

IDENTIFY ESSENTIAL
STUDENT LEARNINGS

REFLECT

STUDY

PLAN

DO

LEADERSHIP AND THE CONTINUOUS SCHOOL IMPROVEMENT PROCESS

As you can see from our model, there is work to be done before launching into the STUDY—REFLECT—PLAN—DO cycle. The first three steps—establishing an inclusive and collaborative process, clarifying mission, core beliefs, and core values, and identifying essential student learnings—are critical to the success of the following steps and to the long-term sustainability of the process. The leader's role, while vital throughout the entire process, is especially critical in these three steps. It is here the leader creates a common vision and a common language, and sets the tone for the entire continuous school improvement process.

In the next chapter we will focus on the personal qualities that have been found to contribute directly to leadership ability. We will look at these personal qualities as they may manifest themselves in the educational setting as much as possible. In addition to reviewing the needed qualities associated with leadership, we have developed and adapted some self-assessment tools to help you to clarify your own vision for educating all children, and your personal core beliefs and values related to schooling.

Also in the next chapter, you will find self-assessments to help you identify your strengths, as well as areas where improvement is needed. This journey toward self-awareness is critical to becoming an effective leader. We hope that this self-reflection will encourage you to develop a personal growth plan to help strengthen your effectiveness as an educational leader.

"I think self-awareness is probably the most important thing in being a champion."

— *Billie Jean King*
American Tennis
Champion

2

BEYOND GOOD MANAGEMENT—
THE ESSENCE OF LEADERSHIP

LET'S GET RID OF MANAGEMENT

People don't want to be managed.
They want to be *led*.
Whoever heard of a world manager?
World leader, yes.
Educational leader.
Political leader.
Religious leader.
Scout leader.
Community leader.
Labor leader.
Business leader.
They lead.
They don't manage.
The carrot *always* wins over the stick.
Ask your horse.
You can lead your horse to water,
    but you can't *manage* him to drink.
If you want to manage somebody,
    manage yourself.
Do that well and you'll be ready to
    stop managing.
And start leading.

A message as published in the *Wall Street Journal* by United Technologies Corporation, Hartford, Connecticut, reprinted in *Leaders: The Strategies for Taking Charge*. The full reference for this book can be found at the end of this book.

This message, originally printed many years ago, highlights two important aspects of leadership. First, people want to led, not managed. They want to be inspired and empowered to accomplish their goals. Second, if you manage yourself well, you'll be able to lead others. That is to say that effective leadership emanates from the interaction of a set of personal qualities with specific behaviors that are appropriate to a particular context. That's what this chapter is all about: describing the best thinking on the personal qualities that make a leader effective, helping you assess your personal vision, values, beliefs, and abilities, and hopefully, inspiring you to make a personal plan for improving your leadership skills. This will set the stage for the following chapters in which we focus on the actions the leader should take within the context of continuous school improvement.

LEADERSHIP VS. AUTHORITY

Leadership is often confused with authority, but in fact they are very different concepts. Within the context of education we can say, for example, that a local school board can give a person the *authority* to be the principal of a school, because authority tends to be delegated from above. However, the school board cannot make the principal the instructional *leader* of the school. The staff, parents, and students

choose whether or not to follow the new principal based on their perceptions of this individual and his/her actions. This discussion leads us to a very significant truth about leadership: *leadership is delegated from the followers*. We might even say that the followers "elect" their leaders. It goes without saying that this is a core value and belief in our democracy. Given this insight, we define the essence of leadership as follows:

Leadership is the ability to take a "followership" to a place they have never been, and are not sure they want to go.

In examining our definition, we can make several noteworthy observations. First, and perhaps most importantly, leadership *by definition* requires a "followership." As noted above, the act of following is a choice. However, the ability to inspire people to follow, in and of itself, is not inherently moral and good.

Throughout history there have been individuals with the ability to attract and sustain a loyal followership and lead them to a place they have never been or are sure they want to go. Most would agree that Hitler's skill in attracting followers demonstrates effective leadership, even though most would agree that the place he led his followers was morally wrong on virtually all counts.

Thus, in addition to the leadership/followership requirement, one must always examine and judge the place to which the leader would have his/her followers go. In our view of leadership, a correct moral purpose is an essential aspect of an effective educational leader.

Further examination of our definition reveals that the leader is deliberately seeking to take the followers to *an unknown place*. That place that may seem idealistic, abstract, even scary. Because the leader is not describing current reality, which all can see, but a preferred future, which few can even imagine, the leader's personal qualities are essential for the followers.

The late Ronald Reagan is commonly recognized as an effective leader by friends and foes alike. History will be left to judge the rightness or wrongness of the "places" he wanted us to go, but few would challenge his skill in creating and maintaining a loyal followership. What personal attributes of President Reagan are most often cited as being critical to his effectiveness as a leader?

President Reagan's direct and inspirational style of speaking to the American people earned him the accolade of "The Great Communicator." He spoke simply and clearly. He often used images and stories to clarify his vision. When President Reagan spoke of the "shining city on the hill," he painted a picture of what the future could be in such a vivid and compelling way that his followers could accept that the direction he wanted to go was the right one, despite their uncertainty. Reagan also conveyed a "we're-in-this-together" approach and an unwavering confidence that, if the American public would follow his lead, together they could and would accomplish great things. As President Reagan demonstrated, a leader's ability to project confidence and reassurance enables followers to overcome the anxiety they experience when facing the unknown and unfamiliar.

QUOTES OF "THE GREAT COMMUNICATOR"

Below are some of Ronald Reagan's most famous quotes. Notice what they have in common: each conveys a sense of camaraderie, optimism, and a call to action in a down-to-earth, jargon-free manner.

- *With our eyes fixed on the future, but recognizing the realities of today . . . we will achieve our destiny to be as a shining city on a hill for all mankind to see.*

- *I'm not running for the presidency because I believe that I can solve the problems we've discussed tonight. I believe the people of this country can. And together we can begin the world over again. We can meet our destiny—and that destiny is to build a land here that will be, for all mankind, a shining city on the hill.*

- *We are the showcase of the future. And it is within our power to mold that future—this year, and for decades to come. It can be as grand and as great as we make it . . . . No crisis is beyond the capacity of our people to solve; no challenge too great.*

- *The history of our civilization, the great advances that made it possible, is not a story of cynics or doom criers. It is a gallant chronicle of the optimists, the determined people, men and women, who dreamed great dreams and dared to try whatever it took to make them come true.*

- *I believe that if we work together, then one day we will say, "We fought the good fight. We finished the race. We kept the faith." And to our children, and to our children's children we can say, "We did all that could be done in this brief time that was given us here on earth."*

What Followers Expect

The realization that leadership is delegated from the followers leads us to the next question: *What are the personal qualities that followers tend to look for in deciding who will be selected and supported as a leader?* In 1987, James Kouzes and Barry Posner published the first in a series of books based on their research on leadership, *The Leadership Challenge*. Through their extensive research, they have identified four cornerstone personal qualities that followers look for and expect from their leaders. While these qualities reach across virtually all situations, we will attempt to place them within the context of education. The four qualities are rank ordered from most to less important according to Kouzes and Posner's research findings.

> *"Leadership is practiced not so much in words, as in attitudes and actions."*
>
> — *Harold S. Geneen*
> *Former CEO, ITT*

1. Trustworthiness

Followers expect leaders to be trustworthy; that is, they expect leaders to say what they mean and mean what they say. The followers may not always agree with the leader but, agree or disagree, the followers need to feel that they can depend on their leader to be consistent regarding his/her beliefs, values, and direction.

Our experience in working with schools and districts over the years has led to the conclusion that, all too often, school administrators flunk the trustworthy test. They tend to fail for two main reasons.

First, most administrators have neither thought deeply about what they believe and value, nor have they spent much time attempting to articulate their core beliefs and values to the followers. Administrators without a clear idea of their own beliefs and values lack the foundation from which consistent and trustworthy behavior emanates. When administrators don't articulate their beliefs and values, followers have no idea what to expect from the leaders. Those interviewing potential administrators should ask them to discuss their core beliefs and values—not only to those with the authority to appoint them, but also to those with the power to select them as their leader.

The second way administrators flunk the trustworthy test is to fail to "walk the talk." False starts, promises with no follow-through, and committee reports that are essentially ignored are all typical ways in which school administrators flunk the trustworthy test. If that weren't bad enough, many times when the leadership of a school or district opens up and a new appointment is made, the person selected deliberately conducts a "clean sweep with a new broom" of the former leader's initiatives. This process happens independent of whether or not the earlier initiatives were effective. The resulting increase in cynicism throughout the organization makes it very difficult, if not impossible, for a leader to secure the broad-based commitment required for sustainable change.

"Trust is the highest form of human motivation."

— *Steven Covey*
Author, The 7
Habits of Highly
Effective People

How Administrators Undermine Trust

A few years ago, a school principal attended a workshop on effective schools conducted by one of the authors. Feeling inspired, he went back to his school and announced that the school was going to move toward planning and implementing improvements based on the effective schools framework. Soon after, the superintendent—for reasons unimportant to the story—informed the principal that the schools would not be going in that direction and demanded that the effort be called off. The next summer, the superintendent attended an effective schools workshop, became inspired and announced that the district and each of its schools were now going to proceed with that framework. Our principal then had to announce that effective schools initiative was once again "on." It's not difficult to see why the staff would be skeptical and doubt whether the administration is trustworthy.

2. Competence

Followers expect leaders to know what they're doing and bring a cadre of knowledge and skills to the organization. That doesn't mean the leader "knows it all." Obviously, one individual can't be an expert in all facets of a complex organization like a school or district. On the other hand, when the leader has set the direction and is now determining what needs to change, followers have the right to expect their leader to be both a co-learner, and to be visible and present throughout the change conversation.

One of the key responsibilities of the leader is to model the behaviors of a learner. Why? Because if we want our followers to approach continuous improvement as an endless journey with frequent adjustments—for many an uncertain journey—leaders must demonstrate confidence in the process by constantly learning and changing themselves.

One challenge to a leader's role of co-learner has to do with the many competing demands for the leader's attention. As a result, leaders often resort to what we have come to call the "leader roll-out." For example, a school district schedules a recognized consultant or speaker to present to the entire faculty of the district. The leader warmly introduces the visiting speaker and "rolls out" the upcoming program or initiative. Once the workshop is underway, the leader then "rolls out" to attend to other matters, believing that his/her presence is unnecessary to the program. However, any outside observer will notice that, once the leader leaves, the "body language" of the staff has changed and that many participants have

High school principals sometimes tell us that they ought not be directly involved with the school improvement team. They often suggest that an assistant principal for curriculum might be better suited for the task. Our response has always been this: participation in school improvement meetings is not only good for the principal's reputation, **it reinforces the value of the effort itself***.*

clearly become less engaged and concerned with the presentation. Why?

Right or wrong, fair or unfair, the followership in an organization infers the vision, values, and priorities of the organization by where its leaders spend their time. The importance of this concept cannot be overstated.

Don't misconstrue our discussion. We are keenly aware that school leaders are not "goofing off." They are extremely busy and often feel as if they can turn

this follow-through aspect of leadership over to others. But as they say, the best generals fight side-by-side with their troops. Over the years, we have found that anytime you see a school or district moving forward, you can bet that the school or district leader is up to his/her elbows in the change process. If anything, these leaders tend to delegate more of the routine business of the organization to trusted supporters so they can give the change process the time and attention it demands.

> *"You can't lead anyone further than you've gone yourself."*
>
> — *Gene Mauch*
> *Major League*
> *Baseball Player*
> *and Manager*

3. Forward Looking

The forward-looking leader isn't precognitive or clairvoyant. The attribute of being "forward looking" simply means being able to choose an appropriate direction for the organization. According to Kouzes and Posner, "Followers ask that a leader have a well-defined orientation toward the future. We want to know what the company will look like, feel like, be like when it arrives at its goal in six months or six years."

To meet the followers' standard of being forward-looking, the educational leader must constantly examine new research, best practices, and new systems to see how the school can become more effective. To be forward-looking for new ideas and new possibilities is not an admission that the school or district is "broken" or "failing." It is just good practice to be constantly looking for ways to improve. Continuous improvement is not just a set of operating principles; it is also a mindset. To initiate, plan, and implement effective and sustainable school reform that will lead to improved student learning, the educational leader must establish, nurture, and maintain a cultural mindset of continuous improvement among the followers.

Unfortunately, this is far easier said than done. It is all too common for leaders to get themselves bogged down in yesterday's problems. Getting bogged down like this makes matters worse because it tends to come at the expense of time spent pursuing tomorrow's opportunities. Warren Bennis, in *Why Leaders Can't Lead*, summarizes this situation in his "First Law of Academic Pseudodynamics: Routine work drives out nonroutine work and smothers all creative planning, all fundamental change in . . . any institution."

What does this mean in the context of education? Virtually everyone recognizes that the job of school leader (principal or superintendent) is much too vast and complex to be effectively performed by one individual. Because management demands occur in the here-and-now and leadership tasks generally focus on the future, the management routines of the job can easily drive out the tasks required to be a leader *if you let them*. Therefore, to be effective in leading change and survive, school leaders must *intentionally decide* what they will and will not do themselves. They must then make a plan to delegate or otherwise handoff those tasks to someone else. We call this "Organized Abandonment."

Leader Assignment:

To determine where you spend most of your time as an educational leader, carefully document for a day or two the various activities in which you are engaged. Then, imagine you are the captain of a ship. How many of your documented activities could be described as standing on the bow of the ship (your organization), scanning the horizon for tomorrow's opportunities? How many of your activities could be described as standing on the stern of the ship of the organization, studying the wake of yesterday's problems?

In a September 2004 issue of *Education Week*, there appeared an article titled "Tackling An Impossible Job," written by Jeff Archer. The article begins with a brief job description of Kelly Griffith, principal at Easton Elementary School located in Talbot County, Maryland. What was astounding about the description of Ms. Griffith's job was the list of "essential tasks" for which she, as principal, is *not* responsible. She doesn't handle maintenance, arrange field trips, oversee the building's cafeteria workers, or supervise busses before and after school.

In place of these tasks, Kelly Griffith spends the "found time" in classrooms, observing teachers, showing them new methods of instruction, analyzing test scores, and planning professional development—in other words, serving as the instructional leader. This is quite a contrast from the story we so often hear from principals who are inundated with compelling tasks that are vital, but relatively unrelated to student learning and achievement. As a matter of fact, a study published by Jack Bowsher in 2003 found that the typical principal is responsible for over 120 different tasks, all important, but only a small number of which directly impact student learning and performance. Compared to middle-management jobs in the private sector, or even in government agencies, the principal's job is far more demanding than most. No wonder principals are overwhelmed; by any standard the position is "unembraceable."

Confronted by the new reality for education created by the standards and accountability movement, the responsibilities of the principal must be restructured. The model at Easton Elementary School would be a good place to begin by creating the educational equivalent of the COO—Chief Operating Officer—to be responsible for the various management tasks so that the principal can truly function as the CEO—Chief *Education* Officer (a.k.a., the instructional leader) of the school.

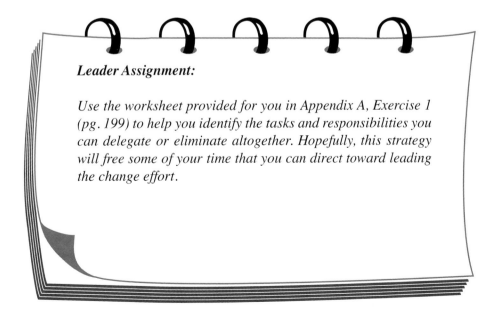

Leader Assignment:

Use the worksheet provided for you in Appendix A, Exercise 1 (pg. 199) to help you identify the tasks and responsibilities you can delegate or eliminate altogether. Hopefully, this strategy will free some of your time that you can direct toward leading the change effort.

4. Enthusiastic

Followers expect leaders to be cheerleaders, and offer encouragement and optimism, even in the face of bad news. Given the wide range of pressures and challenges facing today's educational leaders, it is often difficult to be positive and enthusiastic. Nevertheless, do not underestimate the positive difference enthusiasm can make when it comes to inspiring the followership in an organization. Educational leaders often stumble upon this dimension as the result of an encounter with followers, one that prompts a startling realization of the impact they have on others.

> *"Enthusiasm releases the drive to carry you over obstacles and adds significance to all you do."*
>
> — *Norman Vincent Peale*
> *Clergyman & Author*

The principal of the school has just spent time locked in his office dealing with a knotty budget problem. He decides to take a walk down the hall for a break and one of the staff members approaches him and asks, "How's it going?" The principal responds by essentially suggesting that the staff member take a seat so he can explain just how bad things are. In this scenario, you will see the energy visibly drain out of the staff member. Now suppose the principal responds positively and hopefully, despite looming problems. In this case, you will see that same staff member become energized and engaged. Leaders, in spite of the problems and challenges they face, must remain positive, hopeful, and upbeat. Not everyone can or would choose to be this way. Remember, you are free to not be positive, hopeful, and upbeat. You only have to behave this way if you wish to be the leader.

Leader Assignment:

How do others see you? Solicit feedback from others on how they perceive you by conducting an anonymous survey on each of these critical qualities.

"Good character is more to be praised than outstanding talent. Most talents are to some extent a gift. Good character, by contrast, is not given to us. We have to build it piece by piece, by thought, choice, courage, and determination."

— *John Luther*

WATCH YOUR LANGUAGE: USING THE INTERROGATIVE

Leading continuous and sustainable change that effectively engages the followers in the effort often requires the leaders to change the way in which they communicate with others in the organization. In the old, top-down, command-and-control organizational structure, the dominant form of communication took the declarative form: you should do this, or you should not do that. In the contemporary collaborative organization, the preferred form of language is the interrogative form. Effective leaders in collaborative organizations, especially in schools and districts, must become skilled at asking the right question, in the right way, at the right time, for the right reason. When colleagues are asked the right question in a respectful way, followed by a demonstrated willingness to listen, trust and confidence in the leader grows.

As the response to one question inevitably leads to another, the leader begins to get a clear idea of the issue or problem at hand. This is similar to the "drilling down" method for getting to the bottom or root cause of an issue. However, you'll want to be careful to avoid coming across as "grilling" staff and colleagues by asking questions in a way so as to positively engage even the most reticent staff member and obtain the information you need.

EFFECTIVE LEADERS LISTEN EFFECTIVELY

A big part of being an effective leader is being a good listener. The acronym LADDER is a good way to remember the components of effective listening.

Look at the person speaking to you. Give the speaker your undivided attention (no multi-tasking). This encourages the speaker to open up and allows you to observe nonverbal cues, as well.

Ask clarifying questions. Occasionally, rephrase what the speaker says to clarify what you're hearing.

Don't interrupt.

Don't change the subject. Changing the subject indicates that you're not concentrating on what's being said at that moment, and this makes the speaker feel insignificant. The speaker might also get the impression that you're avoiding the topic and may be hesitant to bring it up again.

Empathize and Acknowledge. When staff members share information with you, acknowledge their point of view and try to see things from their perspective.

Respond verbally and non-verbally. Use an enthusiastic

tone. Smile when appropriate. Avoid crossing your arms and other negative body language (yawning, frowning, tapping). If you're speaking with someone who's seated, you should also sit to avoid making the other person feel uncomfortable.

> *"If there is any great secret of success in life, it lies in the ability to put yourself in the other person's place and to see things from his point of view—as well as your own."*
>
> — *Henry Ford*
> *Industrialist &*
> *Philanthropist*

Leader Assignment:

After your next meeting or conversation, take a moment and evaluate how well you listened using the LADDER acronym to guide your reflection. Did you stop what you were doing and eliminate all distractions? Did you face the person speaking to you and maintain eye contact at all times? Did you focus on what the person was saying or did you spend much of the time preparing what you were going to say next? How many times did you interrupt? If you're unsure, during your next conversation, discreetly make a harsh mark on a scrap of paper each time you interrupt the other speaker. You might be surprised.

(LADDER acronym adapted from EffectiveMeetings.com, "Are You A Good Listener?")

CONFIDENT UNCERTAINTY: AN ENGAGING CONTRAST

In the *Leaders* book mentioned earlier, Bennis notes that one of the ironies of leadership for sustainable change is that the leader has to demonstrate "confident uncertainty." Although seemingly at odds with one another, confidence and uncertainty are essential components for engaging the followers. When President Kennedy spoke of putting a man on the moon by the end of the decade, he said it with great confidence. On the other hand, if he had been asked at that moment how this monumental task was to be accomplished, he probably would have said, "I have no idea." The fact that the leader is willing to express both confidence that a goal can be accomplished *and* uncertainty about how it can or will be done recognizes the follower as an essential partner in figuring out how to achieve the goal. Otherwise, if the leader has both the vision and the means to achieve it, what possible role will the followers play? Having been deprived of an important, creative, and dynamic role in the process, the followers become simply "cogs in the wheel." Without a reason to engage, the followers will make merely a shallow commitment. If problems arise (as they undoubtedly will), the followers—being neither engaged nor committed—will quickly place the problems at the feet of the leader rather than work to find solutions. Clearly, if the leaders have all the answers, the followers will have no reason to be committed to or invested in the effort. Conversely, inviting people to be a part of the process because they have a unique contribution to make, and communicating that, without *them,* the effort may fail, are powerful strategies used by effective leaders. Richard Axelrod, author of *Terms of Engagement,* addresses this when he speaks about building a deeper and more lasting commitment by enlarging the circle of involvement.

> *"No man will make a great leader who wants to do it all himself, or to get all the credit for doing it."*
>
> — *Andrew Carnegeie*
> *American Industri-*
> *alist*

A LEADERSHIP PARADOX

Finally, no listing of personal qualities of effective leaders, no matter how brief, would be complete without at least mentioning Jim Collins, author of the best-selling book *Good to Great*, and his concept of the "Level 5 Leader." Based on his extensive research, Collins reports in *Good to Great* that companies that demonstrated remarkable change over an extended period of time were always led by a Level 5 Leader. These leaders were notable for the fact that they achieved their greatness through the paradoxical blend of both personal humility and professional will.

Collins found that Level 5 Leaders, when compared to other CEOs of large companies, exhibited **personal humility**, that is, *they always put the mission of the organization above their own personal ambitions*. As a matter of fact, many of these leaders actually put their personal careers *at risk* rather than back away from their commitment to the organization's mission. This would be a far cry from those school leaders who put their own career ambitions above doing what needs to be done to assure that all students learn.

Level 5 Leaders demonstrated **personal will** in that they did not and would not take no for an answer. They may have had to adjust tactics and strategies to achieve their goals, but they were determined to find a way; failure simply was not an option they would entertain. One of the qualities that is most needed in the current context of school reform are leaders who are willing to put their career on the line if need be, and who are unwilling to give up on the notion of successful learning for all.

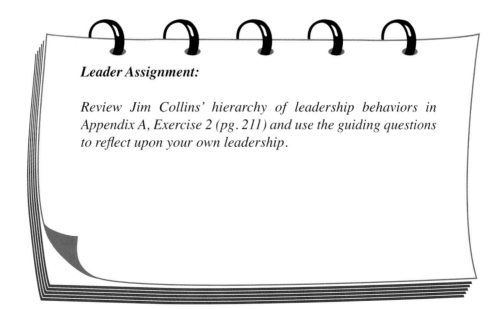

Leader Assignment:

Review Jim Collins' hierarchy of leadership behaviors in Appendix A, Exercise 2 (pg. 211) and use the guiding questions to reflect upon your own leadership.

LEADERSHIP AND LEGACY

Individuals who aspire to leadership do so because they *want* to make a difference and they believe that they *can* make a difference. They want to have a lasting impact on their area of endeavor; that is, they wish to leave a legacy. Legacy is about what remains of the leader's vision and values once the leader has departed from the scene. When speaking of a leader's legacy, observers and followers generally focus on two aspects: *what* the leader accomplished and *how* the leader went about doing it.

When referring to how a leader went about accomplishing his/her vision, comments usually revolve around the nature and tenor of the relationships that the leader built with the followership. Leaders that leave a lasting impression on the followers are those that were able to build and sustain positive relationships with and among people during their tenure. This doesn't mean that the leader must surround him/herself with like-minded individuals, never make unpopular decisions, or engage in conflict. It does mean, however, that effective leaders always treat followers with respect, clearly articulate their expectations, and create a camaraderie or esprit de corps with and among the followers.

Individuals who are remembered as great leaders did not avoid conflict. In fact, according to Bennis, effective leaders encourage followers to offer contrary points of view and honest criticism without fear of reprisals. Conversely, leaders who leave a lasting legacy and positive image are not "wishy-washy" about the direction of the organization. They know how to guide the discussion; what ideas, concepts, behaviors, and goals are nonnegotiable; when to conclude the discussion and make a decision; and how to motivate everyone—even the dissenters—to work together toward the specified objectives. The fact that a leader accepts both input from the followers and the ultimate responsibility for decisions and their implementation inspires confidence and trust among the followers.

The personal attributes we have discussed that are associated with effective leadership provide a map of what leaders can do to establish those positive relationships. For example, there are many ways in which individuals can establish themselves as trustworthy. No single personality type has an advantage when it comes to being judged trustworthy. As Stephen Covey states in his latest book, *The 8th Habit*, each of us must find our voice when it comes to inspiring our colleagues' trust.

How a leader acts toward others in pursuit of the mission or goal and whether or not the leader creates positive relationships are also important aspects of a leader's legacy. However, while positive relationships are necessary to a favorable legacy, they are not sufficient.

The other way we speak about the legacy of the leader is in terms of the *lasting* changes the leader was able to bring about.

Over the years, we have found leaders who were able to get short-term changes in their school or district, but once they left the organization, the followers soon abandoned the leader's vision. What effective leaders do and how they do it lives on because the leader sees to it that the organization as a whole internalizes the vision and the means used to achieve it. This is where the critical difference between being an effective manager and an effective leader is most apparent.

According to Warren Bennis, the problem with many organizations—especially those that are struggling—is that they are over*managed* and under*led*. Let us be clear, despite this chapter's opening message of "Let's Get Rid of Management," every organization needs to be managed well. But good management alone will not take a school or district in need of significant, sustained, and continuous improvement where it needs to go. Only strong and effective leadership can provide the catalyst needed for change.

> *"Management is efficiency in climbing the ladder of success; leadership determines whether the ladder is leaning against the right wall."*
>
> — *Stephen Covey*
> *Author, The 7*
> *Habits of Highly*
> *Effective People*

The difference between managers and leaders is reflected in their actions and behaviors, and directly relates to how individuals in leadership positions construe their roles. Bennis clearly differentiates these behaviors in his book *On Becoming A Leader* (1994) and is reproduced for you on the next page:

Differences between Managers and Leaders
taken from *On Becoming a Leader*
by Warren Bennis (1994)

Managers		Leaders	
• The manager administers.	• The manager has his/her eyes on the bottom line.	• The leader innovates.	• The leader has his/her eyes on horizon.
• The manager is a copy.	• The manager imitates.	• The leader is original.	• The leader originates.
• The manager maintains.	• The manager accepts the status quo.	• The leader develops.	• The leader challenges the status quo.
• The manager focuses on systems and structures.	• The manager is the classic "good soldier."	• The leader focuses on people.	• The leader is his/her own person.
• The manager relies on control.	• The manager does things right.	• The leader inspires trust.	• The leader does the right thing.
• The manager has a short-range view.	• The manager asks how and when.	• The leader has the long-range perspective.	• The leader asks what and why.

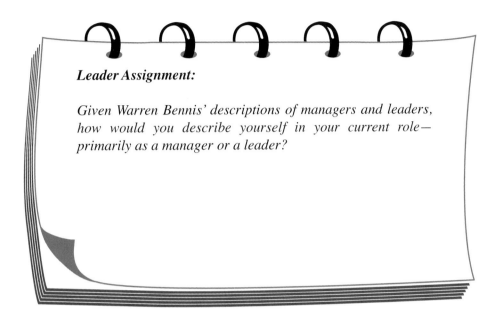

Leader Assignment:

Given Warren Bennis' descriptions of managers and leaders, how would you describe yourself in your current role— primarily as a manager or a leader?

As Warren Bennis noted when he contrasted management with leadership, effective managers manage "things" and the status quo effectively. On the other hand, effective leaders work for change— first in people, who will then help change the system, the culture, and the nature of the work itself. And these are the changes that "stick," that become integrated into the everyday routine to create a better system, and thus a better result. In the case of public education, a better system will produce the result society now demands: *learning for all*. What better legacy can a leader leave behind?

Throughout this book we will constantly strive to weave together the idea that sustainable school and district reform demands that leaders do the "right thing" in the "right way." If you, in your role as a leader for change, meet this standard, your legacy will take care of itself.

Leader Assignment:

Envision that in 5 or 10 years you leave a leadership position (either your current one or one you aspire to); what would you like your legacy to be? What would you want your stakeholders—teachers, parents, students, etc.—to say about you as a leader?

"The only thing you take with you when you're gone is what you leave behind."

— *John Allston*
Author

3

LAYING THE GROUNDWORK FOR LEADING CHANGE

Most of us have heard the expression, "If you don't know where you're going, any road will get you there." Here are some interesting variations on this same theme: *If you're not clear about where you're going, how will you know if or when you get there? If you aren't clear about where you're going, every intersection represents a temptation to change direction.* Surely, there are more variations on this theme, but these are sufficient to make the point that the first requisite of leadership is to "know thyself." Perhaps, then, the second requisite of leadership is to "know the terrain." In this chapter, you will have the opportunity to do both.

To assist you in "knowing thyself," we will challenge you to clarify and articulate your personal philosophy, values, and beliefs about the nature of education and schooling, as well as your vision for your school or district. We then offer you various perspectives on leadership in relation to change, and give you the opportunity to assess your own attitudes toward both.

The second part of this chapter will focus on getting to know the system-in-place. Because, as previously noted, leadership always occurs within a specific context, it is critical that you go into the change process with "eyes wide open." That is to say, you must know the current reality of your school or district's situation: its people, its resources, its strengths and weaknesses.

> *"Creating a new theory is not like destroying an old barn and erecting a skyscraper in its place. It is rather like climbing a mountain, gaining new and wider views, discovering unexpected connections between our starting points and its rich environment."*
>
> — *Albert Einstein*
>   *Physicist & Nobel*
>   *Prize Winner*

First "I," then "We"

Let's imagine three different scenarios. First, imagine that you have applied for and have been invited to interview for an educational leadership position. The school board or search committee is sure to ask you questions like, "Why do you want this position?" "What would you change in the school or district if you were the leader?" "What do you believe is the primary mission of public education in our democracy?" These and similar questions are designed to give you an opportunity to communicate your sense of mission or moral purpose, what you believe and value. Would you have a ready answer to each of these questions?

Second, suppose it's your first day as a new principal and you are standing before the school's faculty for the first time. They would expect you to communicate why you decided to come to their school, your sense about what the mission or moral purpose of the school is or ought to be, and how you plan to approach changing the school and the people who work there. What would you say? Here again, this leadership role requires that you be crystal clear as to who you are and what you stand for, and have the ability to articulate those beliefs and values. In one sense, this is your first "campaign speech" on your way to being "elected" the leader.

Third, suppose you have been the leader for a while and you and your staff begin to sense that something is not "right" with the school or district. Against what "ideal" would you measure "what is"? How would you determine what's working and what's not, and what needs to change? This conversation must begin with a discussion of what is or ought to be our mission, our core beliefs, and our values. Once again, you must be clear and confident in your own vision to be able to facilitate this discussion among the followers.

> *"A man should first direct himself in the way he should go. Only then should he instruct others."*
>
> *— Siddhartha Gautama, Buddha*

CLARIFYING YOUR CORE BELIEFS AND VALUES

Why is it crucial to clarify your core beliefs and values? Because these determine how you will approach your leadership role, and how you will interact with colleagues, parents, students and other stakeholders, both professionally and personally. You may say, "I know what I believe and value." And perhaps you do. But unless we take the time to think about them, our beliefs and values are often only vaguely understood.

This is particularly important in the context of education today, because there are so many differing opinions as to the role of schooling.

One significant conflict is between what John Goodlad and Timothy McMannon call the private and public purposes of schooling. Goodlad and McMannon, in *The Public Purpose of Education and Schooling*, assert, "As the rhetoric of school reform continues to focus on the private purposes of schooling, the critical role of schools in promoting the ideals of our American democracy has all but been forgotten." In his earlier book, *What Schools Are For*, Goodlad suggests, that to preserve our democratic society, we must revisit why we educate our children and what they must ultimately know, not only to become employable, but to become *educated*.

Leader Assignment:

Go to Appendix A, Exercise 3 (pg. 213), and review the list of goals taken from Goodlad's book, What Schools Are For. This exercise will help you clarify what you believe are the fundamental purposes of public schooling, and determine which of those are the most important. This exercise will give you a solid foundation for your "moral purpose"—a powerful force in creating change.

THE RELATIONSHIP BETWEEN VALUES, BELIEFS, VISION, AND LEADERSHIP

Your values and beliefs are the cornerstone of your worldview. Beliefs center around what you think is true. Values are grounded in beliefs about the way the world *should* be, rather than assumptions about the way the world *is*. For example, if you believe that all children can master the essential curriculum, then a core value that would likely emanate from that belief is that all children should have an equal opportunity to learn. As we cognitively compare what we believe should be to our assessment of what is, we then identify areas of dissonance, that is, where the reality of a situation falls short of what we believe it should be. If our belief is a strongly held core belief, this dissonance creates an emotional response of discomfort. The effective leader translates this discomfort into behaviors designed to align what is with what should be.

Creating a positive culture of learning is a fundamental role of the educational leader. But what does that mean? The culture of a school is grounded in its values. Core values define how we will act toward one another in our organization. For example, some schools embrace competition as a motivating factor for their students and teachers; some embrace a collaborative approach.

Some schools stress individuality, while others stress community.

As a leader, you are responsible for guiding your school or district in creating a climate and culture conducive to learning. To do this, you must first clarify your personal values in relation to schooling and learning. In his book, *The Moral and Spiritual Crisis in Education*, David Purpel states that "all meaningful schooling and school improvement is first a moral act designed to advance one's vision of the good person functioning in a good world." Do you agree with this statement? What do you think Purpel is implying about what students should learn in school? How is this different from traditional attitudes and beliefs about schooling? What values do you think your school or district should embrace and convey to your students?

Whether you are an aspiring or new administrator, or a seasoned veteran, take some time, find a quiet place, and think about these issues of mission, beliefs, and values. Don't return until you are satisfied that you can articulate those educational values and beliefs for which you are willing to "fall on the sword." Ordinarily the list is not that long; it doesn't have to be. But each item on the list must be a driving force in every decision you make and every action you take. Then, at the first opportunity, you should communicate your beliefs and values to your staff. Furthermore, you should encourage the staff to "step up" and challenge you if they perceive you as behaving inconsistently with your stated beliefs and values. Inviting staff scrutiny will reinforce both your perceived and actual commitment to "walking the talk."

> *"Setting an example is not the main means of influencing another, it is the only means."*
>
> — *Albert Einstein*
> *Physicist & Nobel*
> *Prize Winner*

Leadership has been often referred to as a "risk" game. This means that, in endeavors that require significant change and represent a perceived personal risk to those being asked to change, the leader has to "ante up" first. One of the first risks the leader has to take is to put forth his/her answers to the lofty questions of "What do I believe?" "What do I value?" "What are the steadfast, nonnegotiable principles by which I live and act?" Unless you take the lead in this effort (hence, the moniker "leader"), it is unlikely that your colleagues will be quick to put themselves in a vulnerable position.

Leader Assignment:

Go to Appendix A, Exercise 4 (pg. 219) and review Purpel's list of values concerning what schools should emphasize when teaching children. You'll quickly see that the fundamental values people have toward schooling will impact the structures, processes, and culture of the school in which they work. After reviewing the list, turn to the next page and rate the degree to which you think schools should emphasize one value over another. Finally, you'll be given a chance to rate each set of values according to the importance you believe it has to your vision of a successful school.

BEYOND A REACTIVE-RESPONSIVE ORIENTATION: VISION AS A CREATIVE FORCE FOR CHANGE

In an earlier chapter, we highlighted Ronald Reagan's ability to paint such a clear and inspiring picture of the future that an entire nation could envision and embrace it. One reason he could do this, besides his natural talent as an orator, was that he was crystal-clear on his vision for the future. To effectively lead change in your school or district, you must be just as clear about your vision for a preferred future.

Through years of research, Robert Fritz, author of *The Path of Least Resistance: Learning to Become the Creative Force in Your Own Life*, found that the most successful individuals in any discipline applied their efforts to creating a preferred future, as opposed to reacting to outside forces. Fritz, a musician and a composer who became a consultant for individuals and organizations seeking change, suggests that the fundamental underlying structure of a person's life determines his/her "path of least resistance." Human nature being what it is, everyone goes through life taking the path of least resistance; an individual's current situation is a result of moving along that path. The structures that most influence your life are your desires, beliefs, assumptions, aspirations, and objective reality itself. Some

structures are more useful than others in leading to desired results. Some lead only to temporary change. One such structure is the "reactive-responsive" orientation.

Individuals with a reactive-responsive orientation take action based on the circumstances in which they find themselves, or might find themselves in the future. They may *react* to circumstance (reject and rebel—be the "last angry man") or *respond* (accept and obey—be the "fair-haired boy"). The reactive-responsive orientation emanates from a presumption of powerlessness, that external circumstances are in control. Those with this orientation develop behavioral strategies—often dysfunctional ones—to avoid negative consequences.

Regardless of whether the situation is a success or a failure, people in the reactive-responsive orientation always feel incomplete and unsatisfied. Why? Because people who focus all their energy on what they *don't want* continually compromise whatever they *do want* in their lives for the sake of safety, security, and a sense of peace. However, they never actually experience these things, and instead attain only mediocrity and complacency with an undercurrent of dissatisfaction, a lack of fulfillment, and a feeling of vulnerability to circumstances beyond their control.

The reactive-responsive orientation arises from the competition between two or more tension-resolution systems. For example, a tension of hunger wants the resolution of eating, but the tension of being overweight wants the resolution of not eating. The two tensions have conflicting resolutions. According to Fritz, structural conflict is _not_ resolvable. Fortunately, you can learn to recognize the structures at play in your life and change them so that you can create what you really want to create.

Fritz suggests that you must create a new structure, one that will take precedence over the old. This, in turn, will alter the path of least resistance and energy will move easily along that new path. *The new structure must contain one major structural tension that will be formed by a vision of a desired result transposed against a clear view of current reality.* Once this structural tension is established, the natural tendency will be to generate actions to resolve that tension. From the inception of the creative process to its conclusion, the actions taken by you and the organization toward the vision will be supported by the structure. And every action taken to create the vision will move you toward the result you want, including the ones that are not directly successful.

The process begins, says Fritz, by asking this question: *What do I want?* This simple question will yield a vision for a preferred future. Vision has power, and "can help you organize your actions, focus your values, and clearly see what is relevant in current reality." To clearly develop this vision, Fritz cautions, you must not get sidetracked by considerations of process or questions about what is or isn't possible. People are often stymied when faced with deciding what they want. They become indecisive because they are afraid that, by making one choice, they may lose out on a better one. Fritz outlines eight ways to undermine effective choice:

- Choosing only what seems possible or reasonable.
- Choosing the process instead of the result.
- Eliminating all other possibilities so that only one choice remains.
- Choosing by default (no choice is a choice).
- Imposing conditions on choice— placing the power to organize your life in certain arbitrary conditions.
- Making a choice to reduce discomfort or eliminate pressure, not to initiate a creative process.
- Choosing by consensus: following what everybody else wants or does.
- Choosing based on a hazy metaphysical notion about the nature of the universe.

Fritz also outlines three types of choices. *Fundamental choices* are not subject to changes in internal or external circumstances. Actions are always based on what is consistent with your fundamental choice, regardless of circumstances. *Primary choices* are about major results. It is designed to be an end in itself and not a "step" to another result. *Secondary choices* are those that help you take steps toward your primary result.

Robert Fritz proposes a powerful paradigm for change, one that is supported by the work of Peter Senge and others. The idea that the structure, or system, will reclaim the process every time, both within ourselves and within our organizations, has been around for some time. And still, more than a decade after this book was written—and supported by an entire genre of writing since—this basic premise is often overlooked.

The accountability and standards movement, embodied by NCLB, is prompting a reactive-responsive change from educators because of the negative and punitive consequences attached to the failure to meet specified benchmarks. While the reaction to NCLB and the accountability and standards movement has jumpstarted the change process in many, if not most schools, *sustainable change will only come from the collective internal commitment of educators and other stakeholders to a common vision, a moral imperative of "learning for all."*

Individually and organizationally, we must make fundamental choices about what we want. As Fritz says, these fundamental choices—like "learning for all…whatever it takes"—will not change in response to circumstances. They comprise the foundation upon which all other choices rest, a choice in which we commit ourselves to a basic life orientation or a basic state of being.

By adopting a creative orientation as opposed to a reactive-responsive orientation, we become bolder, less constrained by convention and cynicism. Why? Because, as Fritz points out, "creating is an art, it deals in approximation. There are no formulas to follow, no hard rules to apply. Creating is, at its roots, improvisational. You make it up as you go along. You learn to break ground. You learn to learn from your failures as well as your successes."

Your role as leader is to inspire a creative orientation to change and the internal commitment to the foundational choice of leaving no child behind within the context of the external mandates for change. It is crucial, therefore, that your vision for change is well-defined and compelling, for yourself and your followers.

Leader Assignment:

Follow the steps outlined below to help you create your vision.

Create a mental image: *Envision you are a stranger walking down the hallways of your improved school. What does it look like? What do the classrooms look like? What are the children doing? Are parents in the picture? Are the children working in small groups? In what types of activities are they engaged? If you are imagining a high school, how is it set up? How about the "feel" of the school? Is there a sense of camaraderie? Are people energized and excited to be there? Write down your description in as much detail as possible.*

Write a headline: *Imagine a reporter has come to write about your improved school. Outline a newspaper story about your school, its struggles, and its successes. What will be the headline of the story?*

Quote your stakeholders: *What do you want your teachers to say about your improved school? Your students? Their parents? The community? Write a quote from each point of view in the first person highlighting the specific things that make them happy to be part of your improved school.*

Now, write your vision for your improved school.

ASSESSING YOUR ATTITUDES TOWARD CHANGE

The challenge of managing change, according to Professor Edward O'Neil, Director of the Center for Health Professions at the University of California, is the paramount issue facing leaders today. Change is not easy; it is dynamic and chaotic, emotionally charged, and stress inducing. An important precursor to leading successful change in your school or district is a realistic view of what that change will mean, as well as a clear understanding of your own attitudes toward the change process.

> *"It's not so much that we're afraid of change or so in love with the old ways, but it's that place in-between that we fear....It's like being between trapezes. It's Linus when his blanket's in the dryer. There's nothing to hold on to."*
>
> — *Marilyn Ferguson*
> *Author, The Aquarian Conspiracy*

Leader Assignment:

Consider the following statement:
> *"I am committed to improving student learning in my school through the adoption and implementation of a continuous improvement process."*

- *List all the pluses and positives this statement suggests to you.*
- *List all the negatives and minuses this statement suggests.*
- *How do you feel about the upcoming changes implied by this statement?*
- *What worries or concerns do you have about change?*
- *What energizes or excites you about these changes?*
- *How do these issues affect your approach to initiating and leading the continuous improvement process?*

PARADIGMS FOR CHANGE AND YOUR LEADERSHIP STYLE

Approaches to change have evolved as organizations have increased in both size and complexity. According to Richard Axelrod in *Terms of Engagement: Changing the Way We Change Organizations*, the earliest leadership paradigm for organizational change consisted of leader-driven efforts to create change from the top using a command-and-control approach. As organizations became larger and more complex, leaders began to seek guidance from experts beyond the boundaries of their own organization. Axelrod refers to this approach to change as "process-driven." As this approach became popular, the "team-approach" model also emerged. These two models have since become integrated into a single "change-management" paradigm.

Each subsequent approach to leadership increased the involvement of others beyond the leader in the change process. However, Axelrod found that the level of involvement in any of these paradigms would be insufficient to assure sustainable change. As a result, he formulated a new change paradigm, one that he and his colleagues have found to be more effective in promoting sustainable change. He calls this approach the Engagement Paradigm.

The Engagement Paradigm is based on four key principles: *Widening the Circle of Involvement; Connecting People to Each Other; Creating Communities for Action; and Embracing Democracy*. This paradigm builds on the successes of past efforts to create sustainable organizational change, while seeking to solve the problems created by the earlier approaches. It also requires a dramatically different approach to leadership. Widening the circle of involvement to build support for change takes patience and persistence. Creating communities for action and allowing people to connect with each other and with a compelling purpose may seem risky to many leaders who fear that doing so will allow the resisters to get organized and, therefore, more powerful. Embracing democratic principles means sharing control. This can be particularly challenging for individuals who are accustomed to the "command-and-control" structure common in bureaucracy, and for those who believe control and leadership are synonymous. It's no wonder that many leaders prefer to operate under one of the more traditional change paradigms.

Research has consistently shown that the most effective school-change strategies have been created and sustained when the leaders risk trusting those closest to the teaching-learning process. It requires patience, persistence, and faith...in people, in the cause, and in the process.

Leader Assignment:

How we view leadership and the role it plays in our schools, by definition, affects how we lead others. In the Appendix A, Exercise 5 (pg. 225), we outline and summarize Richard Axelrod's three leadership paradigms. Review these paradigms and reflect on your own leadership style using the guiding questions.

"The task of leadership is not to put greatness into people, but to elicit it, for the greatness is already there."

— *John Buchan*
Scottish Author

ADAPTING YOUR
LEADERSHIP STYLE

As noted previously, leadership—by definition—requires followers. An appropriate bumper sticker might be "Leaders never do it alone!" As we begin to describe the skills and strategies effective leaders use to create and sustain the followership, we need to reiterate an important truth: the act of following is ultimately a voluntary one. People *choose* to follow a leader. There are as many motivations for choosing to follow a leader as there are individuals. Most, however, can be attributed to three fundamental driving forces: fear of sanctions or reprisal, anticipation of reward, and moral purpose.

Many years ago, Kenneth Boulding, an internationally recognized economist and award-winning author, wrote *The Three Faces of Power*. This book offers valuable insight into the leader/follower relationship and can provide a useful perspective for leading sustainable change. Setting the stage for his ideas, we must remember that the current system of education has an enormous amount of inertia to do again tomorrow what it did today. This inertia is analogous to a boulder rolling down a hill. The boulder has its trajectory and is unlikely to change course on its own. If we want to alter the boulder's course, we will have to leverage a significant force upon it. Likewise, if our goal as a leader is to overcome the system's inertia and get it to do something different tomorrow than it did today, we will need to exert a significant force or "power" upon it.

In *The Three Faces of Power*, Boulding provides the change-oriented leader with the three "power" options: "stick power," "carrot power," and "hug power."

- **Stick Power**. The leader says to the followers: "I want you to do something you don't want to do. If you don't do what I want you to do, something that you don't want to happen will happen." It's an example of leading through the power of threat. Followers choose to follow based on fear.

- **Carrot Power**: Here the leader says, "I want you to do something that you don't want to do. If you do what I want you to do, I will give you something that you do want." The leader attempts to leverage change by using the power of incentives. Followers comply in hopes of a reward.

- **Hug Power**: This is the power that is tapped and realized when two or more people come together around a commitment to shared vision, values, and beliefs.

Throughout the book, Boulding describes examples of these three kinds of power as they have been used in international relations, organizational relations, and even interpersonal relationships. Boulding concludes the book with this statement: *"the stick, the carrot, and the hug may all be necessary, but the greatest of these is the hug."*

Over the years, the most effective educational leaders we have known excelled at getting a critical mass of the followership to share and commit to a common vision and a set of values and beliefs. In other words, these leaders seemed to be masters of the "hug power." It is unlikely that many, if any, of these leaders ever read Boulding's book or ever thought they were using "hug power" to create energy for sustainable change. Nonetheless, they seemed to have a gift for approaching change in that special way. How should the leader proceed to build the shared vision, values, and beliefs among a critical mass of potential followers?

A common mistake aspiring leaders often make when it comes to articulating the need for school reform is to present it as simply a technical adjustment in the way the school or district currently works. For example, unwitting school and district leaders often describe the requirements of NCLB as a call for higher test scores. It is difficult, if not impossible, to sustain high levels of energy and commitment to a change effort if it only amounts to a technical adjustment. Such changes do not inspire because they do not speak to the heart. At best, they speak only to the *head* or *hands*.

On the other hand, people are energized by the call for school reform when it is presented and understood as a *moral journey* (much like Fritz's vision as a creative force for change, discussed earlier). In this way, the change process begins in the *heart*, moves to the head, and finally settles in the hands.

Thomas Sergiovanni, in his article "The Leadership Needed for Quality Schooling," categorizes leadership into two approaches: *transactional* and *transformational*. He defines transactional leadership as the more traditional view, with its emphasis on rules, procedures, and job descriptions to accomplish identified goals and objectives. Transformational leadership, according to Sergiovanni, relies on shared purpose, beliefs, and values, empowerment, and a team-orientation. Transformative leaders are more concerned with results than process, and give people a great deal of latitude in accomplishing stated goals as long as their efforts are aligned with the organizational beliefs and values. Sergiovanni reinforces our earlier premise: that developing a shared purpose among the faculty, parents, students, the community, and other stakeholders results in increased motivation and commitment.

Transactional leadership, with its emphasis on how tasks are accomplished, is by its very nature, directive. It is more concerned with coordinating staff efforts based on rules, procedures, and job descriptions. The directive approach is not, in and of itself, "bad." In fact, a certain level of transactional leadership will always be necessary, even in the most collaborative and enlightened learning community, simply because not everyone on your staff will buy in to the stated mission, beliefs, and values, or have the same sense of passion, despite your best efforts. It's only reasonable to believe that there will be differences. In some schools, where cynicism and frustration are so entrenched, you may initially face either apathy or active resistance from most of the staff. In this case, you may have to resort to a directive approach to get things moving. However, effective leaders adapt their leadership styles over time, with the goal of inspiring and empowering colleagues to take ownership of the change process in pursuit of a common vision. This is the only way to integrate continuous improvement into the school's culture, so that the process becomes bigger than any one individual. That way, the progress

made along the way won't be lost when the formal leader leaves the organization.

There may be times when Boulding's "hug power" or Sergiovanni's transformational approach won't be enough to inspire the action needed to change the trajectory of the "boulder racing downhill" and you will need to resort to another form of power or leadership style to "un-stick" the system. But these actions and approaches must also always reflect and reinforce your stated vision, beliefs, and values, as well as build and support the understanding and commitment of the followers to the organization's moral purpose. Further, you must be sensitive to changes in context and adjust your behaviors to meet the needs of the situation and the followers as they evolve, change, and grow.

The diagram on the following page shows how your leadership style should evolve as the school moves from a group of autonomous individuals to a collaborative learning community committed to the continually improving instruction so that all may learn.

THE EVOLUTION OF LEADERSHIP IN A CHANGING ORGANIZATION

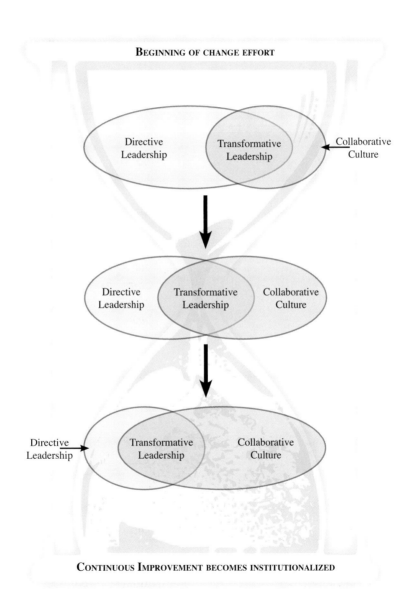

BEGINNING OF CHANGE EFFORT

CONTINUOUS IMPROVEMENT BECOMES INSTITUTIONALIZED

Leader Assignment:

Where do you think your organization is in terms of your leadership approach? Does your current leadership style match the organization's needs? Think about the challenges inherent in moving along the continuum and the interaction of leadership with the evolution of the organization. The organization's culture impacts your leadership style, while your leadership will help the culture evolve.

"Leadership is a serving relationship that has the effect of facilitating human development."

> — *Ted Ward*
>   *Consultant &*
>   *Speaker*

UNDERSTANDING THE SYSTEM-IN-PLACE: STRUCTURE, HISTORY, CLIMATE, AND CULTURE

STRUCTURE: ANCHORS OF THE SYSTEM

In his book *Restructuring Our Schools: A Primer On Systemic Change*, W. Patrick Dolan not only clearly articulates what is meant by "systemic change," he also provides a workable game plan for creating sustainable systemic reform. In his lucid description of the system-in-place, he reminds us that, since the second day of creation, all attempts to bring about change have had to work against a "system-in-place."

Dolan notes that those who occupy critical roles within an existing system can describe its pathologies, express their rage against them, and yet be nearly powerless to change the system—especially working alone.

Why is the system so difficult to change? It's partly because the system-in-place is maintained by several anchors, each with a vested interest in maintaining the status quo. If you want the system to change—and surely the educational system must change—then you must get the permission and support of the anchors to be successful.

Dolan identifies three anchors for our public education system: the elected school board; the administrative leadership team; and the organized labor leaders. According to Dolan, "Each of the three anchor positions. . . represent distinct legal and moral obligations. Often the full achievement of one group's goals may appear to be at the expense of another." This is because changing the structure of the system-in-place represents significant risk for each anchor as they must give up a certain level of control.

These anchors are critical to effective and sustainable change, says Dolan. "You must find a way to move these often adversarial relationships toward a more trusting, collaborative, and supportive relationship that frees the rest of the system to act differently, even as they retain their separate functions."

Dolan offers many process strategies and structures for unsticking the system-in-place. But he cautions us not to underestimate the enormous power of the system to actively resist change and maintain itself—even to the point of self-destruction.

Leader Assignment:

Reflect on the anchors in your own school system.

- *Are there other anchors holding your system-in-place that are not listed here? What are those groups?*

- *Think about Fritz's ideas about changing the structure by using a common vision of a preferred future as the basis of a creative process. How does this apply to Dolan's assertion that you must move the anchors from an adversarial relationship to a more trusting, collaborative, and supportive one? How might you approach these diverse anchors and begin a conversation around a common vision?*

- *Identify individuals in specific leadership roles that you will need to get "on board" to enable your change efforts.*

ORGANIZATIONAL HISTORY

We recognize that many schools have taken at least some steps toward improvement. It is important to acknowledge the work that has gone before, and the results it yielded, both positive and negative.

Otherwise, you may unintentionally convey the message to the stakeholders that history and culture are not important, their past efforts were simply exercises in futility, and that your current "system," like the last, will be swept to the side once the leadership changes.

> *"We can chart our future clearly and wisely only when we know the path which has led to the present."*
>
> — *Adlai E. Stevenson American Statesman*

Leader Assignment:

Research your school or district's history of reform. If you're a veteran, you'll probably have firsthand knowledge of every reform effort made during your tenure. If you're new to the school or district, you may have to ask the informal leaders of the group who've been around awhile. Jot down the different programs and initiatives that have been tried and their results. What worked? What didn't? What impressions did these efforts leave on staff and other stakeholders?

ORGANIZATIONAL CULTURE—FOCUSING ON MISSION CRITICAL

Like all organizations, the culture of a school represents a complex and powerful set of interdependent forces that conspire to assure that the school does again tomorrow what it did today. The school's culture is perfectly aligned to continue to produce the current results. This powerful force and the results that it produces are good things if the *current* results are the *desired* results as set forth in the mission. On the other hand, these forces serve as a major source of resistance or barrier when seeking to *change* the school's current results. In schools and districts where the culture revolves around the traditional way of educating children, you will find that your success at initiating and leading a continuous improvement process will depend on how successful you are at changing certain aspects of the school's culture.

Even though school culture is a complex, multidimensional, and highly interdependent system, changing it may not be as daunting a task as it at first appears if it is approached in the proper way. Only about five percent (5%) of an organization's culture is *mission critical*. That is to say, a few traits of the school culture are important, but most of them matter hardly at all. If school-change efforts can stay focused on the mission-critical five percent of its culture, the change is more likely to be successful and sustained.

Even with the strong push for change that is bearing in on public schools from the outside, recognizing that only a few key mission-critical shifts in the culture need to occur should make the task seem more in reach. The trick is to determine *which* five percent is mission critical. Identifying the needed cultural shifts requires explication and clarification of the school's mission, core values, and core beliefs. Unfortunately, the five percent may be the most ingrained in the culture and the most difficult to change.

As a leader, you cannot afford to let the "vital few" aspects of the culture that are critical to mission attainment get lost among the "trivial many" aspects of culture. Likewise, it would be counterproductive and probably fatal to the change effort to protect the culture of the school at the expense of the mission attainment. Failure to attain the mission, for many reasons discussed earlier, will have a serious impact on the survival of the school.

Leader Assignment:

We've organized various aspects of school (and district) culture using the Correlates of Effective Schools as a framework. The questions under each correlate are meant to get you thinking; they are by no means exhaustive. Feel free to include other indicators as you reflect on your school or district's current culture. Write down your thoughts concerning each aspect of culture. Which of these cultural attributes do you consider "mission critical"? Which of these will most affect your ability to create positive change?

- *Strong Instructional Leadership—Does your school have a history of strong instructional leadership? What was the nature of the previous leader-follower relationship? Are teachers and faculty empowered to perform leadership roles? Is leadership nurtured and developed among the staff and parents? Are mentor relationships in place—principal/teacher, teacher/teacher, teacher/student, etc.?*

- *Clear and Focused Mission—Does your organization currently have a mission statement? If you were to ask 10 people what the mission is, how many of them would know? Is the conversation primarily focused on teaching or on learning? When was the last time the organization as a whole reviewed and reaffirmed the mission statement? Do the programs, curricula, policies, and procedures reflect the mission statement? Are all new initiatives, policies, curricula, and programs evaluated in light of the mission?*

- *Climate of High Expectations for Success—Do all staff members believe that every child in the school can master the standards set before them? Do all staff members believe that they have the capability to help all students achieve mastery? Are teachers and staff committed to doing whatever it takes to ensure that all children learn? Do students know what is expected of them? Do they have a sense of efficacy, that they can achieve their goals?*

- *Safe and Orderly Environment—Is your school a safe place to be? Is there adequate adult supervision? Is there an atmosphere of orderliness and purpose? Is there a sense of respect, teamwork, collegiality, and collaboration among staff? Among students? Among parents? Is the physical plant clean, cheerful, and well-cared-for?*

- *Frequent Monitoring of Student Progress—How is assessment viewed by faculty, parents, and students: as a mandated evil or as an opportunity to identify where students need more help to learn to mastery? Does the school use criterion-referenced, curriculum-based assessment tied to clearly articulated standards? Are students assessed throughout the learning process to identify problems early, or at the end of the learning process? How does your school respond to struggling students?*

- *Opportunity to Learn/Time on Task—Is most of the instructional day actually spent on instruction? Are there continual interruptions for disciplinary problems, administrative issues, noninstructional activities? Is instruction tailored to accommodate specific student needs and different rates of learning? Are additional learning opportunities provided for students who need extra time to learn to mastery? Are enrichment opportunities provided for students who are "ahead of the curve"?*

- *Positive Home-School Relations—Do parents understand and support the school or district's mission? Are they given important roles to play in the school? Are parents visible in the school? Are there significant segments of the student body whose parents are not involved or visible at the school? Does the school or district reach out to parents who may be uncomfortable with their ability to contribute to their children's education? Is there a well-defined 2-way communication process so that teachers, administrators, and parents can work together for the benefit of their children?*

Leader Assignment:

Another aspect of your school or organization's culture that is important to consider consists of the prevailing beliefs and values.

In Appendix A, Exercise 6 (pg. 227), we've created a rating chart similar to the one you used to clarify your own beliefs and values. Here we ask you to rate your school or district's beliefs and values—both where you think they <u>are</u> and where you think they <u>should be</u>.

"Culture is a little like dropping an alka-seltzer into a glass—you don't see it, but somehow it does something."

— *Hans Magnus*
Enzensberger
German Writer

CLIMATE FOR CHANGE

Both within the school itself and beyond the campus, there are many forces at work that will influence your school improvement efforts. Some will facilitate positive change and some that will create resistance. Therefore, it is critical that educational leaders clearly understand the current system-in-place.

When reviewing and analyzing the system-in-place, it is critical, returning to the ideas of Robert Fritz, that we look at current reality clearly and unvarnished. This may be the greatest challenge for educators, since so much is at stake for schools that fail to make adequate yearly progress for any or all students. Schools labeled "failing" may indeed pour their energies into appealing the label and the process (reactive response—avoidance of negative consequences) rather than using the result as a starting point for assessing current reality and creating the preferred future (improved student achievement). And yet, to get to where we want to be, we must clearly see where we are.

Referring back to Dolan and his book *Restructuring Our Schools*, Dolan contends that, "the first issue of systems-thinking is that the critical phenomena are not the individual parts, but how they fit together." Because each part of the system is so integrated with the others, any change in one part of the system will affect every other part. Therefore, you will need to look not only at each segment of the system independently, but also at how the different parts interact with one another. In addition to the parts of the system you can influence, you must also consider the impact of the parts of the system whose influence is beyond your control. You may not be able to control what mandates come from the federal, state, or district level, or whether the number of special-needs students will increase, but you must understand these forces and factor them into your thinking as you plan and implement continuous school improvement.

> *"Whosoever wishes to know about the world must learn about it in its particular details."*
>
> — *Heraclitus of Ephesus*
> *Greek Philosopher*

Leader Assignment:

Use the following list of forces and factors that affect an educational system to help you understand your school or district's particular system-in-place. The list is by no means exhaustive, so feel free to add entities, processes, and forces specific to your school as they come to mind. Remember, at this point you are only trying to clarify and understand the various parts of the system, not address specific problems.

Governmental Mandates
- *What current state and federal mandates are driving your school reform efforts?*
- *Review the standards set by your state and/or district and identify areas of overlap and discrepancy between and among state and federal mandates, the demands of local stakeholders, and the way your school currently operates.*

Changing Societal Context
- *What are the demographics of your current student population? How has the student population changed over the past five years? Based on current trends, project how student demographics will change over the next few years. Will there likely be increases in at-risk student groups: low SES, non-English speaking, minority, special education, transient, or homeless?*
- *Reflect on how these changes, past and future, have affected and will affect how you will educate all children.*
- *How does the community-at-large view your school/district? If there were an editorial in today's paper, what would it say?*

Stakeholders – the Staff
- *Identify the school structures that are currently in place— committees, departments, classrooms, etc.—and how they currently operate.*

- *Is collaboration the norm, or do teachers operate in isolation?*
- *Are committees active? Effective? Nonexistent?*
- *Who are the formal and informal leaders in the school? Are they apt to be supportive or resistant of change?*
- *What is the overall morale of the staff? What is the collective attitude toward school improvement?*
- *Is there a common attitude of high expectations for student success? Do teachers believe that, collectively and individually, they can make a difference and that all students have the capacity to master the essential curriculum?*
- *Is there a teacher's union? If so, is the relationship amiable or antagonistic between administration and the union? Have the two entities collaborated on school improvement in the past? What was the result?*
- *Who among the staff are likely to resist change?*

Stakeholders—Parents
- *Consider the ways and the extent to which parents are actively involved in your school. Is there an active parents' group? Is there a cadre of parent volunteers? Are parent-child activities well attended? Are parent-teacher conferences well attended?*
- *Are parents supportive of homework, projects, performances, etc.?*
- *How do parents, overall, view the school, its teachers and staff, the curriculum, the facility, its resources?*
- *Are parents clamoring for change?*

Information System
- *How does information flow in your organization?*
- *How are information, input, and data collected from teachers, parents, and students?*
- *Assess the openness of information flow in your organization. Do stakeholders feel comfortable discussing problems, issues, and challenges, or is there an atmosphere of blame and fear that discourages honest and open discussion?*
- *Are there currently mechanisms in place to disseminate information to stakeholders? If so, are they used regularly and effectively?*

- *Are there opportunities for stakeholders to review plans and progress and offer suggestions and ideas for change or improvement?*

Available Resources
- *Assess the state of your physical plant. Does it provide an environment conducive to teaching and learning? What areas need immediate improvement? What resources might be available for improving the learning environment?*
- *Assess the school's curricular resources: textbooks, library books, computers, software, other curriculum materials and resources.*
- *Assess the fiscal environment for change. Are your federal, state, and district funding being cut, staying the same, increasing? Are there new programs and initiatives that you might be able to access to support school improvement? Or do you have to do more with less?*
- *Assess your professional resources. Do you have mostly young, inexperienced teachers, veteran teachers, or a balance of the two? What specialists and paraprofessionals are available to deal with special needs students?*
- *Assess your volunteer resources. Does your school have a volunteer mentor or tutoring program? Has your school been "adopted" by a service club or agency?*
- *Assess your community resources. What relationships are currently in place with local social service agencies?*

CURRENT REALITY IN RELATION TO CONTINUOUS IMPROVEMENT

Peter Senge, author of *The Fifth Discipline*, echoes Robert Fritz's two requirements for sustainable change. First, we need to know where we *really* want to go; then we need to have a very clear picture where are we *really*. In the previous exercise, you considered generally the various groups, forces, and factors that will impact your change effort. Now you must consider where your organization is in terms of the continuous school improvement process.

Leader Assignment:

Complete the Continuous School Improvement Process Assessment provided in Appendix A, Exercise 7 (pg. 231) to determine where your school currently is in relation to that process. We have listed the key components to successful, sustainable, and continuous school improvement that are applicable pretty much across the board, from school to school and district to district. We have also left space for you to add indicators specific to your school or district. Feel free to add more on another sheet of paper. This is all about <u>your</u> school's needs.

Next Steps

By now, you should have established a firm foundation for initiating the continuous school improvement process in your school or district. You should have a good understanding of the larger context of school reform and a clear vision for what you want to accomplish within that context. You should better understand and be able to articulate your core beliefs and values, as well as have a pretty good handle on your approach to leadership and change. Finally, you should have developed some insight into your organization itself, so you should be ready for what lies ahead.

In the chapters that follow, we will explain each step of the continuous school improvement process in more depth and what your role as leader should be in guiding and facilitating that step.

> *"They say that time changes things, but you actually have to change them yourself."*
>
> — *Andy Warhol*
> *Artist*

4

LEADING BY DESIGN: CREATING AN INCLUSIVE AND COLLABORATIVE PROCESS

As the old saying goes, you never get a second chance to make a good first impression. And so it is when a leader launches a change effort. How the leader begins the change process will go a long way in determining its success. Thus, leaders need to carefully consider not only what and why change is needed, but also how to increase the chances that the changes will be successfully implemented and sustained in an often emotionally charged, politicized environment.

For many educators, the bureaucratic, top-down, outside-in, standards-based, results-driven call for school improvement may feel like the onslaught of a tidal wave. It may seem as if the advocates of higher standards are at the school's front door unloading the higher standards curriculum, and the assessment and accountability police are standing at the back door, checking to be certain that the school responds. Unfortunately, educational history is filled with evidence that this approach to school change stops at the front and back doors.

On the other hand, organizational research, including research on effective schools, has yielded convincing evidence that the most compelling factor for achieving successful, effective, and sustainable change is a strong commitment from the individuals from whom behavioral change is needed. Research has also revealed that high levels of sustained commitment can only be realized when the affected individuals are involved and engaged in planning the changes they are expected to execute. And the involvement and engagement of others must, in turn, begin with a leader who is personally committed to an inclusive, collaborative process, who is willing to encourage and nurture others to participate and take on leadership roles.

The first essential task, then, is to engage the followers and create the structures that will facilitate their involvement with, commitment to, and collaboration in support of continuous school improvement. This chapter is dedicated to helping you do just that.

STEP ONE: ENGAGING THE STAKEHOLDERS

Systems and organizational cultures are sustained by the people who work in them. These people have a vested interest in what the system produces and how the system operates. For purposes of this discussion, we will refer to this universe of people as the "stakeholders" of the system. A school's stakeholder group certainly includes teachers, administrators, support staff, parents, students, central office staff, the school board, and the tax-paying community. The success of the continuous school improvement process in improving learning and achievement for all children depends heavily on the internal commitment, ownership, and support by the school or district's many stakeholder groups. After all, as the process unfolds they will be the ones who must change as part of the implementation strategy. In addition, each group—indeed, each individual—brings a different perspective to the process, enriching the conversation of change.

While it is true that all stakeholders have the capacity to enhance or impede the change process, the engagement of some groups should precede other groups. As a school principal, you'll not get far with your change vision if you are unable to earn the commitment and support of a critical mass of the teaching faculty and other paid support staff. Once those conversations have been held and the outcome has been positive and supportive, you should, in consultation with the committed stakeholder groups, develop a plan of who should be approached next and formulate a process that constantly enlarges the circle of involvement and commitment among the various stakeholder groups.

Leader Assignment:

The first task of the leader is to identify the various stakeholder groups of the school or district, and then create a plan for engaging them in the change effort. List all the stakeholder groups that will likely have a vested interest in your school or district's reform effort. For each stakeholder group you identify, answer these questions:
- *What is this group's interest in the school (district)?*
- *What is the group's motivation for becoming involved with the improvement effort?*
- *How should you reach out to this group?*
- *How should this group be involved in the process?*

"If we are to achieve a richer culture, rich in contrasting values, we must recognize the whole gamut of human potentialities, and so weave a less arbitrary social fabric, one in which each diverse human gift will find a fitting place."

— *Margaret Mead*
  Anthropologist &
  Scientist

STEP TWO:
FRAMING THE PROBLEM,
CREATING BUY-IN

As mentioned earlier, the path of least resistance for both individuals and organizations is to maintain the status quo of the system-in-place. The leadership challenge, then, is to overcome the inherent inertia of the system and create energy for, and commitment to, school improvement.

If the stakeholders can't say "no," then "yes" doesn't mean anything. If "yes" is to mean anything—that is, if it is to truly signify agreement— the stakeholders must feel empowered. Empowerment means that people feel they have a choice to be engaged in the change process. Therefore, the leader must create a climate where individuals will freely choose to dedicate themselves to creating a new vision for the school or district. The most effective way for leaders to accomplish this task is to clearly communicate the reasons why change is needed. All too often, educational leaders assume that the followers already know. Effective leaders do not trap themselves by making such an assumption. Instead, they anticipate and are prepared to address the question: "Why do schools need to change generally, and why does our school or district need to change in particular?"

It will be the latter part of this question that most concerns your stakeholders. That is why, when it comes to framing the problem for the various stakeholder groups, you should use examples and data that are as local to your school and community as possible. For example, you could say that schools need to change because the global technological revolution requires a whole new set of knowledge and skills in the workplace. True enough, but it focuses on something that is happening "out there." The effective leader will follow such a statement by describing examples of this issue or problem as it is impacting the stakeholders' own community, state, or region of the country.

Former Congressional Leader Tip O'Neal is credited with saying that, in the end, all politics are local. Our version relative to education is that, in the end, all school and district reform is and must be local. Without the local perspective on the problems, it is very difficult to create initial stakeholder buy-in and sustain the energy and commitment needed to reform the system.

Getting People On-Board

Other people's buy-in—their understanding, commitment, and action in support of specific goals—has always been enormously important. But in today's world, it has become the most valuable asset of all. As we suggested in Chapter 2, the ability to influence people's thoughts and feelings, to generate their buy-in, has emerged as the paramount leadership skill. This is especially important when leading others through a change process during challenging times, as is the case with public education.

Creating buy-in goes beyond painting a vivid picture of a preferred future, although that is an important element. The key is to connect that picture with the needs, concerns, and wants of those whose commitment and support we are trying to rally. According to Mark Walton, author of Generating Buy-In, the most effective way to connect our vision with stakeholders is through a story. Why? Because stories are the language of our minds; we "think" in stories.

This is the age-old secret to generating buy-in—to strategically design, target, and deliver a story that projects a positive future. Such stories have been the most powerful language of buy-in since the beginning of recorded time, if not before. Stories create a route to real buy-in—that is, to generating people's understanding, commitment, and ultimately their action—by impacting not just their thinking, but also their emotions (remember Boulding's "hug power"?).

Creating a positive future gives your various stakeholder groups an alternative to dwelling on past failures and problems. It allows your listeners to look beyond the current crisis and controversy and focus on a common vision, something that can easily get lost in discussions around the need for change, which often deteriorate into a "blame game." According to Walton, developing your strategic story provides a framework to "connect the dots" between the future you want (your objective) and the future your audience wants (their agenda). To that end, he outlines a three-step process:

1) Establish your strategic storyline.

2) Develop your storyline in three chapters that target your audience's agenda.

3) Call your audience to action.

Leader Assignment:

For each stakeholder group, think about what action you want your audience to take regarding your idea, proposal, or organization. Then, use the following steps to develop your strategic story.

Establish Your Strategic Storyline: *What is the "big picture" or vision of a positive future you want your audiences to see? Refer back to the exercises you did to clarify your vision, beliefs, and values, and use your notes to create a clear and compelling picture for your stakeholders.*

Develop Your Storyline: *What are these particular stakeholders' needs, wants, and future goals? In the future you are projecting, what are the three most important ways in which this audience's agenda will be fulfilled?*

Call Your Audience To Action: *Ask for a commitment of a first step toward the action you want.*

Most people of goodwill will respond affirmatively to a leader's call for change if it is presented in a compelling way that doesn't "feel" like an indictment of their current efforts. For example, in the current reform environment, teachers tend to resist change when they feel their abilities or intentions are in question, or that their schools are somehow "broken" and in need of fixing. The effective leader will help the staff understand that the call for reform is not about "playing the game poorly," it is about the fact that the game itself has changed, that forces beyond the school are demanding new and different outcomes for teaching and learning. When teachers—or anyone, for that matter—are approached in this manner, they are more willing to commit time and energy to the change process.

Ultimately, exemplary leadership in this environment of standards-based results-driven school accountability will create a sense of excitement about teaching and learning within the school and community by focusing on the hopes, dreams, and expectations of the students, their parents, and the community. The effective educational leader will be able to shift the focus from external mandates to internal commitment for creating an educational system that will enable all students to achieve the academic and personal goals deemed important by their communities.

"There are many persons ready to do what is right because, in their hearts, they know it is right. But they hesitate, waiting for the other fellow to make the first move—and he, in turn, waits for you."

*— Marian Anderson
1st African-American
singer to perform
with the Metropoli-
tan Opera*

STEP THREE: ADOPTING A COMMON LANGUAGE OF CHANGE

Noted author Peter Block says that if you want to change an organization, you must start by changing the conversation within the organization. To create a new conversation, you must achieve two goals: First, you will need to select a model or framework for school reform. There are many different models, and each represents a different "language" that can be used to ground and sustain the reform conversation. The framework we offer within these pages is based on the integration of three languages: effective schools research, total quality management theory, and systems theory. Second, you will need to develop and implement an action plan to ensure that all stakeholder groups are taught the language.

THE LANGUAGE OF CONTINUOUS SCHOOL IMPROVEMENT

Although it is beyond the scope of this book to provide an in-depth look at the theories that comprise the Effective Schools Continuous Improvement Process, we would like to offer a brief summary of each component theory and highlight the key concepts from each that comprise the "language" of the continuous school improvement process.

> *"First learn the meaning of what you say, and then speak."*
>
> — *Epictetus*
> *Greek Stoic*
> *Philosopher*

Theory #1: The Effective Schools Framework. The Effective Schools philosophy provides the *moral imperative* for the continuous school improvement process. This philosophy, based on decades of research on what makes a school effective, embraces these beliefs:

- **All children can learn and the school controls enough of the variables to assure that virtually all students do learn.** This belief does not say that all children can learn the same day, at the same rate, or in the same way. As a matter of fact, a critical component to successful "learning for all" is the willingness of the school staff to customize and differentiate its services to meet the specific needs of each student.

- **There only two kinds of schools, declining schools and improving schools.** This core belief directly confronts an unspoken assumption held by some educators—the "status quo" school. NCLB and other governmental reform policies have virtually eliminated the status quo option. According to author Jack Bowsher in his book *Fix Schools First,* even the highest achieving schools in the United States have upwards of 30 percent of their students failing to meet the grade-level standards of NCLB. Within this context, a status quo school would be described as a declining school and educators clinging to this concept, misguided.

Obviously, most educators would rather be associated with improvement than decline. When a school embraces this belief, the conversation moves from "Should we seek reform?" to "What reforms should we pursue?" Since time is always a problem, this shift in the conversation is significant.

- **School improvement must take place school-by-school, one school at a time.** Collaborative processes associated with schoolwide configurations work best. While there is a place for districtwide and grade-level conversations, they do not substitute for the school-level conversation. We believe that educational reforms must always be adapted to fit the context of the individual school and its students if they are to be successful and sustained. The need for schoolwide conversation is especially important when schools are struggling to create the vertical and horizontal curriculum alignment demanded by the standards and accountability movement today.

- **The capacity to improve learning already resides inside the school.** Often schools come to believe that the resources needed to change a school reside outside the school. This belief, when unchallenged, seems to provide a level of comfort to those who hold this view, by placing the responsibility for change beyond their control. Certainly, external resources of one sort or another can facilitate the reform effort. Nonetheless, absent external help, there is still virtually no limit to what schools can do to improve if the stakeholders are truly committed to change

- **There are no unimportant adults in a school.** While no one is more important than the teacher in achieving the school's learning mission, a school's culture is indeed created and maintained through the actions of virtually every adult and every role in the school. As a result, the quality of life in a school community is enhanced when all the members of that community understand and accept their roles, rights, and responsibilities. Therefore, the change process, to be effectively and efficiently implemented, must reach out and give voice to all the keepers of the culture to secure their commitment.

Decades of effective schools research have also found that effective schools—schools where all children learn regardless of demographics or disadvantages— have certain characteristics in common. These characteristics have come to be known as the *Correlates of Effective Schools*, and are a critical component of the "language" of the continuous school improvement process. As such, the educational leader seeking to lead this process would do well to become very familiar with the Correlates. To that end, we have provided a brief description of each in Appendix B.

Theory #2: Total Quality Management. This theory is attributed to W. Edwards Deming, a statistician by training, who became one of the world's best-known advocates for quality. His 14-point management model has been used to transform companies throughout the world. There are striking similarities between Deming's 14 Points and the tenets of the Effective Schools theory. The primary concept incorporated into this model of school improvement is that of continuous improvement. Others that are integral pieces of the model include an emphasis on inclusiveness, a focus on mission, and creating an atmosphere of trust, pride, and continuous learning.

> *"Quality is everyone's responsibility."*
>
> — *W. Edwards Deming*
> *Management Expert*

Theory #3: Systems Theory. A system is a collection of parts or subsystems that work together to accomplish the overall aim of the system. Systems have inputs, processes, outputs, and outcomes that are interdependent. If one part of the system is removed or changed, the entire nature of the system is changed. Systems theory is a way to understand the complex world of systems; its primary tool is "systems thinking."

By incorporating systems thinking into the continuous school improvement process, those involved are able to view the school or district as more than the sum of its parts, to take a broader perspective that includes the organization's structures, patterns, and events, and the interaction among them. This broad view helps the leader and stakeholders identify the *real* causes of issues and how best to address them. This is absolutely critical, because without clear understanding of the "big picture" of an organization, leaders—and therefore their followers—will focus only on the behaviors and events associated with problems in the school or district, rather than on the systems and structures that caused the problems in the first place.

ORIENTING THE STAKEHOLDERS TO THE MODEL

Whatever model or language system you choose, we cannot overstate the importance of giving deep thought and serious effort to its teaching to the stakeholders. In the end, the quality of the change effort will be enhanced or impeded based on the stakeholders' awareness of and comfort with the change framework that is guiding the reform effort.

> *"Never doubt that a small group of thoughtful, concerned citizens can change the world. Indeed it is the only thing that ever has."*
>
> — *Margaret Mead*
> *Anthropologist &*
> *Scientist*

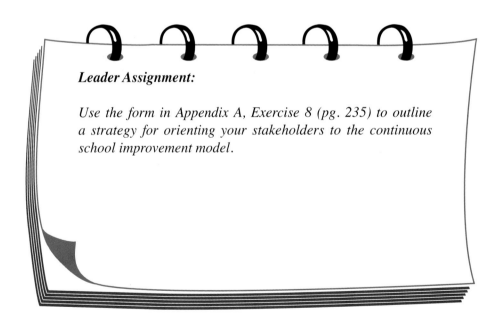

Leader Assignment:

Use the form in Appendix A, Exercise 8 (pg. 235) to outline a strategy for orienting your stakeholders to the continuous school improvement model.

STEP FOUR: STRUCTURING COLLABORATIVE PROCESSES

While engagement, involvement, and collaboration are essential to sustainable school or district change, they do not occur spontaneously. The leader must give serious thought to designing the systems and structures necessary to create and sustain these critical elements to support the reform effort over the long haul. The following process, while oriented to the Effective Schools Continuous School Improvement Process, would be just as applicable if you choose another framework for change.

Create a Leadership Team. Once the stakeholders have become acquainted with the chosen framework and have agreed on the need for change, the leader should now create a structure that gives various stakeholder groups an ongoing voice in the process. An extremely successful strategy has been the development of a leadership team that includes representatives of the various stakeholder groups. The process used to select members of the team should be thought out very carefully, because the leadership team will provide the engine for sustainable change. Its credibility, and the credibility of the process used to select its members, is crucial to the team's ability to lead the change process. If the stakeholders perceive the selection process as suspect, the work of the team will be as well. We would recommend that the leader avoid hand-picking team members, and instead employ a more democratic process.

On the other hand, you will want to have some input into the membership of the leadership team to ensure that the team is comprised of individuals who can take a positive attitude toward the school and a new change effort, is representative of all the stakeholder groups, and include individuals who are the opinion leaders in the school. The aims of stakeholder ownership, representativeness, and effective leadership may seem at cross-purposes, but it is possible to accommodate all these goals.

> *"In the long history of humankind (and animal-kind, too), those who learned to collaborate and improvise most effectively have prevailed."*
>
> — *Charles Darwin*
> *Naturalist*

Leader Assignment:

Use the following process to identify individuals with the skills and interests that will contribute to an effective leadership team, while promoting ownership of the team and the process among the stakeholders.

- *Identify the stakeholder groups that must be represented on the team.*

- *Choose the size of your team (we recommend no more than 8-10 individuals).*

- *Allot a specific number of slots per stakeholder group, making sure that you have included yourself as a member of the team.*

- *Compile a list of potential team members, making sure that all relevant stakeholder groups are represented and keeping in mind the qualities you are looking for in an effective team member and diversity of membership as far as age, race, new/experienced teachers, etc. You may also want to request volunteers or nominations from the "floor."*

- *Contact individuals concerning their interest in being part of the team. Convey the responsibilities and opportunities of team membership. Explain the process and gauge their interests in being on the team.*

- *The resulting pool of individuals would provide a solid slate of "interested individuals" from which stakeholder groups can choose. The stakeholders will then choose the appropriate number of representatives (For example, faculty may have 4 slots on the team and have 7 or 8 interested individuals from which to choose.) As the leader, you are automatically a member of the team.*

Widen the Circle of Involvement.
Depending on the size of the school or district, we would suggest that the leadership team use a professional learning community, study group model for involving additional stakeholders. If the school or district is quite small, the leadership team may wish to involve everyone in all conversations, operating as a "committee of the whole." For more typical schools or districts, the leadership team should consider creating additional stakeholder study groups. In the Effective Schools Continuous School Improvement framework, a study group is formed around each of the seven Correlates of Effective Schools.

Here are a few other procedural suggestions for structuring a collaborative and inclusive process around a leadership team model:

- Make it clear that the leadership team is responsible and accountable for the overall improvement system. As the correlate teams collect data, frame problems, and formulate suggestions, they will take their recommendations to the leadership team so they can coordinate the overall effort.

- The leadership team should design and announce an open, two-way communication system so that all interested parties have up-to-date information on the deliberations of the other correlate teams. Correlate teams should be encouraged to meet with other teams when there is a sense that such cross-team discussions would be beneficial.

- Adopt a policy that all meetings of the leadership team and the correlate teams are to be open to all interested members of the community. The time and place of all meetings should be posted in the school calendar so that interested colleagues can choose to attend.

- Via e-mail or hard copy format, all members of the primary stakeholder community should receive the notes on the deliberations of each correlate team as well as the leadership team. Furthermore, the members of the school community should be given the opportunity to ask questions or otherwise provide comment and feedback to the various study groups.

Create Time for the Reform Effort. One of the common complaints that school staffs make regarding collaborative efforts to create sustainable school reform is that there is no time to meet. As the educational leader, this is the first "test" you will encounter. As we said in Chapter 2, followers look to the leader to determine what's important and what's not. If you do not ensure that time is available for the reform effort, you are sending a message about the importance of the task. Therefore, the leader needs to anticipate and address this concern even before it gets raised.

Leader Assignment:

- *Carefully scrutinize the current school calendar to determine what time is currently dedicated to the school reform process.*

- *If available time is not adequate, carefully study the calendar to see of other time-consuming activities can be abandoned or modified to free up more time that could be dedicated to the school improvement change process.*

- *Finally, it may be necessary for the leader to solicit creative or extraordinary means for creating more time for the teams to meet. Over the years we have been amazed at the creativity that leaders and school staff members when it came to finding time to do the important work of continuous school improvement.*

EFFECTIVE TEAMS DON'T "JUST HAPPEN"

There is a vast operational difference between a committee and a team. Although both are groups of people who are brought together for a purpose, committees often fail to accomplish anything because there are no clearly defined roles and expectations. Therefore, little progress is made, the group flounders, and its members lose interest. On an effective team, however, everyone knows what they are supposed to do and are accountable for getting it done. This means taking the time to establish specific written roles complete with job descriptions. This way, team members clearly understand how their activities contribute to the achievement of the team's mission.

Even with a clear aim and specific roles, many teams falter because the members lacked the skills necessary to work effectively and efficiently as a team, or to lead the school improvement process. Therefore, you as the leader must ensure that team members are adequately trained in both the individual skills necessary to become an effective team participant, and on the continuous school improvement process itself. The individual skills team members should have are further discussed in our previous publication, *Assembly Required: A Continuous School Improvement System*, and exercises are provided for developing team skills in its companion *Implementation Guide*. Both publications also provide an excellent training tool and step-by-step guide for leadership teams as they seek to guide the continuous school improvement process.

> *"The leaders who work most effectively, it seems to me, never say 'I.' And that's not because they have trained themselves not to say 'I.' They* think *'we'; they* think *'team.' They understand their job [is] to make the team function. They accept responsibility and don't sidestep it, but 'we' gets the credit. . . . This is what creates trust, what enables you to get the task done."*
>
> — *Peter Drucker*
> *Organizational*
> *Management Expert*

DISSENSION IN THE RANKS: PERCEPTION IS THE KEY

When it comes to education and the schooling of our children, we are bound to have some level of disagreement among various stakeholders. As we discussed in Chapter 3, it is not uncommon for the anchors of the educational system to have competing and conflicting aims. Leaders who utilize the collaborative process outlined earlier will go a long way toward anticipating and heading off dissension among the stakeholder groups.

A research article published in *The Harvard Business Review* confirmed the importance of process in obtaining and keeping the support key stakeholders, even when they did not "get their way" on certain aspects of the change effort. In their research, the authors, W. Chan Kim and Renee Mauborgne, found that leaders can still count on the support of the followers who didn't get their way *if the process was perceived as fair process.*

The researchers identified three critical attributes that were associated with a fair process. First, the followers expect the leaders to clearly explain why change is needed. Our process discussed earlier addresses this attribute. Second, the leaders must make every effort to describe what changes will be expected of the followers. This attribute cannot be fully addressed until specific change plans are completed and the action plans developed. (More on this point later.) The third attribute judged to be important by the followers is that they had a voice in the discussions.

Democracy is not about always having your way; it is often about having your say. Thus, a key leader behavior is to listen to colleagues as they come to terms with the issues associated with the change. The engagement process outlined earlier is one example of being given "voice" in the change discussion. The continuous school improvement process provides many opportunities for stakeholders to engage in productive dialogue. Such dialogue leads to an increased commitment to change. As we move toward implementation of specific continuous improvement processes and strategies, we will identify additional opportunities for stakeholders to provide input and feedback.

The researchers point out that while fair process is important in any system, "fair process can have an even greater impact on the quality of professional and managerial work. That is because innovation is the key challenge of the knowledge-based economy, and innovation requires the exchange of ideas, which in turn depends on trust." It is easy to see, then, how critical the perception of fair process is in our system of schooling. Successful and continuous school improvement is, by its nature, a collaborative process. Because involvement builds commitment, stakeholders—staff, parents, and students—must be engaged in some way in every step of the process. Changes that are required must be clearly explained so that everyone understands how decisions were made and why. Finally, teachers, students, and parents must know what the changes mean to them, what they will be required to do, and how their performances will be judged.

Unfortunately, many schools and school districts have yet to understand the concept of fair process. Change is still handed down from the central office, or perhaps the principal's office. Why is this so, when the concept of fair process seems so simple? One explanation is that managers often confuse fair *process* with fair *outcomes*. They think that by giving resources or rewards, people will be satisfied. Another is the managerial view that knowledge is power, and to share power is to lose control.

Until schools and school districts embrace the idea of fair process, which in fact mirrors the democratic ideals we are trying to instill in our students, effective and sustainable school improvement will continue to be out of reach.

To do this, everyone involved in the education of our young people must take a "leap of faith" and trust the process of continuous improvement, even if initially stakeholder groups don't trust one another. This research shows that fair process—which is strikingly similar to the continuous improvement process—can bring even traditionally adversarial groups together in pursuit of the common good. As Kim and Mauborgne so aptly point out, "Fair process builds trust and commitment, trust and commitment produce voluntary cooperation, and voluntary cooperation drives performance, leading people to go beyond the call of duty by sharing their knowledge and applying their creativity." And where is this needed more than in our public schools? And what more important role for you as a leader than helping the followership take that "leap" and transcend politics and self-interests to work toward the best interests of our children?

We cannot stress this concept enough: Whoever is not "in" on what you're proposing to do in the beginning, will likely be "down on it" later. In addition, they will "attack" your efforts at a time and place of their own choosing, most likely at the most inopportune time. As an effective leader, you must try to anticipate where the resistance is likely to come from and head it off through involvement processes and other engagement strategies. If the processes you put in place represent a good-faith effort to solicit broad-based input from the full range of stakeholders, most will buy into the process, even if there are still areas where they disagree.

"Public sentiment is everything. With public sentiment, nothing can fail; without it, nothing can succeed. He who molds public sentiment goes deeper than he who enacts statutes or decisions possible or impossible to execute."

— Abraham Lincoln
16th President of
the United States

INTENTIONAL LEADERSHIP

By now you've no doubt ascertained that you must be very intentional in structuring the collaborative processes that are essential to sustainable school improvement. The team approach, while sometimes frustrating and always time-consuming, will yield many benefits that simply handing out assignments and orders will not:

- **Alignment of People.** Aligning people means getting people lined up behind the vision and moving in the same direction. When everyone is aligned, individuals across all disciplines focus their attention and activities on the same goal through different strategies and interventions. For example, in schools with a focus on literacy, every department, grade level, and teacher must do whatever necessary to contribute to the literacy goal. They may use different approaches, but everyone is working on the same goal. Aligning people with the vision, mission, and a set of strategies helps produce the changes needed to cope with the changing environment.

- **Creation of a Positive Culture.** Working together as a team with all the positive connotations that are associated with that term—as opposed to working on a "committee," which, in many instances, may have negative connotations—will produce more positive results. Individuals typically volunteer for a team, are proud to be a member of a team, have a common focus, assume various roles and responsibilities as a member of the team, support each other as team players, and share in the team successes, victories, or wins. Working together as a team to improve student achievement will bring the same satisfaction, gratification, and rewards—not only to the team members, but to the students as well.

- **Leadership Development.** The team approach outlined here gives participants an opportunity to build, expand, and demonstrate their leadership skills. Increased involvement and shared decision-making can help the leader cope with a loss of resources while building a capacity for change through transformational leadership.

> *"I start with the premise that the function of leadership is to produce more leaders—not more followers."*
>
> — *Ralph Nader*
> *Consumer Rights*
> *Activist*

A LEADER OF LEADERS

Hopefully, we've made the case that effective leadership is fundamental to the continuous school improvement process and to successful change. Conversely, there is a strong correlation between the continuous school improvement process and leadership development. As individuals accept leadership roles such as chairing committees or task forces, conducting surveys, writing position papers and reports, or performing other tasks specific to implementing the school improvement process, they are, in fact, developing the skills required to be effective leaders. Leadership development among the staff is especially important, as they are the closest to the "action" and can, through formal and informal means, influence their colleagues, as well as students and their parents.

Teacher-leaders have the ability to go beyond the classroom, to utilize current research, to influence colleagues in the pursuit of positive change, and are teaching advocates. These teachers have the potential for bringing about significant change, literally transforming the school. Teacher leadership ranges on a continuum from formal—such as career ladders, lead teachers, department heads, and mentors—to informal leadership, frequently based on expertise and interests.

Interestingly, as strong an influence as you as leader have on your followers, individuals who rise to the leadership challenge will affect how you lead. Researcher Kirk D. Anderson found that there is a mutual influence between teacher-leaders and their principals. He refers to the effect that principals and teacher-leaders have upon one other—that is, shared leadership with each party influencing the other—as *leadership reciprocity*. Leaders must rely on a follower, which makes them dependent as well as dominant. Yet teachers, and especially teacher-leaders, also influence the principal and rely on the principal for direction and support. There are three models of mutual influence, or leadership reciprocity, which were reflected in the data from this study.

- **The Buffered Model.** In this model, the principal is close to the teacher-leaders, but isolated from the rest of the teachers in the school. In this situation, the teacher-leaders serve as a buffer for the principal, insulating him/her from outside influences. Frequently this is done by representatives of committees, chairpersons, and department heads. This model's sole reliance on a small group of people for vision and feedback limits the engagement and commitment of other teachers, as well as other stakeholders beyond the staff.

- **The Interactive Model.** The Interactive Model of reciprocal leadership is one in which the principal will interact with all staff. It is the principal who distributes decision-making in a manner that is interactive and extensively involves all teachers. Formal and informal teacher-leaders interact successfully. In this model, teachers have broad involvement in school decision-making as teacher-leaders. Teacher-leaders in this type of school recognize the need for many voices to be heard. The principal is visible and accessible to all staff without stifling their creativity or trying to control their deliberations. This model promotes transformational leadership by both formal and informal teacher-leaders.

- **The Contested Model.** In the Contested Model of teacher leadership, the principal is frequently buffeted by formal teacher-leaders, who may also be department heads. These teachers often try to usurp decision-making from the principal. These formal leaders are strong enough to prevent the rest of the staff from challenging them and the principal is unable to resolve this dilemma. This model does not provide a healthy context to initiate change. Furthermore, these formal leaders are of special concern because how they use

their formal leadership roles can in fact constrain teacher leadership. In these schools, informal teacher leadership is discouraged and transformational leadership nonexistent.

Clearly, this study shows that teacher leadership is a complex issue. In this study, some formal teacher-leaders actually impeded the broader distribution of decision-making and teacher leadership by occasionally excluding groups or individuals from leadership roles. This type of teacher-leader behavior may also reflect some of the traditional bias toward women and young teachers. In another study, formal leadership roles were also found to inhibit other leadership potential on the faculty by squelching women teachers and younger, less-experienced teachers, who often possess leader characteristics and behaviors that result in transformational leadership practices.

Does this mean that we should abandon any formal structure for our teaching faculty and the change process? Given that we just recommended creating a leadership team, this may seem contradictory to the research presented here. But remember, our recommended model represents *all* stakeholders and our process of recruiting members asks you look beyond formal titles and roles to ensure a diverse and balanced membership. It also promotes widening the circle of involvement beyond the leadership team.

As a leader, it is up to you to create a process and structure that circumvents the inertia of the system, not further entrenches it. As the leader, it is up to you to draw out the talents of other leaders within the school. This is critical, according to Deborah Childs-Bowen, Gayle Moller, and Jennifer Scrivner, if a school is "to stay afloat, assume internal responsibility for reform, and maintain a momentum for self-renewal." In their article, "Principals: Leaders of Leaders," they suggest that principals can engender leadership by creating opportunities for leadership, building professional learning communities, and providing professional development to help potential leaders develop necessary skills. One often overlooked strategy for encouraging leadership in others is recognition and praise of initial leadership efforts.

As Anderson discovered through his research of teacher-leaders and principals, the principal who adopts the Interactive Model of teacher leadership has the best chance of blending both informal and formal teacher leadership roles, to create a climate of collegiality where leadership is nurtured and encouraged from every individual, regardless of age, title, experience, or gender. To make this form of leadership happen, you must first spend time reflecting on your personal beliefs about leadership and the empowerment of others. You must be comfortable with shared management, open and honest two-way communication, trust building, and the use of personal power to influence others. You must be willing to focus on "we" rather than "I." Your success in doing so will be crucial to successful and sustainable school reform while meeting such challenges as declining enrollment and limited resources.

> *"The key to successful leadership today is influence, not authority."*
>
> — *Ken Blanchard*
> *Management Expert*
> *and Author*

Leader Assignment:

Reflect upon the leadership reciprocity models presented. Which of Anderson's models best reflect how your school operates? Have you surrounded yourself with a few key individuals who insulate you from the rest of the staff? If so, think about the processes outlined above and how you can use them to become more accessible to the staff and other stakeholders. Does the current formal leadership structure impede the leadership initiative of others? If so, think about how the process can help you change or circumvent the structure of the system so that everyone can be involved in the change effort in a meaningful way.

Continuous school improvement based the effective schools research has a long and proud history of improving student achievement when the research and the processes of change are implemented with fidelity and sustained over time. We have found that when schools adopt a common language and take steps to assure that all stakeholders are grounded in that language, the essential ingredients for improvement are at hand. When we empower an ever-enlarging conversation of school change by engaging a leadership team and other "study groups," the essential processes for continuous learning and change begin to stir. Finally, when the system provides the time for the teams to meet and learn how to learn together, the momentum for sustainable change steadily builds.

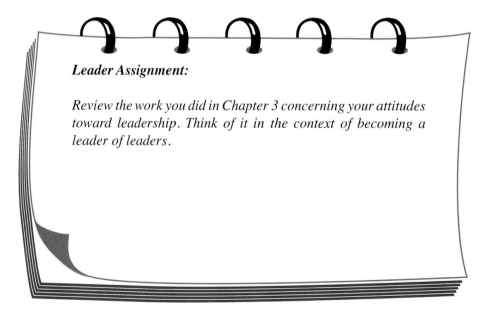

Leader Assignment:

Review the work you did in Chapter 3 concerning your attitudes toward leadership. Think of it in the context of becoming a leader of leaders.

5

CREATING A SHARED VISION AND VALUES BASE FOR REFORM

The stakeholders are now clear about what problems need to be solved and why, the problem has been framed, the language taught, and a collaborative process is in place. The next step will be to bring the stakeholders together to create a common vision of the specific future we are trying to create, and to clarify and articulate the core beliefs and values upon which the school or district will operate.

Effective leaders begin with the end in mind and design down. Because few schools and districts are starting from scratch, we've found that a useful metaphor is that of remodeling an existing home. What would be the first step in remodeling an existing home?

Before the development of new blueprints, the architect will need to clarify and codify what the homeowners want to preserve in the existing home and what new or different features they want to be incorporated into the remodeling. In other words, the architect will elicit the homeowner's *vision* for the home. The experienced architect will guide the homeowners in

their decisions, reminding them of local code requirements, logistics, costs, deed restrictions, and other considerations the homeowners might otherwise forget. If we see the homeowners as stakeholders and the architect as the leader, we can see how critical it is that the leader oversees the clarification and codification of the parameters of the "remodeled" school. As leader, it will be your job to guide the process, reminding stakeholders of issues and requirements they may otherwise overlook, and helping diverse groups find common ground: a vision, a mission, and a set of core beliefs and values around which everyone can focus their efforts.

> "Dream lofty dreams, and as you dream, so shall you become. Your Vision is the promise of what you shall one day be. Your Ideal is the prophecy of what you shall at last unveil."
>
> — James Allen
> New Zealand
> Statesman

95

FIRST THINGS, FIRST: KEEPING ENDS AND MEANS SEPARATE

Peter Senge, author of *The Fifth Discipline*, and other systems theorists speak about the Double-Loop Learning Model. The model resembles a figure eight; the top "loop" is associated with mission, beliefs, and values and the bottom is associated with tactics, strategies, and behaviors. We've adapted that model to incorporate the larger context within which educational leaders must work and have presented it on the following page.

Senge asserts that most of the problems with which organizations struggle are rooted in the top loop. Over the years, our observations of effective and not-so-effective schools agree with Senge's assertion. Most schools that cannot seem to make the needed improvements lack a fundamental vision for change, and a shared foundation of core values and beliefs. For example, many teachers believe that the solution to any learning problem in their school can be found by adopting a new program. A new program represents new tactics, strategies and behaviors. But a program that isn't based on a common vision, or that emanates from a shared set of values and beliefs is doomed to fail.

> *"Where there is no vision, there is no hope."*
>
> — *George Washington Carver*
> *American Agriculturist*

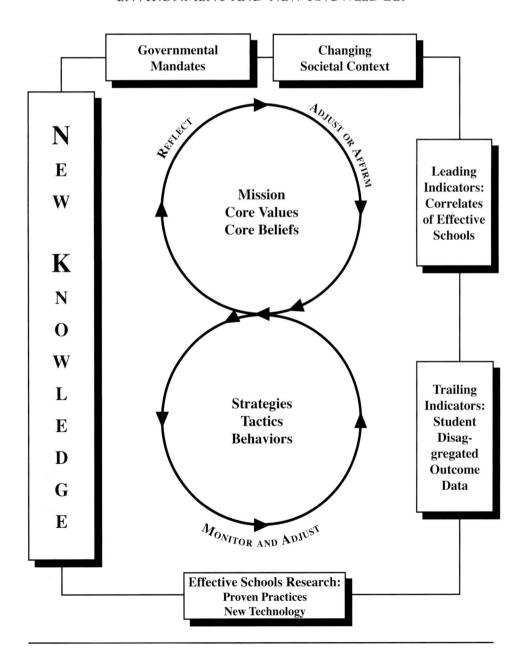

ADAPTED DOUBLE-LOOP LEARNING MODEL WITHIN THE CONTEXT OF THE CHANGING EDUCATIONAL ENVIRONMENT AND NEW KNOWLEDGE.

Without Foundation: Change Without A Shared Vision

A 2003 study published in the *American Educational Research Journal* details how one district and elementary school responded to the pressure to improve student achievement quickly without taking the time to create a foundation of shared values and beliefs, and a common vision for change. In this study, the researcher used a case-study approach to determine how and why an urban Texas district and one of its elementary schools altered their policies and practices in response to the Texas Accountability System's *Student Success Initiative* (SSI), which requires third-grade students to pass a reading test before being promoted to fourth grade.

This study by Jennifer Booher-Jennings took place at Beck Elementary, a pre-K through fifth-grade school located in a poor urban neighborhood in the Brickland Independent School District. Most Beck students are Hispanic and more than 90% qualify for free or reduced-price lunches. Since 1993, Beck Elementary has received an "acceptable" rating." The school's goal was to reach a "recognized" rating, which requires that more than 80% of students pass the state test. This had been a source of great frustration for the teachers and administration.

Since the beginning of the Texas Accountability System, data-driven decision-making has been the distinctive characteristic of school districts that improved their test scores. But for the Brickland School District, only one kind of data mattered: student scores on Texas Assessment of Knowledge and Skills (TAKS) assessment. The Brickland District so emphasized the importance of high passing rates, that "good teaching" became synonymous with the percentage of students passing benchmark and TAKS tests. In fact, to motivate teachers, the district began publicizing individual teachers' class scores. This created a competitive school environment in which teachers began to question their colleagues' competence and commitment, undermining the collegiality and relational trust so necessary to the learning-for-all mission. According to the author of the study, the conflict between raising the school's scores and competition between colleagues "put a very real strain on teachers' relationships and on the school as a community."

The district's emphasis on pass rates also affected teaching at Beck. Students are given three tries to pass the TAKS. Students who score 70% or higher on the TAKS are identified as "passers," students scoring 60-69% are designated "bubble kids," and students who score below 60%

are considered to be "foundation" or "remedial" kids. The researcher describes how, after each benchmark test, Beck teachers established a target of students who would pass the next test and allocated their resources to the students they believed would most likely improve the school's aggregate score: the bubble kids. This is based on the assumption that the bubble kids would become "passers." In addition, low-performing students were tested to determine if they qualified for special education status, which removed them from the "accountability subset." (As a result, the percentage of special education students has doubled since the inception of the accountability system.) The array of strategies used to increase the school's test scores was described as a form of "'educational triage" by the study's author, a practice which resulted in the lowest scoring students receiving the least attention since they were considered "hopeless cases."

How could this happen? Why, the author asks, "would teachers systematically and actively privilege some students at the expense of others. . . . given that no rewards or sanctions were attached to the performance of teachers' classes, nor were test scores an integral part of teachers' annual evaluations?" Both the Brickland School District and Beck teachers responded to

the requirements of the Texas Accountability System *by doing what they thought was right* to achieve high passing rates on the TAKS. However, by focusing solely on aggregate pass rates, the Brickland District ended up creating an institutional culture that embraced data as an end in and of itself, and not simply the means to accomplishing a greater goal. Because the district equated good teaching only with high pass rates, and even went so far as to publicize class scores, teachers who wanted to be viewed as "good" implemented "educational triage," sacrificing some students in the name of improving the school's TAKS scores. This practice, in effect, subverted the real intent of the standards and accountability system—educating all children, regardless of demographics or disability.

It is ironic that the very practice that the Texas Accountability System was designed to eliminate, providing assistance only to certain students, became institutionalized by Brickland's version of data-driven decision-making. Furthermore, as a result of the district's distorted implementation of data-decision making, it's myopic focus on raising TAKS scores, and its emphasis on promoting competition among teachers, collaborative and collegial relationships between and among teachers suffered greatly. This is unfortunate because decades of research shows that to improve student learning—and as a result, student scores on standardized measures of achievement—it is vital that schools appropriately use data-driven decision-making, and work collectively and collaboratively to ensure that *all* students make steady academic progress, not just the "bubble kids." To do so, educational leaders, teachers, and all stakeholders must have a common vision and mission for their students *beyond external mandates*, as well as a shared set of core values and beliefs through which external mandates are interpreted and implemented.

The moral of this story is this: Despite the urgency to improve student scores and the pressure to "do something," you as the leader must resist the impulse to short-circuit the discussions around mission, beliefs, and values and go directly to a discussion of new and different tactics, strategies, and behaviors. Because, as this study shows, only when you and your followers have a shared vision and a core set of values and beliefs to guide our reform efforts, will you be able to do the "right thing" in the "right way" for the "right reasons." Once you are clear about where the organization is attempting to go and the values and beliefs framework to guide the effort is in place, only then will you be able to select the tactics, strategies, and behaviors that are aligned with the organization's mission, core values, and core beliefs.

Leader Assignment:

Reflect on how the standards and accountability movement has affected your school and/or district. How are you, as the leader, interpreting those to the stakeholders? Are you approaching the learning-for-all mission as a mandate imposed from the powers-that-be that requires compliance, or as a moral imperative? Are you focusing on student learning, or on adult teaching?

"Could we change our attitude, we should not only see life differently, but life itself would come to be different. Life would undergo a change of appearance because we ourselves had undergone a change of attitude."

— Katherine Mansfield
Author

CRITICAL CORE BELIEFS AND VALUES

While the core beliefs and values will vary somewhat from school to school, or district to district, certain critical core beliefs and values must underpin the continuous school improvement effort if it is to be successful. Often, they are the most difficult for the school or district to agree upon because they challenge long-held norms of behaviors and beliefs. As the leader, it is up to you to promote the values that will ensure that the change effort is successful.

> *"Out of our beliefs are born deeds."*
>
> — *Henry Hancock*
> *English Surgeon*

All children can learn and deserve the opportunity to do so. It has come to be accepted as axiomatic that low-SES children often begin school at a deficit in comparison to their more affluent counterparts. Particularly for faculties that teach in schools with large numbers of disadvantaged children, it may seem next-to-impossible to overcome the backgrounds of these children. And yet, decades of research show that many schools with high proportions of poor and disadvantaged children have successfully fulfilled the learning-for-all mission. Armed with stories from these successful schools, you as the leader must tell your "strategic story" to get everyone to embrace this belief. Some of the followers may only "go through the motions" and not really believe that all children can learn. For some of these individuals, as they see positive results from their behaviors, they will come to internalize this belief statement. Some will never embrace the learning-for-all mission. Then you will be faced with a different challenge, that of determining whether those individuals can function as part of your organization.

This is the fundamental belief that everyone associated with the school or district must embrace. Without this belief to guide our efforts, some students will be overlooked and left out as a school focuses on the "bubble kids" like in the example presented earlier.

Leader Assignment:

Find research that supports the belief that all children can learn. One study you might review was conducted by Karl L. Alexander, Doris R. Entwisle, and Linda S. Olsen, called "Schools, Achievement and Inequality: A Seasonal Perspective," published in the Summer 2001 issue of Educational Evaluation and Policy Analysis. It is also summarized in the Effective Schools Research LiNK, an online comprehensive archive of school improvement research abstracts. This tool is further described in the Appendix.

Collaboration is "how we do things around here." Research shows, again and again, that in effective schools—schools where all students learn the essential curriculum—administrators and teachers understand the importance of a collaborative culture. Since teaching has historically been an isolated activity, creating a collaborative culture won't happen overnight in most schools. The key to successful collaboration within a school or district is a laser-like focus on meeting student needs and supporting each other as educational colleagues. A collaborative culture is self-reinforcing as teachers form strong bonds with each other as they work to improve curricula and instruction. New teachers find support and guidance, while veteran teachers assist one another with problems, further reinforcing the atmosphere of collegiality and collaboration. It is up to you as the leader to establish and nurture both the expectation and the processes that the followers will work collectively and collaboratively *and* to model this behavior. Remember, the leader has to "walk the talk."

> *"Example is not the main thing in influencing others, it is the only thing."*
>
> — *Albert Schweitzer*
> *Doctor, Theologian*
> *& Missionary*

I can, we can. Everyone involved in the change effort has to feel as though they have the capacity to organize and execute the actions required to ensure that all children learn. Educational researchers call this "individual efficacy." This concept is also a key component of the Effective Schools Correlate of High Expectations for Student Success. A great deal of research has been done on both student and teacher sense of efficacy and the evidence is clear: both have an influence on behaviors, such as level of effort and persistence in the face of obstacles, and ultimately on student achievement. Logic reinforces this idea, that teachers, administrators, parents, and students alike must believe they have the capacity to improve, change, and do the things to successfully fulfill their responsibilities.

There is another aspect of efficacy according to researchers Roger Goddard, Wayne Hoy, and Anita Woolfolk Hoy, and that is "collective efficacy." Collective efficacy is the belief of the school's faculty and staff as to the capability of the school as a whole. It in fact asks this question: Does the school community, as a collective of individuals, believe that they can organize and execute the actions required to produce the expected performance outcomes now and in the future? Using an indicator specific to perceived collective efficacy—"How I feel about the school's ability to accomplish the task."—the researchers found that perceived collective efficacy varied greatly among schools and that this construct was a strong and positive predictor of student achievement.

The importance of a sense of collective efficacy to student achievement makes it incumbent upon you as the leader to consider it in the scheme of things when it comes to the change effort. It is up to you to do whatever is necessary to reinforce the followers' belief that they can, as individuals and as a group, ensure student learning.

> *"If I have the belief that I can do it, I shall surely acquire the capacity to do it, even if I may not have it at the beginning."*
>
> — *Mahatma Gandhi*
> *Spiritual &*
> *Political Leader*

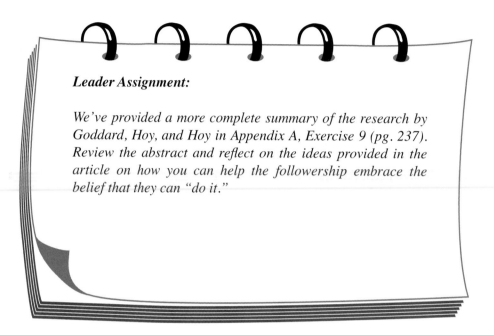

Leader Assignment:

We've provided a more complete summary of the research by Goddard, Hoy, and Hoy in Appendix A, Exercise 9 (pg. 237). Review the abstract and reflect on the ideas provided in the article on how you can help the followership embrace the belief that they can "do it."

CLARIFYING MISSION, CORE BELIEFS, AND CORE VALUES

There are many ways to structure the discussion about mission, beliefs, and values. Surveys are one way to get insightful data from the stakeholders around these issues. This is a first good task for the leadership team. Once data is collected and analyzed, you and the leadership team should plan a series of focus groups with interested stakeholders to discuss the results and "give voice to the data." These discussions will ensure everyone is on the same page, and give diverse groups a way to come to consensus.

The instruments you used to clarify your own vision, beliefs, and values could be adapted to elicit input from the stakeholders. Or, you can create your own surveys and instruments, or use the process and worksheets provided in *Assembly Required: A Continuous Improvement System* and its companion *Implementation Guide*. You can also create surveys using a variety of software products including *Reality Check*, an easy-to-use online survey tool created specifically for schools interested in continuous school improvement. More information on these tools is available in Appendix C.

MORE THAN WORDS

Your role as the leader is not only to guide this process, but to ensure that the mission statement doesn't become just another well-meaning, largely ignored document. Simply by using an inclusive process to create the beliefs and values statement and the mission statement, you will have taken the first step towards this end. Lew Allen, in his article, "From Plaques to Practice: How Schools Can Breathe Life Into Their Guiding Beliefs," makes several more suggestions on how leaders can maintain the mission as a living, breathing, useful document:

- Once a mission statement is developed, leaders should initiate an ongoing dialogue that deepens the stakeholders' understanding about it. Without such conversation, people will believe that their current actions reflect the mission without giving it another thought. Leaders should evaluate every school program, policy, and procedure in light of whether it furthers the school or district's mission.

- Leaders must ensure that the mission guides every discussion and debate among

the stakeholders of the school or district. By using the actual language of the guiding statements (both beliefs and mission), you'll leave no doubt in anyone's mind of their primary importance as the foundation for action.

> *"The strength of a man's virtue should not be measured by his special exertions, but by his habitual acts."*
>
> — *Blaise Pascal*
> *French Physicist*
> *& Mathematician*

This process of clarifying mission, beliefs, and values is an excellent method for you to build energy and commitment around the reform process. However, this process does not—and should not—ask the stakeholders to identify the *means* to achieve the desired ends. Just as the contractor and his/her staff design the specific blueprints for the home remodeling project, the plan to create the desired outcomes will be crafted by smaller, representative groups of dedicated and knowledgeable stakeholders. However, the larger groups should be kept well informed about the development of the reform plans as they evolve and given a myriad of opportunities to review and comment, so that you can keep them both engaged and committed. Following through on your commitment to stakeholder involvement will be seen by the followers as a fundamental test of your trustworthiness as a leader. Therefore, you will need to develop and utilize an ongoing communication system that gives all stakeholders the opportunity to stay informed about and engaged in the reform process.

Now that you've framed the problem, articulated a vision and a set of core values and fundamental beliefs, and earned stakeholder support, you are well on your way to creating a framework for successful and sustainable change that will lead to improved learning for every child. Now you must guide your school or district as they determine what every child should learn.

6

LEADING FOR LEARNING FOR ALL

By this point, you will have engaged the collaborative processes, and guided the followers in defining a common mission and set of core beliefs and values. Now you have come to the point of translating all that has gone before into a curriculum and instructional program. The basic assumption of this next step is that if students master the curriculum they are going to be taught, they will leave the system prepared for success at the next level. In the case of the high school, this would mean that students will graduate prepared for success in either post-secondary education or the world of work. In the case of the middle school, this means that students leave prepared with the prerequisite knowledge and skills for success in high school. In the case of the elementary school, students will leave prepared for success at the middle school. While this seems obvious, meeting these challenges represent one of the greatest leadership challenges that educational leaders will confront.

> *"Leaders establish the vision for the future and set the strategy for getting there. They cause change. They motivate and inspire others to go in the right direction and they, along with everyone else, sacrifice to get there."*
>
> — *John Kotter*
> *Leadership Expert*

The Need for Instructional Leadership

If you look through the existing literature on leadership, you will find that researchers have defined many forms of leadership. Throughout the beginning chapters of this book, we've emphasized transformational leadership—how you as a leader can inspire positive change in and by others, by engaging in certain leader behaviors that cause the followers to commit to a common vision. But what of the concept of Instructional Leadership? How does this concept differ from transformational leadership? Are they mutually exclusive, the same thing, or complimentary approaches that can be integrated? Fortunately, researchers Helen Marks and Susan Pinty help clarify these two leadership concepts and shed light on the role they play in school success.

Marks and Printy describe transformational leadership as providing intellectual direction aimed at innovation within an organization. Instructional leadership involves "the active collaboration of principal and teachers on curriculum, instruction, and assessment." Describing the limitations of both concepts, Marks and Printy suggest that, "while transformational leadership is necessary for reform-oriented school improvement, it is insufficient to achieve high-quality teaching and learning." Yet, in the absence of developing a mission-centered, performance-centered, and culture-centered community by the principal, instructional leadership is rendered aimless or without purpose. Thus, the researchers designed a study to test their hypothesis that an integration of shared instructional and transformational leadership would result in substantial student learning achievement.

Through their research, Marks and Printy found that the most effective schools were characterized by integrated leadership. In these schools, principals provided strong instructional leadership while they facilitated leadership by the teachers, whom they regarded as professionals and full partners in furthering high-quality teaching and learning. Attributing this to a higher degree of engagement and collaboration between teachers and principal, the researchers found that schools with integrated leadership maintained a concerted focus on curriculum, instruction, and assessment, which is central to student learning and achievement. Not surprisingly, the researchers found that in the schools with integrated leadership, school performance, pedagogical quality, and authentic achievement of students were higher.

Researchers Kerri L. Briggs and Pricilla Wohlstetter reinforce these findings. Their examination of effective site-based school management found that struggling schools "were less likely to focus on teaching and learning in their discussions and instead focused on procedures. . . the content of discussions was much more likely to be about the distribution of power and housekeeping issues and less likely to be about curriculum and instruction." Without a focus on student learning and the resources to act collectively, these schools were unable to create meaningful change.

As the researchers note, both shared instructional leadership *and* transformational leadership are necessary if schools are to improve. We've discussed in depth your role as a transformational leader. Now, as the instructional leader, you must work to assure that the conversation is focused on student learning and success.

> *"If you cry 'Forward,' you must be sure to make clear the direction in which to go."*
>
> — *Anton Chekhov*
> *Russian Dramatist*

BEGIN WITH THE END IN MIND

We have long advocated that the primary role of the teacher is to prepare her/his students for success at the next level. To execute this concept, the system must begin with the end in mind and design back from that end. The instructional program will then be expected to "deliver up." For those who have difficulty relating to the concept of beginning with the end in mind, designing down, and delivering up, let us revisit our home remodeling metaphor.

In the last chapter, we asked the question, "What is the first concrete step that must be completed in remodeling a new home?" We answered this as "the homeowner's vision of the remodeled home." This comprises the homeowner's "dream" home, the ideal. The homeowner's vision might include, among other things, that the remodeled home is cozy and welcoming, with good traffic flow, and spacious enough to accommodate the family's needs. In the continuous school improvement process, our "dream home" translates into the school community's vision, core beliefs, and core values about how we will approach educating our children. Some beliefs and values your school community has embraced may include the following, among others:

We will create a school in which all children can learn; where every member of the learning community will be treated with respect; where we recognize and will accommodate individual learning needs.

Now the school community must define more specifically what the students will learn as they progress through our school system. This is akin to the next step in the remodeling process, creating the blueprints for the finished home.

In the early days of the effective schools movement, we thought schools had a clear vision of what they wanted the students to know and be able to do, and simply lacked the necessary teaching strategies to get students to learn. However, the longer we worked with schools, the more it became clear that many educators either did not know or couldn't clearly articulate what students should learn and be able to do as they moved through the system.

> *"When a man does not know what harbor he is making for, no wind is the right wind."*
>
> — *Seneca*
> *Roman Philosopher*
> *& Statesman*

To some degree, the educational leader's burden regarding what students need to know and do has been made easier by the standards movement. However, the state standards only a partial solution for at least four reasons:

1. State standards are written at a level of generality that don't provide enough guidance for teachers and students.

2. Some state requirements are overloaded with too many standards and therefore, are impossible to teach to a level of mastery in the time available.

3. In some states, the standards appear to have been written by one division and the state assessments of the mastery of those standards by yet another. This apparent lack of alignment is a source of great anxiety and frustration.

4. State standards are often silent on many of the most important educational goals of parents and the local community.

Despite these drawbacks, an articulation of what your students must know and be able to do when they leave your school must begin with a review of the state and district standards.

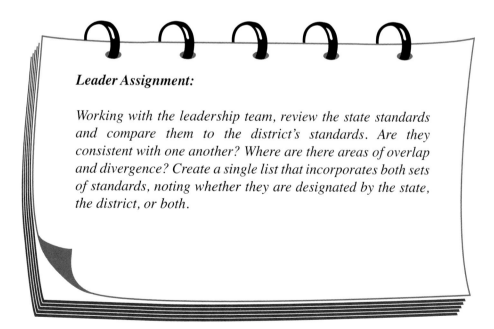

Leader Assignment:

Working with the leadership team, review the state standards and compare them to the district's standards. Are they consistent with one another? Where are there areas of overlap and divergence? Create a single list that incorporates both sets of standards, noting whether they are designated by the state, the district, or both.

Soliciting Stakeholder Input

Once the state and district standards are reviewed, you will need to prompt a discussion with the stakeholders as to their priorities for the students using the collaborative process you've implemented. One school district that we worked with for many years used the following process to find commonalities between and among the district's stakeholder groups. The leader, in conjunction with a collaborative team, invited literally hundreds of parents, educators, business and community leaders, and high school students to a conversation. Heterogeneous groups of six to eight were seated at round tables and asked to answer these questions: *What do the many publics want our students to know, do, and be disposed to do when they graduate from our school system?*

What evidence can or should we collect and monitor to be sure that the students have learned what they need to learn before they graduate?

After gathering, processing, and summarizing the information from these stakeholders, the educational leader not only had a clearer picture of where the system needed to go, but had also earned a great deal of support and commitment from those who were invited to be part of the process. If this sounds like a process of negotiation with and among the stakeholders, you are right. It would be naïve to think that such a diverse group of people will achieve complete consensus. It is not unreasonable, however, to believe that the group will identify areas of common ground, around which there is a high degree of consensus and support.

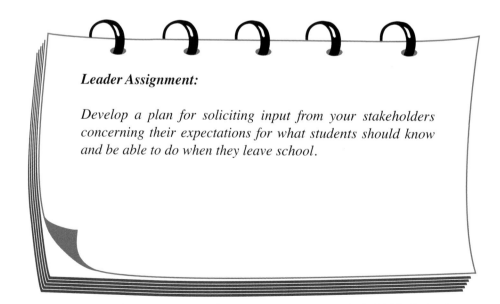

Leader Assignment:

Develop a plan for soliciting input from your stakeholders concerning their expectations for what students should know and be able to do when they leave school.

Merging State, District, and Stakeholder Expectations

State standards generally address content, that is, the core skills and knowledge that all students are expected to attain during their time in public school. Stakeholder expectations generally address issues of character, and are often specific to the community within which the school resides. Stakeholders may want to stress employability skills, or creating well-rounded students, or encourage an appreciation for the arts, in addition to the state-specified content requirements. Like two mountain streams that merge into a larger river, state standards and stakeholder expectations will merge into the intended curriculum.

Going back to our earlier remodeling metaphor, the leader's role here is that of an architect, guiding the process of merging stakeholder priorities with state and district requirements into a coherent set of expectations to which everyone can commit.

"Learning is not attained by chance. It must be sought for with ardor and attended to with diligence."

— *Abigail Adams*
Former First Lady

Merging Expectations

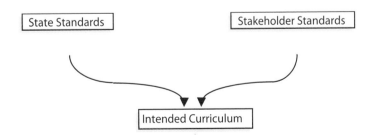

BACKWARD MAPPING OF THE CURRICULUM

Once a consensus has been reached on what the remodeled "home" will look like, the educational leader will trade the architect's hat for the hard hat of the general contractor. It is the general contractor's responsibility to assure that when the carpenters arrive at the job site they have three things. First, the carpenters must have the blueprints that explicitly set forth the job to be completed. Without the blueprints, it would be impossible and unfair to fault the carpenter who chooses to use the raw materials to build bird houses. Second, the carpenters need to have the required knowledge and skills to do the job. Finally, the carpenters need the raw materials needed to do the job.

If we substitute educational leader for the general contractor, and we substitute students and teachers for the carpenters, the identical logic holds. Consider the following statements for their fairness and appropriateness.

- No student in any classroom should have to take up his/her seat without the teacher of that class making it clear what results are expected of that student.

- No teacher in any classroom should have to take up his/her teaching station without the principal of that school making it clear to that teacher what results are expected.

- No principal in any school should have to take up his/her station unless the superintendent, operating as an agent of both the state and the local board of education, has made it clear what results are expected from that school.

Thus, the next step in the process will be to create detailed blueprints for what students should learn from level to level. Creating the blueprints for your school or district will consist of "backward mapping." The following diagram outlines the process beginning at graduation, using the identified standards to determine what a student must learn in 12th grade to be ready for graduation. Once again, your role as leader will be to set up a collaborative process to accomplish this task. One way to do this is to establish committees for each content area and a steering committee made up of representatives from each content area. The steering committee can then deal with issues like literacy or writing across content areas. After the 12th grade knowledge and skills are identified, move "backwards" to the 11th grade to determine what students need to learn to enable them to be successful in the 12th grade. Continue to "backward map" until you have identified what children need to learn from kindergarten through graduation.

BACKWARD MAPPING

Essential Student Learnings

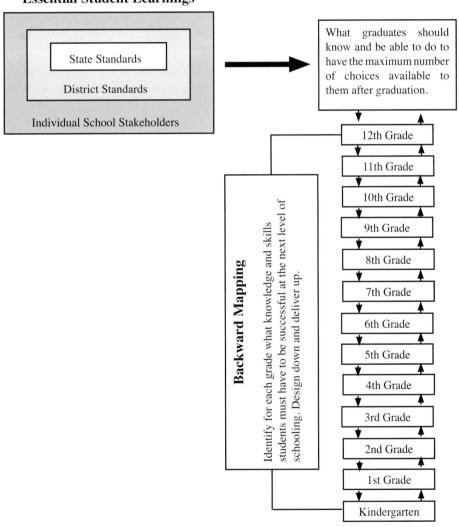

Ideally, all the schools in a district will work together to ensure continuity as students progress from grade to grade and school to school within the system. If this is not the case, and you are the leader of a school, you can still use the process at the school level.

Like the general contractor, the educational leader must have the necessary knowledge and skills required to assure that all "blueprints" are executed properly and the "home" is completed as intended. However, there is a notable difference between the general contractor and the educational leader. For the general contractor, most locales will require that construction be "inspected" along the way to be sure that "building codes" (a.k.a., best practices) are being followed. In education, the leader is left more or less alone to determine whether the appropriate practices are being followed.

> *"Always design a thing by considering it in its next larger context—a chair in a room, a room in a house, a house in an environment, an environment in a city plan."*
>
> — *Eliel Sarrinen*
> *Finnish Architect*

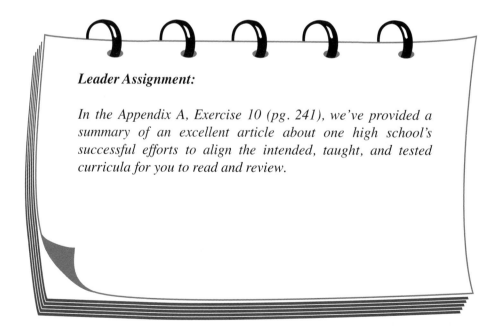

Leader Assignment:

In the Appendix A, Exercise 10 (pg. 241), we've provided a summary of an excellent article about one high school's successful efforts to align the intended, taught, and tested curricula for you to read and review.

ASSURING INSTRUCTIONAL ALIGNMENT: A MORAL IMPERATIVE

Alignment between intended, taught, and tested curriculum not only makes sense from a practical perspective, it also carries with it the weight of a "moral imperative." Let us explain with the following questions. First, who pays the price for adult negligence when there is slippage between the intended, taught, and tested curriculum? The first answer is the students. Even more specifically, "Which students pay the greatest price for the adult negligence?" The answer is that the poor, disadvantaged, often minority students bear the greatest burden. How can we morally justify asking the most educationally vulnerable students to pay the greatest cost for adult negligence around issues of alignment?

Initially, the leader may encounter resistance to the call for careful alignment because some teachers may feel that tight alignment between the intended, taught, and tested curriculum encroaches on their freedom as a classroom teacher. The educational leader must convey this unequivocal reality of today's education: individual teachers cannot operate as autonomously as they did previously since the accountability movement necessitates that the scope and sequence of learning be coherent and cumulative. The fifth-grade teacher, for example, must be able to depend on the fourth-grade students who come to his/her room being ready for the fifth-grade curriculum. Too often, the receiving teacher has to go back and re-teach critical concepts or skills, thus reducing the time needed to teach that to the fifth-grade standards. If this phenomenon occurs over a couple of years, one can quickly see where we get the phenomena known as *cumulative deficit*. This process of cumulative deficit, if not addressed, makes it virtually impossible for a student to "catch up" and eventually meet the requirements for high school graduation.

Since more and more states are requiring students to pass an exit exam before getting a high school diploma, this issue becomes critical to the success of our students, and to the schools, districts, and states that must show adequate yearly progress. Recently, one state was so concerned about the number of students who would not be able to pass the state test and thus not receive a diploma, that they considered eliminating the state test. We would encourage these well-meaning educational leaders and policymakers to reframe the discussion and focus on the root problem of cumulative deficit.

Leader Assignment:

A little research will help you better understand the concept of cumulative deficit. First, go back to the year this graduating senior class entered high school (presumably four years ago). Based on the best available data at the time, disaggregate the then freshmen into two groups: group one, the freshmen who entered high school performing at or above grade-level standards; and group two, those who entered high school performing below grade-level standards. Now, fast forward to this year and examine the students' performance on the high school exit exam with these questions in mind:

1. How many of the students who entered above grade level did not pass the exit exam?

2. How many of the students who entered below grade level did pass the exit exam?

3. How did so many students get to high school performing below grade-level?

While the profile described above would differ from place to place, we would wager that you will discover how cumulative deficits take a very significant toll on the students who have been sent forward without the prerequisite knowledge and skills necessary for success.

Too Many Apples, Too Small a Bag

We have all heard a version of the expression, "You can't put ten pounds of apples in a five-pound bag." Confronted with this dilemma, one has only a few options:

- Get a ten-pound bag.

- Buy fewer apples.

- Get a somewhat larger bag <u>and</u> select fewer apples.

What does this all have to do with educational leadership? Teachers often say that they have too much to teach and not enough time to teach it to a level of reasonable mastery. The teachers have too many apples for the size of the bag. And, in fact, the process outlined above will no doubt yield an overwhelming list of things to be taught and learned—far more than can be done in the time allotted for teaching and learning.

In the past, educators facing this situation were encouraged simply to do their best; if some of the students didn't master the curriculum, little could be done about it. But with the advent of NCLB, no students can be left behind. Therefore, you must find a way to change the time and opportunity structures so that all students can master the intended curriculum. Here is where effective leadership is required.

It is up to you as leader to ensure that the standards and stakeholder priorities are interpreted within the context of your students' needs and your school or district's mission, beliefs, and values. Using a variety of collaborative approaches, you must thoughtfully engage in a process of organized abandonment of selected portions of the curriculum—including selected state standards. The aim of this process is to reduce the amount to be taught to give the teachers more time to teach the remaining curriculum.

Noted author Doug Reeves, in an article entitled "Standards are Not Enough: Essential Transformations for School Success," suggests that educational leaders seeking to pare down the curriculum identify the "power standards"—those that meet three criteria:

- **Endurance**: Does the standard provide students with knowledge and skills that will be of value beyond a single test?

- **Leverage**: Will the standard provide knowledge and skills that are applicable across a wide spectrum of other disciplines?

- **Readiness**: Will the standard provide students with the knowledge and skills necessary to be successful at the next level of learning.

According to Reeves, power standards sort the "wheat" from the "chaff" and provide the building blocks for students to be successful at each subsequent level of learning. And yet, giving teachers permission to omit selected aspects of the curriculum in an effort to make the instructional program better fit your students' needs and the opportunity structures currently available is risky. The leader must be prepared to "take the hit" if someone is called to accounts. Here is an example of the expression noted earlier: Leadership is a risk game and the leaders have to ante up first.

> *"It takes a lot of courage to release the familiar and seemingly secure, to embrace the new. But there is no real security in what is no longer meaningful."*
>
> — *Allen Cohen*
> *Author & Inspirational Speaker*

LEADERSHIP AND THE HARDBACK TEXTBOOK

In the recent past, one of the authors was conducting a teacher workshop in a high school room in which a student had left his/her American Literature textbook on the shelf. The book was more than three inches thick and contained over 1,700 pages of small print. The course met 50 minutes a day, everyday, for the full school year (approximately 36 weeks). If the literature teacher believes—as many teachers do—that his/her job was to "cover the content," the students would have to process the equivalent of one page of small print every five minutes!

We hope and want to believe that most teachers are not tethered that closely to the hardback textbook any longer. However, the educational leader must be prepared to challenge the content coverage mission of those who still cling to it, and move these staff to the mission of having the students learn the content that is covered. Once they embrace that

mission, the teachers will quickly realize that they must abandon some of the content. This represents yet another variation of the challenge noted earlier.

The hardback textbook has a long and proud place in the history of American public education. So did the one room schoolhouse with its pot-bellied stove. As time moves on, however, aspects of yesterday must inevitably give way to today and tomorrow. Curriculum and instructional systems must be uncoupled from single-source materials. Given the mission of learning for all and leaving no child behind, teachers must customize and differentiate instruction. The one-size-fits-all instructional model so characteristic of the hardback textbook makes the customization challenge even more difficult. It is your job as leader to encourage teachers to "think outside the box"—or in this case, the hardback textbook.

> *"There is a danger as well as appeal in the glamour of the past. But, the past is for inspiration, not imitation, for continuation, not repetition."*
>
> — *Author Unknown*

Is there a place for the publishers of the hardback textbook? Modern technology has made it possible to create instructional modules that can be customized to align with the particular standards and priorities of the state or school district. Two desirable outcomes would result if publishers adopt this approach to school instructional materials. First, by design this would assure better alignment from the outset of the process. Second, local committees of educators would have ownership of the curriculum if they were permitted to set the scope and sequence of instruction, and even the pacing charts, to assure that it fit the opportunity structures of the school day and school year. Imagine the success of the textbook publishers who decide to create a modularized curriculum, as well as identify or develop "world-class" lesson plans for delivering the program. Furthermore, suppose the publishers used the Internet and continued to add more and more model lessons that their customers could access on continuing basis as part of the contract. Without a doubt, teachers would welcome the chance to be guided by excellent lessons.

> *"The vision is really about empowering workers, giving them all the information about what's going on so they can do a lot more than they've done in the past."*
>
> — *Bill Gates*
> *Founder & CEO*
> *of Microsoft Corp.*

LEADERSHIP AND THE INTENDED AND ACTUAL SYSTEM

One Total Quality concept states that a system consists of two parallel systems—the intended and the actual. How does this notion apply to education and the leader's responsibility? If you ask the curriculum office whether the intended, taught, and tested curricula are aligned, they will probably respond affirmatively. If you press them for supporting evidence to their claim, they may show various curriculum maps, grade-to-grade alignment of standards reports, and even grade-level pacing charts. In other words, they may claim that the intended curriculum is aligned to a "fault." However, if you observe the day-to-day life of the school and classroom and observe what *actually happens*, you will realize that there is often a disconnect between the intended curriculum and what is actually taught.

How does this slippage occur? A typical example would be the situation where the school lost three days of instruction due to snow or other acts of nature. Was the intended curriculum designed so that such loss of instructional time would not cause a problem toward the end of the school year? Experience suggests that the intended curriculum fills each day to capacity and any such loss will affect the actual curriculum that is delivered. Another scenario would occur when a teacher, for the best of motives, slows the instructional pace down for disadvantaged learners. As a result, less content will be covered. Because the current time for learning for children is pretty much fixed, disadvantaged students are ultimately denied an opportunity to learn those aspects of the curriculum that were not taught. We will never close the actual learning gap until we close the opportunity-to-learn gap for all children.

> *"The power to question is the basis of all human progress."*
>
> — *Indira Gandhi*
> *Former Indian*
> *Prime Minister*

The tasks for the leader are obvious. First, as we outlined earlier in this chapter, the leader must take the necessary steps to assure that the intended curricular system is aligned with the state and district standards and is perceived as fitting into the opportunity structures of the schools and classrooms. Second, the leaders must develop a feedback metric that provides ongoing information regarding the alignment between the intended and actual curricular systems. Finally, the leader must constantly work with teachers to be sure that when there is slippage between the intended and actual systems, the school formulates a plan for assuring that all students have an equal opportunity to learn the entire intended curriculum. We believe that most district and school leaders would be amazed to see how much slippage actually occurs in the day-to-day happenings of the school. Remember, this slippage is not the fault of bad educators intentionally aiming to do a poor job. Rather, most of the slippage occurs because of exigencies that are beyond the control of the school or the teacher. The leadership challenge is to assure that the school and teachers have action plans for responding to these unavoidable intrusions into the best of intended curricular plans.

> *"That which we persist in doing becomes easier—not that the nature of the task has changed, but our ability to do has increased."*
>
> — *Ralph Waldo Emerson*
> *American Philosopher & Writer*

> *Ask your teachers whether they believe—in their heads, hearts, and guts—that if they teach the intended curriculum and the students master it, the students will do well on the required assessments. To the extent that there is a perceived disconnect between the intended, taught, and assessed curriculum, the leader's work is not finished.*

7

FRAMING THE PROBLEM, CHOOSING THE VITAL SIGNS

> *"The mere formulation of a problem is often far more essential than its solution."*
>
> — *Albert Einstein*
> *Physicist & Nobel*
> *Prize Winner*

The vision, values, and mission have been identified, and student skills and knowledge defined. Now, the educational leader must ask the critical question: *How are we doing?*

This is the foundational question for improving student learning. Its answer will highlight your school or district's specific strengths and weaknesses, identify problems that must be addressed, and provide the overall framework within which the improvement strategies will be developed. To answer this question, you and your followers will need accurate and relevant data.

Using data as a tool in the diagnosis of learning problems, and the planning and implementation of school improvement is essential. As Ted

Creighton, in his scholarly article "Data Analysis and the Principalship," contends, "Data-driven decision making and instructional leadership must go hand in hand." Educational leaders must use data and data analyses to both communicate the vision of where they are trying to take the school, and as a means of monitoring progress toward the vision.

As we noted in earlier chapters, changing the culture in any organization starts by changing the conversation in the organization. Creating conversation around data is one of the surest ways to change the culture of schools and their decision-making processes.

To create that conversation, the leader and members of the stakeholder groups should work together to identify what data have been or need to be collected. Clearly, a critical indicator of how we're doing will be the outcome measurements required by the state. Such indicators should be treated as nonnegotiable. But beyond mandated test scores, what additional data need to be collected to determine how well the system is doing on its mission and its core values?

There are numerous student outcome measures that can provide valuable information to your analysis: student achievement data taken from state, district, school-level, and classroom-level tests, both norm-referenced and criterion-referenced, grade distributions, etc. Student affective data is another source of data, and might include student conduct reports, attendance, observations, student awards, participation rates in AP or honors classes, and extracurricular activities, among others. The data you choose will depend on the questions you're asking. For example, while most states measure achievement on literacy and mathematics, parents, employers, and educators are also interested in students learning self-discipline. You will need additional measurements—or metrics—when you ask: *How are we doing in effectively teaching students to be self-disciplined?*

The heart and soul of continuous improvement is the ability and willingness of system leaders to "monitor and adjust." Monitoring requires *data*—reliable and valid indicators of both the outputs and the processes of a system. While the continuous school improvement process in no way limits the metrics you may choose to assess student performance, it does demand that you are *explicit* and *intentional* about what you plan to measure and monitor to judge mission accomplishment. That is why one of the essential leader behaviors is to preside over a process that defines the measurements for monitoring both the relevant outputs and core processes of the system. In fact, a leader's legacy of success is directly tied to his/her ability to select the appropriate metrics and use the data to adjust the system over time.

> *"The temptation to form primitive theories upon insufficient data is the bane of our profession."*
>
> — *Sherlock Holmes (Sir Arthur Conan Doyle, Author)*

Wrong Measurement, Wrong Conclusions

Here's a story that will underscore the importance of the indicators that characterize a system and its efforts to improve. Up to and including the Vietnam War, field generals used "land taken" from the enemy to measure the progress of the war effort. The upper levels of command, political leaders, and citizens alike could relate to this "metric" as a way of showing progress. Unfortunately, the Vietnam War was unlike earlier conflicts in that the enemy's tactics were that of "guerilla warfare." That is, our troops would take an area one day and, a week later, the enemy would circle back, and retake the area, and our troops would have to recapture it. As a result, the "land taken" metric no longer proved to be effective in demonstrating progress. The Secretary of Defense at that time decided to change the progress metric to that of enemy body count. The body count compared how many of our troops were killed to the number of the enemy killed. Unfortunately, this body count metric was misleading at best. Using this metric, we could say that, up to the day we finally withdrew from Vietnam, we were winning the war!

Leader Assignment:

Identify the current sources of data that are available to assess where your school or district is in relation to the mission. Include direct measures of student mastery, as well as process and organizational measures. What "gaps" in the data exist? Where can you get the needed data? If not currently available, think about how it could be collected.

QUALITY, NOT QUANTITY

Effective leaders tend to become identified with a few vital measurements. Why? Because, generally speaking, followers find it difficult to maintain a clear and focused sense of mission if the number of vital signs to be monitored is too large. The education of children is a complex undertaking. As a result, it may be difficult to select the critical few measures that will serve to characterize the system. Doing so, however, is necessary. Therefore, it behooves the leader to choose the metrics carefully (not too many, not too few) that can serve as the "telemetry" for monitoring and continuously improving the system.

Ensuring multiple perspectives is another thing to keep in mind when choosing the metrics by which to assess school performance. This point is aptly stated by Margaret Heritage and Raymond Yeagley in the chapter they wrote for the 2005 NSSE Yearbook, *Uses and Misuses of Data for Educational Accountability and Improvement*: "To draw valid inferences about overall school and individual performance, and to provide a sufficiently detailed picture of student achievement to make decisions about school improvement, it is essential for educational practitioners to use evidence from a range of measures." They also suggest that you look at the quality of the data in terms of completeness and accuracy.

If this seems overwhelming, perhaps a medical metaphor can serve to illustrate the process, and give hope and guidance to the leader facing the difficult task of choosing a few vital signs from an endless laundry list of possibilities. During an annual physical for a patient, a physician checks only a few vital signs. If the data falls within "normal" parameters, both the patient and physician are willing to "bet the patient's life" that the patient is healthy. While many more tests could be given, most of us would be content to draw this conclusion based on a few major indicators of our health. However, if one of the vital signs suggests that there may be a problem, our physician will no doubt recommend more tests to confirm the existence and specifics of a problem. In this case, the physician is attempting to get to the "root cause" of the problem by "drilling down" for more specific data. School leaders should follow the same path.

Giving Voice to the Data

No doubt, you've heard people refer to "the facts." They might say, "The fact is…" or "The facts speak for themselves." And underlying "the facts" are data. This inspires us to collect data, all kinds of data, in copious amounts, in hopes that the data will magically inform us of what we want to know. What educators must recognize is that data are only useful in the right context; data out of context are at best unhelpful, at worst misleading. Effective leaders develop an instinct for knowing which data are useful and relevant, and which are not.

> *"Data is not information. Information is not knowledge. Knowledge is not understanding. Understanding is not wisdom."*
>
> — *Cliff Stoll*
> *Astrophysicist &*
> *Author*

As leader, you must be personally and directly involved in the selection of the metrics or vital signs that will be used to guide the continuous school improvement process. Once selected, you must constantly use and refer to these critical metrics, communicating their meaning and application to the continuous improvement process. You must also guide your school or district through the process of collecting, interpreting, and using data to improve instruction and, as a result, student learning. Throughout this chapter, we will refer to this constellation of proactive, reactive, and interactive references to these vital signs as "giving voice to the data."

In the context of continuous school improvement, it is critical that we make it clear that giving voice to the data is a much broader concept than simply looking at student achievement scores. Make no mistake, in today's standards and accountability world, school leaders must incorporate these test scores into their array of vital sign or critical metrics. On the other hand, these indicators represent only one of the critical metrics that will come to be associated with the leader. As we proceed with the discussion of the vital signs of a continuously improving educational system, we will continue to emphasize vital signs that are inclusive of, but go beyond mandated test scores.

TREND ANALYSIS: THE KEY TO CONTINUOUS SCHOOL IMPROVEMENT

Continuous improvement implies change over time. While monitoring the selected vital signs will be of some value as "stand alone" data, the real value in the various vital signs comes when the leader and followers are able to examine trend data and ascertain changes from Time 1 to Time 2, and so on. When we look at the data from a single school or district, trend analysis allows the stakeholders to use their own history as the reference for improvement. While it is useful to see how a school or district is performing relative to other schools and districts, ownership and commitment builds when we see improvement within our own context.

Recognizing the value of trend analysis, plans must be made to evaluate the same metric and collect the same data over time so that it can be determined if the improvement efforts are having the desired effect. This will require you to discuss with the relevant stakeholders the monitoring cycle that will be associated with each vital sign, keeping in mind that the shorter the monitoring cycle and the more frequent the monitoring, the easier it becomes to improve the system.

The leadership challenge that must be confronted regarding the monitoring cycles has to do with cost, time, and ability of the system to adjust in the face of the data. The longest cycle that seems to be of value would be the annual assessments of student achievement required by most states. Such measures are not on shorter cycles (e.g., every semester) because they are costly in terms of both dollars and time. Furthermore, teachers and parents would balk at taking more time from classroom instruction for testing, especially when the results are not back in time to be useful for improving instruction.

Many schools are going in the direction of curricular benchmark testing several times during a school year. Generally, teachers and school-level administrators favor these shorter benchmark assessment cycles for two reasons. First, if designed properly, these benchmark tests are tightly aligned with the essential curriculum and therefore have more face validity to the curriculum. Second, the results of these assessments are available to the teachers much more quickly than the annual measures. The timely feedback allows teachers and school staff to make needed adjustments such as regrouping students, re-teaching essential curricular standards, or providing tutoring or other interventions.

So the question then becomes, "How frequently should a school monitor its chosen vital signs?" There are two answers to the question. First, a school should monitor as frequently as time and money permit. Second, a school should not monitor any more frequently *than they are prepared to adjust what the school or teachers do*. In the context of continuous improvement, the primary rationale for monitoring vital signs is to provide a basis for adjusting the system. If the school or its teachers are not inclined to change their way of doing things regardless of what is learned from the assessment, monitoring will be a waste of time.

> *"Knowing a great deal is not the same as being smart; intelligence is not information alone, but also judgment, the manner in which information is collected and used."*
>
> — *Carl Sagan*
>   *American Astron-*
>   *omer, Writer, &*
>   *Scientist*

DRILLING DOWN ON THE VITAL SIGNS DATA

"The goal is to transform data into information, and information into insight."

— *Carly Fiorina*
Former President
& CEO of Hewlett-
Packard Co.

We began the chapter with the general question, "Given our mission and core values, how are we doing?" One of the unique contributions the effective schools research has made to the general conversation on continuous school improvement has been to ask two, more specific questions:

- At *what* are we effective?
- For *whom* are we effective?

The first question requires leaders to look beyond broad measures of student achievement, particularly for student performance on standardized achievement tests. While these tests provide information about how schools and districts are doing generally, they aren't too helpful in showing you how to improve student learning. The ability to improve the system would benefit from having data that are more closely tied to specific aspects of the curriculum and instructional program. Generally, subscale scores are more useful in providing a clearer answer as to what is working and what needs to change.

The effective schools research movement deserves the credit (or blame) for encouraging schools to ask the second question. In the very early days of the effective schools research, schools typically examined their performance data by looking only at the measures of central tendency (mean, median, or mode) for the total student population. If performance data were disaggregated at all, it was only by gender. The effective schools advocates encouraged schools to disaggregate their performance data on the basis of both race/ethnicity and socioeconomic status, in addition to gender. The rationale for focusing on these three variables was based on the observation that they accounted for the preponderance of the observed variability in student achievement. Our logic was that if schools could close the gap associated with these variables, most of the gap in achievement would be gone and one would be hard-put to find another sociodemographic variable with such major subgroup differences.

Based on the best available data, these sociodemographic variables remain the major sources of observed variability in student achievement. However, the increasing diversity of the student population has prompted NCLB to include these variables and to add the categories of migrant status, English language learners, and special needs status.

Regardless of one's personal feelings about the mandated disaggregation of student data, it is clear that simply examining the average scores of diverse groups of learners is no longer an option when it comes to accountability. Nor is it helpful in supporting continuous improvement. School leaders who were willing to disaggregate student performance data long before the current mandate have found that looking at the data this way truly and irreversibly changed their perception of the school. Leaders should be encouraged by this, and by the fact that technological advances make it much easier to conduct disaggregation analyses than in the past, and to chart and graph the results for interpretation and meaningful conversation.

Remember—disaggregating student achievement data is not a problem-solving strategy. Effective leaders realize that disaggregating student achievement data is a problem-finding strategy. Nevertheless, no apology seems necessary since all problem-solving models begin with a description of the problem. The disaggregation process allows leaders to describe, in data terms, the problems that we must solve if we are to make progress on our mission.

LEADERS GET TO ROOT CAUSES

"There is nothing like looking, if you want to find something. You certainly usually find something if you look, but it is not always quite the something you were after."

— *J.R.R. Tolkien*
Author

While disaggregating the data will highlight which subgroups are struggling to meet the standards, the simple correlation between achievement and a single demographic variable cannot tell the whole story. Heritage and Yeagley assert that "deeper levels of disaggregation are essential for determining the effectiveness of school practices and the equity of services for different populations within a school and district, and educators should look at subgroups within the major categories. For example, academic achievement over time…may be more effective for students whose native language is Spanish than for those whose native language is Chinese." Heritage and Yeagley are suggesting a process we call "drilling down" on the data. Many have come to call these processes "mining the data." Whether we use these processes

to drill down or mine the data, the aim is the same: to identify the root causes of the learning problems we observe in our schools and districts.

Root causes are the underlying primary factors that contribute to an identified problem. Root causes are seldom readily apparent, and thus, are often overlooked. In addition, our existing "mental models" may cause us to jump to the wrong conclusion as to why a problem exists, which will lead us to apply the wrong solution. Not only will this not solve the problem, but may in fact exacerbate the existing problem or even create an entirely new one.

Root cause analysis is somewhat like going from a telescope view down to a microscope view. Both views are valid, but from very different vantage points. To find root causes, leaders must become skilled in a particular question: *Why?* This deceptively simply question is an invitation to develop and test different hypothesizes or different "theories of cause." For example, let's suppose that, based on our analysis of the disaggregated data, we identify that our lower-SES students are performing well below their higher-SES counterparts on a specific measure of learning. This would prompt us to ask: *Why do lower-SES students in our school do less well than the higher-SES students on the performance measure?* Our first theory may suggest that lower-SES students do less well because they miss a lot more school than their middle-SES counterparts. Do the data support this as a plausible contributor to the observed gap? If the answer is "yes," the leader will be prompted to ask another question: *Why do lower-SES students miss more school than their middle-SES counterparts?*

Root cause analysis is a process that should engage the stakeholders, including those from the larger school community. This gives the leader a chance to solicit multiple perspectives on the data and prevents "tunnel vision." As Paul LeMahieu, a participant in an Annenberg Institute colloquium, *Using Data for School Improvement*, so aptly states: "We need both internal and external viewpoints. Without the internal viewpoints you lack compassion, you lack the ability to really understand what those data are really saying to you. But without the external view, you lack perspective. You lack the wherewithal to see important interpretations and questions that don't occur to the people who are working too close to the situation."

Root cause analysis is an especially powerful strategy for addressing the educator's tendency to see the solution to an achievement gap problem as purchasing a new program. Using the earlier example, staff seeking a new reading program for underperforming low-SES students, once confronted with the underlying cause of poor attendance, can be asked how the new program will address the underlying problem for lower-SES students.

> *"Men give me credit for some genius. All the genius I have lies in this: when I have a subject in hand, I study it profoundly."*
>
> — *Alexander Hamilton*
> *American Statesman*

LEADERS FOCUS ON THE LEADING INDICATORS OF LEARNING

As important as the disaggregated analyses of student performance data are, they are limited in what they can do to assure continuous improvement. They are limited because they are an after-the-fact or *trailing* indicator of learning. Experts who work with the concept of continuous improvement understand that you cannot improve the performance of a system by simply studying the results. To truly improve our schools and our students' learning, leaders need to become advocates and champions for the *leading* indicators of learning.

Leading indicators are those variables that impact learning. They include processes, attitudes, perceptions, skill levels, time spent, and other factors that interact with one another to affect whether and to what extent students master the intended curriculum. Any change in a leading indicator will, by definition, result in changes in learning. For example, increasing the amount of time spent on a core subject will positively affect the performance of the students. Conversely, there is no doubt that reducing the time spent teaching core content will lead to reduced achievement.

An effective leader will assure that the array of vital signs to which their leadership is tied includes leading indicators. This may represent a greater challenge than it may first appear. Why? Because focusing on leading indicators implies a transition from a teaching-centered orientation to a learner-centered orientation. This means that the conversation must now focus on student learning, not simply what is being taught. Perhaps the most critical role of the educational leader is to orchestrate and guide the staff in the transition to a learner-centered orientation.

A variety of different frameworks can be used to give insight into the leading indicators of learning in the school. Here, we recommend two frameworks to help you identify leading indicators for your school.

The Correlates of Effective Schools represent an excellent source for the organizational leading indicators of learning. A full discussion of the correlates as leading indicators is available our previous book, *Assembly Required: A Continuous School Improvement System*, and need not be repeated here. A brief discussion is also presented in Appendix B. However, the key idea that leaders seeking to create sustainable change in their organizations need to know is this: decades of effective schools research have found that the extent to which these correlates or characteristics are strong and present in a school is strongly related to how successful a school is in educating all of its students. Effective leaders use this research-based framework to assess leading indicators, and encourage the followers to adopt a set of processes by which the organizational leading indicators can be monitored on a reasonably regular basis. Some indicators will require quantitative data, while some will require qualitative—or "soft"—data.

Many indicators will rely on survey data from staff, parents, and even students. Many technological tools are available to assist with this task. Reality Check™ is an example of one such tool. Reality Check™ includes over 2000 survey questions that have been used over time and place to determine staff, student, and parent perceptions within the framework of the Correlates of Effective Schools.

A second set of leading indicators of learning can be found in the literature on how humans learn. An excellent resource for vital signs based on human learning is a document published by the American Psychological Association entitled "Learner-Centered Psychological Principles: A Framework for School Redesign and Reform." Data drawn from these leading indicators can be used to identify problems, rule out other problems, and provide guidance for what ought to be changed so that student learning improves. For example, one principle of human learning states that learning is enhanced when the learner has the opportunity for guided practice with precise feedback. The leader's question, based on this principle, would then be: *How much time and effort is being devoted to guided practice with precise feedback in our classrooms and schools?*

LEADERS MUST MANAGE LEARNING

W. Edwards Deming stated that an effective system must have three qualities. First, the system must have a clear aim. Second, the system must have a broad-based commitment to the aim. Third, a system must be manageable. In the past, improvement strategies usually focused on establishing a clear aim, and building and sustaining broad-based commitment to the aim. More recently, educational leaders have recognized the importance of being able to manage the mission of learning.

Historically, educational systems have developed and managed fairly elaborate systems for managing the financial aspects of the system. In addition, most schools and districts have developed intricate systems for capturing and reporting student attendance, since it has been closely tied to budget allocations. With the new aim of "learning for all," school leaders must now develop and implement a system for managing the mission of learning in the schools. What would such a system look like?

Let's imagine that a parent in the district were to call the superintendent and ask how well his/her child was doing in mastering the school system's intended curriculum. If the superintendent is able to turn to a computer, call up the child's record, and answer the question, the school district has an effective and comprehensive system for managing learning. Such a data system provides leaders at all levels of the system with the capacity to ask and answer questions with data. Such a system would also make it possible to more easily complete the many leader tasks presented throughout this chapter. This is emphasized by the National Research Council, which outlines the characteristics of an integrated assessment and reporting system in a 2001 report titled *Investigating the Influence of Standards*. They suggest that an effective system is comprehensive, coherent, and has a level of continuity to that provides information on student progress over time.

> *"The art of progress is to preserve order amid change and to preserve change amid order."*
>
> — *Alfred North Whitehead*
> *British Philosopher, Physicist, & Mathematician*

BEING THE (DATA-DRIVEN) WORLD YOU WANT TO SEE

Historically, the culture of education has not emphasized the ongoing collection and analysis of data. Therefore, leading with and through data, central to a continuous improvement system, represents a major departure from past practice. And yet, as Heritage and Yeagley assert, data analysis tools and skills "will remain largely ineffective if teachers and administrators are unwilling or unable to use them." As leader, it is up to you to initiate and nurture a school culture that embraces data as a vehicle to improve student learning. In pro-data culture, there is a common commitment to using data, within the context of the organization's mission, as the basis for day-to-day decisions about instruction, policies, and procedures.

Changing to a data-driven system and an organizational culture that will support it will take time, patience, and training. Although we have touched on many of the challenges leaders encounter in creating such a culture, we recap them below:

- Educators are often suspicious of data, and afraid that "bad news" will lead to sanctions and punishment. This is where you must cultivate one of the essential attributes discussed in Chapter 3: trustworthiness. It is up to you as the leader to instill a sense of trust in the staff and to convey your intention to utilize data for constructive purposes.

- Teachers may also see data collection and increased assessment as an intrusion on and a diversion from teaching. As we said earlier, one of the greatest challenges you may face as a leader will be to change the collective focus from teaching to learning. But once teachers and administrators accept and embrace the notion that they are no longer in the "teaching business," but in the "learning business," they will quickly recognize that learning can be significantly enhanced by careful monitoring and assessment.

- Data collection and analysis are often far removed from the people who must respond to it. The closer the collection and analysis of the data are to the end users, the more likely the data will be meaningful, timely, and trusted.

- Few educators are trained in the collection, analysis, and the application of data in their day-to-day practice. The effective leader will see to it that teachers receive the training they need to gather, understand, and use data to improve student learning.

Referring back to Warren Bennis and his book *Leaders*, you'll remember that he described effective leaders as manifesting "confident uncertainty." Both the confidence and the uncertainty have a role to play in creating a data-driven culture and a continuous school improvement system. The leader must be confident, and communicate that confidence, that such a system will produce the success that all are seeking. Likewise, the leader's uncertainty represents an invitation to the followers to help define the system and its critical dimensions. Involving stakeholders in developing the vital signs that make up the metrics of the system will go a long way in securing their trust, ownership, and commitment to using data for continuous improvement.

> *"There are no experts with 'the answer'—we will have to invent the future ourselves together as we go along."*
>
> — *Tom Sergiovanni*
> *Professor of Education & Author*

Leaders committed to continuous school improvement realize the importance of vital sign data and their place in the ongoing continuous improvement discourse. Effective leaders are well-prepared and passionate about the data that is needed to guide and direct school improvement, and model data-driven decision making in their own practice. Effective leaders understand and appreciate the concept of root causes and are comfortable with drilling down on the data to get evermore specific descriptions of what is and isn't working, and for whom. Effective leaders encourage teachers to use data to evaluate their own instructional practice.

As a leader, you will need to learn the ins and outs of data gathering and analysis, and become skilled at explaining the results simply and clearly so that all stakeholders can draw meaning from the data and use it to improve student learning. You must make data a priority as a means to mission accomplishment: ensuring there is time for staff and stakeholders to work with data, and providing training to teachers and other stakeholders in data interpretation and application. Most of all, you will need to model data-driven decision making, to become the world you want to see.

8

LEADING THE SEARCH FOR SOLUTIONS

In addition to using data to identify the root causes of the achievement problems in the school, the continuous school improvement process creates the opportunity for leaders to use research and effective practices to help set improvement goals and to frame the improvement strategies for the school.

Often, school improvement efforts proceed directly from identifying the school or district's problem list to developing strategies and action steps. At this point, the leader must intervene to prevent the stakeholders from skipping an essential step in the continuous improvement process: the "ritual of reflection." In this step, the leader engages the faculty and other relevant stakeholders in two activities: 1) a discussion designed to prioritize the problems to be addressed, and collectively decide on a few critical improvement goals to which everyone can commit; and 2) an internal and external scanning process designed to uncover the best possible solutions tailored to the school or district's needs. Such a thoughtful, deliberative, research-based process is far more likely to develop better plans—plans that address causes, not symptoms. Hence, the solutions formulated through this process are more likely to raise the level of student learning. This process requires not four or five days, but several months— perhaps even a semester or more.

> *"Whatever failures I have known, whatever errors I have committed, whatever follies I have witnessed in public and private life, have been the consequences of action without thought."*
>
> — *Bernard Baruch
> American Finan-
> cier & Presidential
> Advisor*

NARROWING THE FOCUS

Taking an honest and thorough look at the data in relation to the mission, identifying gaps in learning, and drilling down to determine root causes often yields a lengthy "laundry list" of problem statements. Since most schools and districts do not have unlimited resources, not all problems can—or should—be tackled at once. Therefore, before launching into the solutions-seeking process, you and your colleagues will need to settle on a manageable number of improvement goals.

> "Never try to solve all the problems at once—make them line up for you one-by-one."
>
> — *Richard Sloma*
> *Attorney & Management Expert*

Experience has taught us that doing a few things well is going to produce greater improvements than undertaking several goals and implementing them in a haphazard and shallow manner. There are several things to keep in mind when choosing your improvement goals:

- In general, it's better to choose no more than three improvement goals. Any more than that and your efforts will be scattered in too many directions.

- Use the SMART acronym when choosing improvement goals. Make sure they are Specific, Measurable, Attainable (but challenging), Relevant, and Time-based.

- Continuous improvement theory suggests that 80 percent of improvement will result from 20 percent of the changes you make. Therefore, it behooves the leader to consider which improvement goal, once met, will yield the greatest impact on overall student achievement in terms of equity and equality. For example, focusing on reading and comprehension can reach across all other content areas.

- Choosing what to work on is an opportunity to build commitment to the reform effort. This should occur as an open and honest discussion in which the leader clearly articulates the context within which the goals will be set. That context will include the agreed-upon mission, core values and beliefs, and external forces at play. This said, we do offer one note of caution. While stakeholder participation can play a valuable role in choosing the appropriate goals, it does not substitute for your engagement in and leadership of the process. As we discussed early in this book, human beings often opt for the path of least resistance, and, given the option, may choose more "do-able" goals over the most urgent.

> *"Efforts and courage are not enough without purpose and direction."*
>
> — *John F. Kennedy*
> *35th President of*
> *the United States*

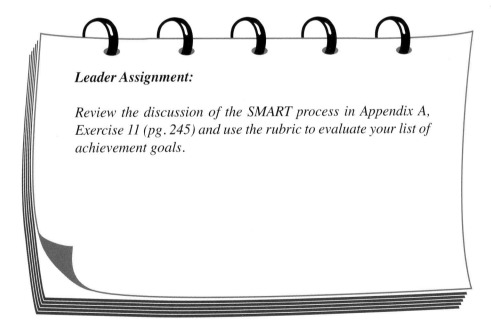

Leader Assignment:

Review the discussion of the SMART process in Appendix A, Exercise 11 (pg. 245) and use the rubric to evaluate your list of achievement goals.

FRAMING THE SEARCH FOR SOLUTIONS

Now that the improvement goals are chosen, we now turn our attention to identifying possible solutions. The leadership tasks associated with finding solutions are based on two assumptions:

Assumption # 1: You and your colleagues are already doing the best you know how to do, given the conditions in which you found yourselves.

The vast majority of workers in any system behave in accordance with their mental model of the work to be done and the training that they received. Furthermore, most of the individual worker's behavior is aligned with, and supported by the context in which they find themselves. In other words, educator behaviors are aligned with and rewarded—or at least not sanctioned—by the system of which they are a part.

If this assumption is true and still we are not successfully accomplishing our learning-for-all mission, then what needs to occur if we are going to find effective solutions? *New knowledge* must be brought into the system. That is to say, the workers need to know something *more* to impact the problem. It should come as no surprise to anyone that solving the learning problems of a school is going to require learning on the part of the crucial stakeholders of that school or district system.

For reasons that are not obvious, workers often interpret the call for improvement as an indictment of their work, that it suggests they have not been doing a good job. If you acknowledge your belief that everyone is doing the best they know how given the current conditions, your stakeholders will be less likely to see the call for change as implying their negligence. And if you empower the staff to work collaboratively to find the required new knowledge, their commitment to and ownership of the changes will increase dramatically.

Assumption #2: Leaders must model the world they want to see.

Any effective continuous improvement system is based on *learning*. If schools and school districts are to distinguish themselves as learning organizations, the leader must be seen as the first learner among a community of learners. In the last chapter, we identified one of the leader tasks as "giving voice to the data." As we move into the arena of searching for solutions, the leader as "first learner" must give voice to the research and best practices.

EXTERNAL AND INTERNAL
SCANNING STRATEGIES

As the trustee of the organization's mission, the leader has two broad responsibilities: to scan the outside world for new ideas, research, and best practices; and to engage in an ongoing process of internal scanning to determine what is working and what's not.

Our experience with effective school improvement over the years has revealed that when a school or district demonstrates continuous and sustainable school improvement, its leaders are "up to their elbows" in the research and proven practices literature. These leaders identify research or best practices that might help the school or district, and have a strategy for bringing it in for a closer examination. This doesn't mean that every new idea gets implemented, but it does suggest that effective leaders are always on the lookout for strategies that could, if implemented, make things better—after all, that is what continuous improvement is all about.

The internal scanning process being envisioned here takes on the form of program and process evaluation called "action research." Educational organizations, as a rule, implement a new strategy and spend few resources and little time collecting feedback as to whether or not it's working. Without a program evaluation framework and the accompanying data it is intended to examine, one of two things are likely to happen: 1) the program or process, regardless of its effectiveness, will be abandoned if the "champion" of that program or process moves on; or 2) an ineffective program or process will be retained. The leader needs to strive for both effectiveness and efficiency. Educational institutions cannot afford to use scarce resources on efforts that aren't working. We can do better and leaders need to assure that we, in fact, do better.

While effective school and district leaders do as much as they can to keep "on top of things," this doesn't mean that they do it all alone. Both the internal and external scanning processes open the door for engaging the staff and other stakeholders in the continuous improvement process.

TOGETHER, WE LEARN

Just as the collection and analysis of data are more meaningful and accurate when all relevant stakeholders are involved, so will the solutions formulated through an inclusive and collaborative process be more meaningful and inspire more commitment to their implementation. As leader, it is up to you to create such a *collaborative learning environment*. Unfortunately, the historical culture of most schools and districts is not one of collaborative learning and educators often do not know how to learn efficiently and effectively *together*. Educational leaders committed to making schools and school districts as effective as they can be in assuring success for all must give thought to how the stakeholders and the system can become better collaborative learners.

Currently, the concept of the school as a *professional learning community* is very popular. A professional learning community is based upon a collegial relationship between the leader and stakeholders, and is focused on professional inquiry around data and research. This is where the concept of shared leadership comes in. This is where you as the leader will have to empower your staff to adopt leadership roles, because the demands of continuous improvement means everyone will at times be a learner and, at others, the teacher. One way to do this is to form collaborative learning teams and charge them with the task of seeking new and useful knowledge that can be used to solve the identified problems.

> *"I never teach my pupils; I only attempt to provide the conditions in which they can learn."*
>
> — *Albert Einstein*
> *Physicist & Nobel*
> *Prize Winner*

For schools and districts that have used the effective schools framework to guide their search for solutions, establishing and empowering "Correlate Teams" has proven to be a particularly successful collaborative learning strategy. In this approach, study groups are formed around each of the seven correlates of effective schools—safe and orderly environment, clear and focused mission, etc.—and charged with investigating the available research around that correlate in relation to the problem being studied. Teams become both learners and teachers as they investigate the research and proven practices around each correlate and then convey that information to the other members of the learning community.

Another form of research is to send a team of teachers and administrators to visit other demographically similar schools that are successfully teaching all students. Armed with a common interview form and observation guide, visiting teams can then return and report information that can be compared across sites, and with existing research. This process of reflection better equips the school to draw conclusions about what works and why. Unfortunately, sending a team to observe similar successful schools seldom happens, despite the research evidence that reinforces that this is a very important part of the change process. If teachers and principals see a practice being successfully implemented in a similar school, they are more likely to believe that it is appropriate for their school and recognize that they can do what is needed to achieve similar or better results.

"Nothing has such power to broaden the mind as the ability to investigate systematically and truly all that comes under thy observation in life."

— Marcus Aurelius
Roman Emperor

Teachers as Action Researchers

In their article on teacher involvement in action research, researchers John Ross, Carol Rolheiser, and Anne Hogaboam-Gray, found that while the process of action research can be quite involved and requires a long-term view, it promises to be a fulfilling, effective professional growth path for the teachers who participate.

In their case study, teacher-researchers first learned to study the research by working with university personnel. They were then able to use the results of their inquiry to design individual action research projects to improve their teaching. The authors found that collaboration with supportive peers and professional researchers proved to be an important element, building the teachers' confidence while simultaneously building knowledge and skill. Partnerships between university members and school staff can benefit all, as the academics offer research expertise and the teachers identify questions often neglected by the researchers. The conclusion of the authors is borne out by decades of research on teaching and learning: wherever teachers are actively involved in identifying problems in their classrooms, seeking alternative approaches, evaluating the outcomes, and making appropriate adjustments, students are the ultimate benefactors.

SYSTEMS APPROACH TO APPLYING THE RESEARCH

A common mistake school leaders make is to assume that if the teachers attend a workshop or conference and gain useful new knowledge, they will return to the classroom and implement that knowledge without further guidance and support. This rarely happens without changing the system to support the new behaviors based on the newly acquired knowledge. Organizational researchers have long known that individual workers, no matter how dedicated, cannot and will not go to work everyday and "swim up stream" against the system-in-place. Smart leaders recognize that sustainable change requires both new knowledge *and* systemic change and address both the knowledge acquisition and system changes in a carefully coordinated way. Therefore, in addition to finding relevant information on promising strategies, you must ask the teams to consider the system changes that will be required to support the successful implementation of the new knowledge.

LEADERSHIP THROUGH ORGANIZED ABANDONMENT

In his writings, Peter Drucker, internationally recognized management scholar, draws a parallel between a complex organization—of which educational institutions are an example—and the human organism. Both represent complex systems. In humans, two of the vital signs that characterize our health as human beings have to do with our ability to "eliminate." If we lose those two vital functions, we become sick. If we don't recover these functions, we die! Organizations, like people, need to abandon aspects of yesterday if they are going to be ready for tomorrow. However, according to Drucker, organizations often lack systematic procedures for the abandonment of anything. That is to say, while most complex organizations have procedures to establish a new process or program, most do not have similar processes in place for eliminating a program when the mission and organizational priorities change.

As noted earlier, the mission of public education has changed. The current system-in-place—whether classroom, school, or district—was never designed or intended to do what it is now being asked of it. Therefore, current policies, procedures, and practices—even those that have been around "forever"—must be reexamined to be sure that they enhance rather than impede the mission of "learning for all." When new strategies are implemented, they must be evaluated in terms of effectiveness.

An example might help you to see the importance of the concept of organized abandonment. Initially the one-room schoolhouse, by necessity, simultaneously dealt with students of varying ages. As the population grew, schools grew from one room to many, and it was decided to assign students to classrooms based on chronological age. Placing students on the basis of age probably made sense when the mission was compulsory attendance with learning being optional. However, the new mission of public education rules out the optional learning. We know that children start school with significant variation in readiness. Does it still make sense to place children in learning groups based on their age and continue to disregard their readiness for the curriculum associated with that particular age group?

Some schools have had the courage to examine this educational "sacred cow" and as a result, have abandoned the concept of age-to-grade placement. They have replaced the old model with an ungraded, continuous progress system for assigning students to flexible learning groups, with significant success. Evidence shows that such a school organizational model, if implemented with fidelity, enhances student learning and assessed performance.

> *The moral of this story is that every system, policy, program, and practice should be critically reviewed as potential candidates for organized abandonment, even those that we take for granted because "we've always done it this way." Leaders need to initiate and sustain an ongoing discussion on candidates for organized abandonment.*

LEADER AS "CRITICAL FRIEND"

Ron Edmonds, recognized leader and founder of the effective schools research movement, was often heard to say that effective schools spend as much time avoiding things that *don't* work, as they do searching for things that *do* work. Therefore, leaders must both model and support the concept of organized abandonment. They must step back and become the "critical friend" of their own organization, and have the courage to take a long, hard look at some of the core structures that we take for granted in our system of schooling and ask the question: *What should go and what should stay as we pursue our mission?*

Most leaders would be surprised by the number of candidates for organized abandonment that would be suggested by the stakeholders of a system if they were invited to do so. What do we say to the leader who says that they know that certain policies and practices should be abandoned, but they can't see what will take their place? If leaders never make the decision to abandon practices that don't work, they will never have to take the risk to find a replacement. And, as we've said before, effective leaders must be risk-takers. Remember the story of the general who, after the soldiers landed on the beach in a battle to take the island, burned the lifeboats! Going forward and winning rather than retreating was the only option in the battle. Leaders must project that "confident uncertainty" that we will find a better way.

> *"Progress always involves risks. You can't steal second base and keep your foot on first."*
>
> — *Frederick B. Wilcox*
> *Author*

Leader Assignment:

Authors David Tyack and Larry Cuban refer to preexisting ideas about how schools "should be" as the "grammar of schooling." Review the discussion on this concept in Appendix A, Exercise 12 (pg. 247) and reflect upon the guiding questions.

WHEN TO LET GO

Marketing experts often grapple with when to discontinue the production of a particular product or service. They suggest that the leader, when evaluating whether something should stay or go, ask the following question: *Knowing what we now know about the product or service, if we were not already producing the product or offering the service, <u>would we start</u>?* If the analysis leads to the answer of "no," then the decision should be to stop.

If we return to our example of age-grade placement and ask the question: *Given the mission of leaving no child behind, if we were not already placing students in age-based learning groups, would we start?* If we listen to teachers as they struggle with the large and increasing variability in readiness among students, most reasonable people would say "no." If that is true, then the leader will have to step up and initiate the conversation that will lead to a new and more effective system of student placement.

Like any change in a system, organized abandonment will require careful logistical planning. Further, there are limits as to how many changes—additions or eliminations—that a system can handle at one time. Leaders must be both courageous and judicious when initiating change.

LEADING THROUGH HIGH-YIELD STRATEGIES

Leaders often fear two undesirable possibilities when it comes to searching for solutions to identified problems. The first possibility is that no solution will be found. Experience suggests that this fear is ungrounded. When it comes to school reform the knowledge base of better ways to assure learning by all students is well developed and relatively easy to find, if the leader is determined to do so.

The second fear often expressed by leaders is that too many possible solutions will be found, and the leader and the collaborative groups will not be able to choose the correct one. The concept of high-yield strategies can serve as a guiding principle when considering various directions. When examining the research, you and your colleagues will find that some strategies have a greater impact on learning than others. Other things being equal, leaders should encourage the selection of the strategies that will produce the *highest possible yield* when it comes to improving student learning.

To isolate the likely yield associated with a particular strategy, you will need to become familiar with a few key principles of research design. The quality of research and program evaluations can be scaled

in terms of the rigor of the research design. Some research makes it possible to attribute causality to a new strategy or practice. This requires the presence of a randomly assigned experimental and control group. Absent the rigor of the true experimental design, other less-rigorous methodologies can still be very powerful in identifying high-yield problem-solving strategies.

One option that leaders can and should use to help guide study groups and solution teams in their work is called a meta-analysis. Without getting into the technical aspects of the meta-analysis process, it is sufficient to say that scholars who use the method attempt to gather all the relevant studies on a particular topic to determine what has been found across many studies. Robert Marzano and his colleagues published a monograph in 2001 titled *Classroom Instruction That Works*. This monograph and many others are good examples of meta-analyses that can help leaders make good choices about the strategies they adopt to solve the identified problems.

Leaders Consider Levels of Support

The leader should also take into account the level of support for various solutions among those who will ultimately have to change their behavior if the solution is to be implemented successfully. In the short term, the leader probably has enough power and authority to mandate that a particular strategy or practice be adopted. Unfortunately, those who must implement the strategy or practice may sabotage the effort unless they come to embrace the effort. Few effective strategies are powerful enough to be "teacher proof." Therefore, leaders must remember that the sustainability of any change effort requires some level of ownership by those that implement the changes day to day.

We aren't suggesting that you should abandon a solution because of a lack of support. Rather, we are saying that if some of the implementers are resisting a high-yield solution, you will need to engage in further conversation to find out the source of the opposition. It may well be that the implementers believe in and support the strategy conceptually, but have misgivings regarding how it will be implemented. Further conversation may well produce a compromise that causes the leaders to reduce or eliminate their resistance.

Leaders who adopt new strategies against the support and will of the implementers must realize that their innovation is only a heartbeat away from extinction—if the leader's heart stopped today, tomorrow the innovation would go the way of the dinosaur.

LEADING THROUGH PILOT PROJECTS

It would be ideal if, once a high-yield solution has been found, we could see to it that it was implemented school- or district-wide immediately. However, a more realistic strategy would be to design and implement a pilot project in which only a few classrooms implement the change, and its impact carefully studied. Although more time consuming, pilot projects often save time and resources in the long run, since ineffective strategies are identified before being adopted by the entire school or system.

The pilot project model for selecting solutions also allows the leader to field-test more than one idea at a time. For example, some classrooms could be assigned to test a new approach to classroom instruction, while other classrooms field-test a tutoring model. Eventually, both ideas may prove themselves and ultimately be integrated and implemented systemwide. However, the comparison of the two pilot projects will identify the highest-yield strategy so that limited resources can be used to get the most benefit to student learning and school improvement. The resulting high-yield strategies that are ultimately implemented system-wide will then become "the way we do things here!"

"Theory guides. Experiment decides."

— *Izaak Kolthoff*
Chemist & Nobel
Prize Winner

LEADERS USE
TECHNOLOGY AND NETWORKS

Obviously, school and district leaders are very busy people. Asking them to keep current on a wide range of research and best practice literature may seem unrealistic. In the days when doing research meant hours at the library, thumbing through the indexes of scholarly journals and other publications, research was indeed out of reach for most practitioners. But with today's technology, it has become much more feasible to keep up with the current literature.

One way effective leaders "keep current" is to subscribe to one or more of the available online services that are designed to provide book reviews, summaries of new research, and descriptions of practices that work. One example of such a service is *Research LiNK*, an online subscription service that contains an expanding and searchable archive of over 1,500 research summaries on every aspect of school improvement, from the classroom to the district level. Many of the national professional organizations have similar services, all of which recognize the leader's workload and attempt to provide useful, just-in-time information. Subscribing to, reading, and distributing summaries of research and proven practices and discussing them with the stakeholders will go

a long way toward modeling the leader as first learner—an essential attribute of an effective continuous improvement system.

Effective leaders also learn from one another. Historically, educational institutions could be criticized for doing a poor job of capturing and sharing the wisdom of the educational practitioners. Consequently, local school and district leaders found themselves having to constantly "reinvent the wheel." Today, however, information technology provides a means to overcome this unfortunate tradition. The Internet itself makes it possible for school leaders to share what is working for them with other leaders anywhere in the world.

One online tool, the *Effective School League*, represents an example of how research and best practices can be shared among educational leaders who are seeking solutions to similar problems. Although web sites that attempt to bring professional educators a comprehensive resource for improving teaching and learning are in their infancy, we believe that great and powerful changes in this domain are just around the corner.

LEADERS CREATE A COMMUNITY OF CONTINUOUS LEARNERS

Underlying the research process is the notion that no individual leader, no single faculty, no one school improvement team has all of the accumulated wisdom of the profession. For faculties, schools, and districts to learn, to grow, and to succeed, they must reach out. It is your role as leader to create a culture of collaborative inquiry in which faculty and other stakeholders thoughtfully read and discuss the research pertaining to identified problems, visit similar schools that are successfully teaching students, and feel safe in trying out new strategies based on their findings. You must also have the courage to ask the difficult questions about long-held practices and programs, and to make the difficult choices and decisions, if necessary.

> *"Again and again, an impossible problem is solved when we see that the problem is only a tough decision waiting to be made."*
>
> — *Dr. Robert Schuller*
>   *Motivational*
>   *Speaker*

Continuous school improvement based effective schools research has a long and proud history of improving student achievement, when the research and the processes of change are implemented with fidelity and sustained over time. We have found that when schools adopt research on effective schools and effective teaching as a common language and take steps to assure that all staff members are grounded in that language, the essential ingredients for improvement are at hand. When we empower an ever-enlarging conversation of school change by engaging a leadership team and other "study groups," the essential processes for continuous learning and change begin to stir. Finally, when the system provides the time for the teams to meet and learn how to learn together, the momentum for sustainable change steadily builds. This is the job of an effective leader.

9

BUILDING THE BRIDGE FROM GOALS TO ACTION

> *"The secret of getting ahead is getting started. The secret of getting started is breaking your complex overwhelming tasks into small manageable tasks, and then starting on the first one."*
>
> — *Mark Twain*
> *American Humorist,*
> *Writer, & Lecturer*

Having communicated a compelling vision, inspired the commitment of the stakeholders, guided the stakeholders through the processes of gathering and analyzing relevant data and research, and clearly articulating improvement goals, the leader and followers should have a good idea of where they are going. But even the most laudable, knowledge-based change goals will not make a dime's worth of difference if they are not implemented in an effective and sustainable manner. The leader's responsibility in building the bridge from change goals to action steps is as critical to overall continuous improvement as any other step in the process.

A popular expression that leaders often hear is to "plan the work and work the plan." Selecting improvement goals that are based on comprehensive data analysis is certainly a vital step in planning the work. Selecting solutions based on sound research and proven practice is another vital step. Though necessary, these activities are not sufficient. The goals and chosen solutions must be translated into feasible action plans that set forth the logistical steps needed to make the goals a living reality in the system.

Action plans that lead to ongoing improvement in student learning must meet three criteria: they must be *feasible*, *sustainable*, and *adaptable*. It is the leader's responsibility to see that any action plans meet these standards.

Leaders Ensure Feasibility

Oftentimes, planning committees become overly enthusiastic and try to commit the school to a level of effort and an implementation schedule that is simply unrealistic given all the other activities that must continue to go on at the same time. To be feasible, the action plan must address a variety of logistical questions. Some of the questions that must be addressed include: *Can we do what needs to be done in the time available to us (e.g., this school year)? Do we have or can we find the resources needed to pay for the actual costs associated with implementing the action plan (e.g., training materials, substitute teachers?) Do we have the human resources and the "talent" (e.g., internal expertise or outside consultant) required for the needed staff development?*

There are many other considerations when considering feasibility, some not as obvious as others. And yet, if any critical element is overlooked, the successful implementation of the action plan will be "stalled" and the cynicism of the staff will increase since, from their perspective, we have once again invested in another change effort where there was no follow-through. As the leader, it falls to you to anticipate and address these issues as much as possible in the planning stage.

Given the complexity of a school or district, how can you "get a handle" on the critical interrelated issues? Effective leaders recognize that a change in one part of the complex school or district system will affect every other part of the system, in both intended and unintended ways. This recognition leads them to adopt a systems approach to planning. One way to think about the complex system of the school is by using the Four Common Places of Education, a concept first described by Joseph J. Schwab in 1962. Schwab identified the Four Common Places as the learner, the teacher, the classroom, and the curriculum. We have combined this systems consideration with Schwab's Four Common Places to create a model that will help you to take a comprehensive approach to action planning. We present this model on the following page.

While these areas are crucial to consider, you will also need to consider what structures, policies, and aspects of the culture must change to support the implementation of the action plan.

A Systemic Approach to Creating A Comprehensive Action Plan

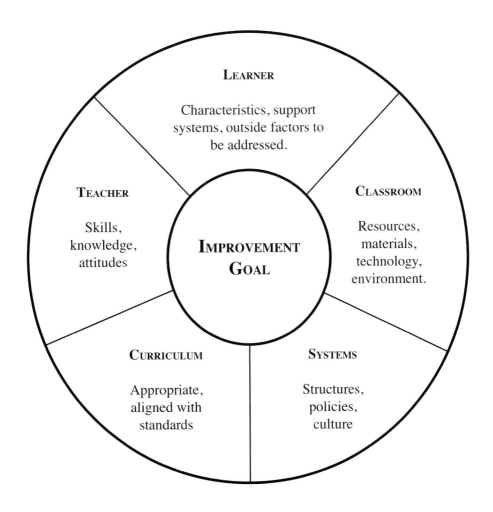

LEARNER

Characteristics, support systems, outside factors to be addressed.

TEACHER

Skills, knowledge, attitudes

IMPROVEMENT GOAL

CLASSROOM

Resources, materials, technology, environment.

CURRICULUM

Appropriate, aligned with standards

SYSTEMS

Structures, policies, culture

This model incorporates Joseph Schwab's Four Common Places of Education.

Leader Assignment:

Review our example of taking a systems approach to planning in Appendix A, Exercise 13 (pg. 249). Then use the model to review and reflect on your school or district's action plan, if one already exists; if no plan currently exists, consider how you would apply it within the context of your school or district as you plan your tactics and strategies.

"The ultimate test of practical leadership is the realization of intended, real change that meets people's enduring needs."

— *James MacGregor Burns
Professor &
Leadership Expert*

LEADERS ENSURE SUSTAINABILITY

In many ways, the sustainability criterion represents a logical extension of feasibility. The primary difference is that the sustainability criteria requires the leader to take a longer view—to look "down the road"—to be sure that the change effort can be supported on an ongoing basis. Here is a typical scenario. The leadership team of stakeholders designs an action plan that the school or district leader indicates can be implemented because s/he was able to secure a grant from an outside agency to underwrite the initial implementation costs. However, sustaining the effort in year two and beyond will require a continuing dollar and time investment.

System scholars such as Patrick Dolan caution leaders need to be very cautious in taking and using grant money to underwrite long-term change efforts, since grants are usually not sustainable. Unless additional funding is secured, many grant-initiated programs or projects will have to be eliminated or severely curtailed, which will again contribute to the cynicism of the stakeholders. We are not suggesting that you should never incorporate activities into an action plan paid for by grant money. We are suggesting that careful foresight and planning by the leader will be needed to look beyond the grant period to determine what time, talent, and dollars will be needed to continue the effort and find ways to secure those resources.

Some leaders have found it useful to approach the action planning process with the collaborative stakeholder groups by asking them to consider that the change process must ultimately be "revenue neutral." To be revenue neutral means that an existing activity, program, or process must be abandoned so that resources can be reallocated to the improvement effort. Throughout this book, we've drawn parallels between school improvement and home improvement. At this point, we find another comparison appropriate to illustrate this concept. When it's time to remodel or renovate our home, we generally don't develop our plan and place it on a shelf until enough "new money" comes along to implement it, especially if the renovations aren't optional (e.g., the roof is leaking). Rather, we are forced to find the needed resources by reallocating existing resources. We may dip into our savings, forego this year's vacation, or put off another, less-urgent repair to another time. Like the leaking roof, improving student achievement is not optional. It is up to the leader to ask the collaborative group to explore what could be abandoned to free up resources to support the continuous improvement process.

LEADERS ENSURE ADAPTABILITY

Intentional change in the system-in-place is both difficult and often "messy." Change in a complex system is difficult because it requires the coordinated efforts of many people, some of who may not be convinced that all this individual and organizational effort will make any difference in student learning. It is messy because even the best action plans will encounter unintended roadblocks, disruptions, and delays.

High-quality action plans reflect the leadership's best thinking at the time, based on the best information available at the time, on how to go about the intended change process. However, circumstances change, sometimes in such a way as to render an action plan, which was feasible and practical when it was designed, impractical and unsuitable. A good analogy would be the popular online mapping program, Mapquest.™ This and other online services designed to provide directions and maps are generally very accurate in indicating how to go from point A to point B. But, as good as they are, such programs cannot anticipate detours due to road construction or accidents that may occur along the route. Likewise, leaders must be vigilant and be prepared to make adjustments and midcourse corrections to timelines, resource allocations, pace, etc.

> *"I can't change the direction of the wind, but I can adjust my sails to reach my destination."*
>
> — *Jimmy Dean*
> *Actor and*
> *Entrepreneur*

In addition to unforeseen events, as time goes by, new knowledge about new and better ways to do things may become available. As a result, an action plan that will be useful throughout the change effort, even in the face of unforeseen events and new knowledge, must be what systems theorist Russell Ackoff calls "adaptable"—that is, able to learn from experience. Adaptability, according to Ackoff, is an essential requirement of a sustainable system.

A Systems Approach to Monitoring

The willingness to adapt to changing circumstances and new knowledge is really another way to say that effective leaders are willing to "monitor and adjust." Regardless of what we call it, the heart and soul of continuous improvement is the ability and willingness of system leaders to change direction in ways that further the vision and mission, and are consistent with our core beliefs and values. The ability to do so is dependent on having a method in place for obtaining information on the changing environment, internal processes, and results of the reform efforts. It is critical, then, that the leader makes sure such a system for obtaining pertinent information, both from within and outside the organization, is created as part of the action plan.

In the context of continuous school improvement, a leader must be mindful of various types of information as the basis for adapting the action plans. The leader must find a way to gather relevant information from sources both external and internal to the organization. To create a systematic and systemic approach to monitoring, we'll refer back to the Adapted Double-Loop Learning Model (located on the next page).

"Information is a source of learning. But unless it is organized, processed, and available to the right people in a format for decision making, it is a burden, not a benefit."

> — *William Pollard*
> *CEO of Service-*
> *master Corp.*

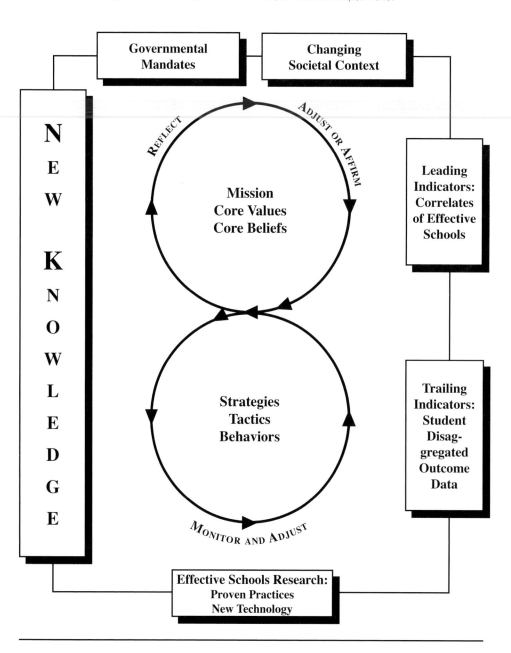

ADAPTED DOUBLE-LOOP LEARNING MODEL WITHIN THE CONTEXT OF THE CHANGING EDUCATIONAL ENVIRONMENT AND NEW KNOWLEDGE.

The double loop in the center of the diagram represents your school. The boxes that surround the double loop represent the factors that may impact the strategies, tactics, and behaviors that are part of the action plan. You should consider these factors as the action plan is being created, and monitor changes in these areas so that the action plan can be adjusted in a timely and appropriate manner when necessary:

Governmental Mandates. Since NCLB was instituted in 2001, there have been many policy and procedural adjustments handed down from the Department of Education. In addition to responding to these mandates, schools and districts contend with changes and demands set forth by their respective states and communities. Effective leaders have "their ears to the ground" so that they can adjust the action plan if necessary.

Trailing & Leading Indicators. We have already addressed the issues around choosing appropriate metrics for measuring student outcomes and indicators of learning, as well as the frequency of monitoring, in Chapter 7. How student learning responds to the action plan will constitute

the primary reason for adjusting the action plan. As we said in Chapter 7, the more frequently you monitor learning, the easier it will be to adjust the system.

New Knowledge, Research, & Technology. The leader should be on the lookout for new research and descriptions of proven practices that may be incorporated into the action plans, even if the plan is being implemented. This doesn't mean that entire action plans should be changed midstream every time a new approach is found. It does mean that research can help us refine and hone our existing plan, making it more efficient and more effective.

Strategies, Tactics, & Behaviors. Monitoring the tactics, strategies, and behaviors associated with the action plan is a complex undertaking. However, the sustainability of the change effort requires ongoing engagement by the leader. Like other aspects of continuous improvement, sustainability is helped when the leader constantly monitors the processes, collects and analyzes process data, and routinely provides progress reports throughout the system.

Progress of Implementation.
One of the best ways to monitor how well the action plan is being implemented is the Gantt chart (see example on the following page). A Gantt chart represents a matrix of tasks to be completed on the vertical axis and a timeline on the horizontal axis. The responsible individual or group is listed within the cells of the matrix. A Gantt chart should be developed for every improvement goal and the leader should have the chart enlarged and displayed in a place where the staff and other stakeholders can see it. The Gantt chart will serve as a reminder of their commitments to continuous improvement. As tasks are completed, the leader should check them off, giving everyone a sense of progress and accomplishment. The Gantt chart, as a public display of the work to be done and those designated to do it, also represents a powerful accountability system. Most people do not want to be seen by their peers and colleagues as the individual or group that impeded progress by failing to complete their responsibilities.

Response of the System. Leaders must be attentive to how the system responds to the implementation of the action plan and, if appropriate, modify the action plan to incorporate the new knowledge. As we suggested earlier, virtually any change in the system-in-place will create unintended consequences elsewhere in the system. Positive unintended consequences are generally welcomed and celebrated. It's the negative unintended consequences that leaders must be prepared to address as soon as they appear. For example, the new student report card represents a more accurate reporting system for student learning. The teachers are initially very excited about the new process. After having worked with it, the teachers find the extra time, effort, and paperwork required a burden. Report cards are turned in late, and morale at the end of the marking period plummets. It is the leader's responsibility to use this new knowledge to adjust the system to address this unintended consequence. This will no doubt require creativity on the leader's part, since each situation that arises will be different.

> *"Enjoying success requires the ability to adapt. Only by being open to change will you have a true opportunity to get the most from your talent."*
>
> — *Nolan Ryan*
> *Baseball Hall of*
> *Fame Pitcher*

EXAMPLE OF A GANTT CHART

	Activity	Who's Responsible	Sept.	Oct.	Nov.	Dec.	Jan.	Feb.
Action Plan 1: Develop Dropout Intervention System	Action Plan 1 Task 1		▬					
	Action Plan 1 Task 2		▬▬	▬			▬	
	Action Plan 1 Task 3				▬	▬		
	Action Plan 1 Task 4						▬	
Action Plan 2: Expand College Prep Course Offerings	Action Plan 2 Task 1			▬	▬			
	Action Plan 2 Task 2							▬
	Action Plan 2 Task 3				▬	▬	▬	
	Action Plan 2 Task 4		▬					
Action Plan 3: Expand Service Learning Opportunities	Action Plan 3 Task 1		▬	▬	▬	▬	▬	
	Action Plan 3 Task 2				▬	▬		
	Action Plan 3 Task 3					▬	▬	
	Action Plan 3 Task 4				▬			

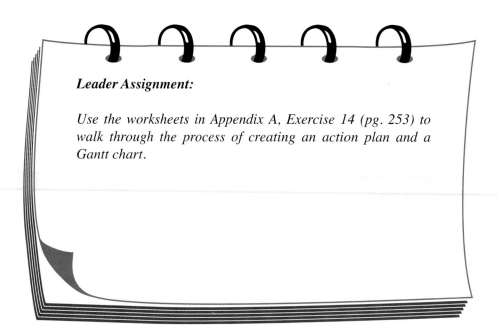

Leader Assignment:

Use the worksheets in Appendix A, Exercise 14 (pg. 253) to walk through the process of creating an action plan and a Gantt chart.

LEADERS STAY ENGAGED

The leader may or may not be singled out for specific tasks that are outlined in the action plans and Gantt chart. Nevertheless, the leader has an obligation to oversee the implementation of all the tasks in a timely fashion. Therefore, in your role as leader, you should develop a parallel chart that specifies how you intend to be engaged in monitoring each and every step and stage of the implementation process. This could be as simple as adding a column to the Gantt chart that will track what you will do to monitor and, where necessary, adjust each step on the timeline.

> *"One of the true tests of leadership is the ability to recognize a problem before it becomes an emergency."*
>
> — *Arnold H. Glasgow*
> *Author*

BRINGING CONTINUOUS IMPROVEMENT PLANS TO LIFE

The primary purpose of the logistical action plan document is to provide all stakeholders, and other interested parties for that matter, with a clear overview of how the improvement goals will be translated into the ongoing reality of the school or district. Beyond this, however, the document can be useful in communicating to any number of publics. Community groups, parents, policymakers, and the public at-large will react favorably knowing that "their" school or district has thought deeply about doing better on the learning-for-all mission and core values. State agencies and private foundations will no doubt want to receive a copy of the plan.

Leaders should think about the many and various publics that would have an interest in the plan document. They should make it attractive and have multiple copies available for distribution. They should be creative and proactive in brainstorming additional ways the document can be used.

One sure way to just about guarantee no change will occur as a result of the planning process is to take the planning document and hide it in the bottom drawer of your desk. Remember: This is not a classified document! Make it public! Make it a living document that gets discussed with folks at every opportunity. As the plan is successfully implemented and desired changes begin to appear, use the document and the accomplishments it has wrought as a source of celebration. Imagine the power that will be generated when a group of invested people, led by a committed individual, says they are going to do something, actually does it, and the predicted improvements in learning become apparent!

Effective Leaders, Effective Plans

It has been said, "Failing to plan is planning to fail." It would logically follow, then, that the better we plan, the more likely our success. In the end, leaders who are seeking to create action plans that will yield sustainable improvement in student learning must be able to answer "yes" to three big questions:

- Can we successfully achieve the goals we have set for ourselves in the short run given the time and resources we have with which to work?

- Have we incorporated a way into the action plan for successfully supporting and maintaining the changes over the long run?

- Are we prepared to change our action plans and/or the substance of an improvement goal if new knowledge becomes available along the way?

Although a collaborative and inclusive process is key to the success of the continuous school improvement process, it is ultimately the leader's responsibility to ensure that every action plan is related to a specified improvement goal and incorporates a comprehensive monitoring process. If the monitoring component is missing, accountability will be lacking, and it is likely that the action plans will not be properly implemented. After all, "What gets measured, gets done." If the action plan never "gets done" and school improvement is not forthcoming, all eyes will turn to the leader for an explanation. Therefore, it behooves the leader to be very vigilant and engaged in the process of translating improvement goals into a set of feasible and sustainable action steps.

> *"It is not only what we do, but also what we do not do, for which we are accountable."*
>
> — *Jean-Baptiste Moliere French Playwright*

10

MAKING IT HAPPEN

"Knowing is not enough; we must apply. Being willing is not enough; we must <u>do</u>."

— *Leonardo da Vinci*
Italian Scholar,
Philosopher,
Inventor & Architect

The word "execution" has two meanings. The first means to end someone's life for crimes committed; the other is the act of doing something successfully. Given the pressure for school reform, and the demand that every school and district meet annual yearly progress goals, both meanings have currency for today's educational leaders and their careers. It is the latter definition, however, upon which this chapter will primarily focus.

All too often, school improvement plans fail to have the desired effects, not because they were bad or ineffective plans, but because they were never implemented or "executed." The reasons for this lack of execution are many; lack of commitment, resources, knowledge, training, time, and accountability are just a few. However, if the leader has carefully attended to the steps of the continuous school improvement process and the required leader behaviors outlined throughout this book, many of these causes will have been already addressed and, hopefully, prevented. Even so, the continuing engagement of the leader throughout implementation of the plan will be essential to its success.

Leaders Take Action

Larry Bossidy and Ram Charan, in their book titled *Execution: The Discipline of Getting Things Done*, assert that successful execution is not just happenstance. In fact, the thesis of their book is twofold, that 1) the skills necessary to successfully execute and sustain organizational change represent a discipline; and 2) leadership without the discipline of execution is incomplete and ineffective. They go on to describe seven essential leader behaviors associated with the successful execution of organizational change. Many of these leader behaviors have been discussed in some detail in previous chapters. Here we will describe each briefly, and expand on those that have not yet been addressed.

1. **Know your people and your "business."** In organizations that don't execute, the leaders are usually out of touch with the day-to-day realities. All too often, this observation is true for principals and superintendents—not because they are indifferent to the learning mission, but because of the number of different functions for which they are responsible.

2. **Insist on realism.** Many organizations are filled with people who are unrealistic about the strengths and weaknesses of their organization. It's amazing to see the extent to which some people will go to avoid having to confront reality. Effective leaders use relevant data and appropriate questions to circumvent denial.

3. **Set clear goals and priorities.**

4. **Follow through.** Failure to follow through on plans is widespread in change-oriented organizations. Over the years, the number of schools that labored to develop improvement plans only to let them sit on a shelf unused is legion. As we discussed in the last chapter, a publicly displayed Gantt chart outlining the what, who, and when of task accomplishment will go a long way in assuring follow through.

5. **Reward the doers.** It seems obvious, but if you want people to produce specific results or do things in a specific way, you need to reward them accordingly. The current culture of education tends to avoid anything that smacks of merit pay. Nonetheless, when it comes to school change, individuals tend to vary in the amount of time and effort they are willing to expend in the name of continuous improvement planning and implementation. Recognizing and rewarding extraordinary effort can be a powerful force for sustaining the change effort. One of the most powerful strategies that school districts use is to recognize and

reward the entire staff of a school if improvement goals are met. This strategy can strengthen the sense of community within a school, and the idea that "we're all in this together."

Recognition and reward can take many forms, some tangible and some subtle. Some of the obvious forms would include financial awards for individuals, teams, or the whole staff. Others might be to provide the "doers" with an opportunity to attend professional conferences or access to other special "perks." Less tangible, but equally important, includes public recognition by the leader. Sometimes a simple "thank you" by the school leader is as powerful as anything. Here again, the leader needs to think about the issue of rewards and recognition, and be very intentional in recognizing those key individuals whose heroic efforts have contributed significantly to the change effort.

6. Expand people's capabilities.
We have emphasized throughout this manuscript that sustainable change requires new knowledge and skills on the one hand and changes in the system on the other. Good leaders know that one of their most important tasks is to assure that staff have the skill sets and capabilities they need to successfully execute the action plan. Effective leaders are sensitive to training and technical assistance needs at the launch of the change effort and throughout the implementation process.

The leader can fulfill this function in a variety of different ways. Training and retraining of staff may be central to the change process. Coaching with support will be more effective in many situations. Collaborative inquiry and action research are excellent tools for developing staff expertise.

Asking for change without assuring that the needed knowledge and skills are in place is a formula for resistance and failure. Author and organizational change scholar Phillip Schlechty has said that educators are not so much change _resistant_ as they are change _inept_. For example, many of the most effective improvement strategies require teachers to work together in teams. Yet, since most teachers work alone most of the time, they may not be skilled in teamwork and collaborative decision-making. These individuals would benefit from training on team building, shared decision making, and collaborative problem solving. Leaders must be able to ascertain when progress is being slowed or stifled because of the absence of necessary skills and take appropriate action.

7. Know yourself. Earlier we addressed some of the personal attributes that are associated with successful leadership. While needed character dimensions are critical throughout the continuous improvement process, some take on special significance at this stage. For example, leaders always have to be seen as trustworthy, but it is especially important at the point when you are asking individuals to let go of past behaviors and "grab" new behaviors. The followers need constant reassurance that the change effort and their risk taking will not be abandoned in midstream.

Bossidy and Charan also list three personal qualities that leaders especially need at the execution stage of the change process: emotional fortitude that gives the leader the courage to proceed; the ability to live with and adjust to ambiguity in a fast-moving and complex organization; and the ability to hold people accountable and be firm with those who are not performing. A leader who accommodates individuals who cannot or will not meet the standards discourages those who do.

Some schools are "can-do" schools, while others are "no-can-do" schools. School leaders must take a large share of the credit—or blame—for the prevailing attitude in their school. The leader behaviors specified by Bossidy and Charan and throughout this book, coupled with a positive can-do attitude, will help you ensure that the action plan will be implemented and that continuous school improvement becomes "how we do things around here."

> *"If your actions inspire others to dream more, learn more, do more, and become more, you are a leader."*
>
> — *John Quincy Adams*
> *6th President of the United States*

STAY CLOSE

Leaders need to stay as close as possible to the change process once it is launched. Day-to-day engagement in the implementation process will allow you to observe the implementation of the change process for an "up close and personal" perspective. This is much different that looking at the Gantt chart or reading a report. By being "in the trenches," whether at school improvement meetings, in a study group, or observing classes, you will learn firsthand what's working and what's not. You'll get a sense of individual and collective attitudes toward the change effort, and be able to identify existing and potential obstacles to implementation.

Being close to the implementation effort offers additional benefits. Continued visibility and engagement in the implementation phase is one way leaders "walk the talk." Remember, fair or not, the stakeholders will judge what you as the leader value by where you spend your time. If you delegate the oversight of school improvement activities to someone else, it will appear to the followers that the implementation of the action plan is not your priority. Conversely, personal involvement will convey your commitment to the continuous improvement process and communicate the feeling that "we're all in this together." All these benefits serve to reinforce your trustworthiness as a leader.

> "The day soldiers stop bringing you their problems is the day you have stopped leading them. They have either lost confidence that you can help them or concluded that you do not care."
>
> — Colin Powell
> Former U.S.
> Secretary of State

ASSURING IMPLEMENTATION BY GIVING VOICE TO THE DATA

The second strategy the leader should use to the greatest extent possible is to monitor the implementation by "giving voice to the data."

In the previous chapter, we introduced the concept of the Gantt chart as a way of summarizing who is supposed to do what, by when, as a way to ensure the successful execution of the action plans. The Evaluation Gantt chart is a similar idea, but with a little different focus. The Evaluation Gantt chart is designed to set out what data will be collected by whom, from whom, and by when, to determine the effectiveness of the effort. This will incorporate many of the metrics you and the stakeholders specified earlier in the process. The data gathered along the implementation journey will allow the leader and others to know what midcourse corrections are needed and whether the intended outcomes of each step and stage in the action plans are being realized.

When developing the Evaluation Gantt chart, we recommend that the leader start with the assumption that each and every action plan will have both positive and negative outcomes, some of which can be anticipated and others that cannot. If you set out a data-gathering net that does a reasonably comprehensive job of monitoring the change process, you and your colleagues will have the data needed to increase the likelihood of success.

> *"When it is obvious that the goals cannot be reached, don't adjust the goals, adjust your actions."*
>
> — *Confucius*
> *Chinese Philosopher*

THE LEADER AS CRITICAL FRIEND

Some school improvement efforts falter because those implementing them lack an in-depth understanding of effective change. Everyone associated with a change effort, including the leader, has a personal map or mental model of how change does, or should, proceed. These personal maps guide individual behaviors. If a map is built on incomplete or incorrect information, it won't provide reliable guidance. Many failed attempts at school reform can be traced back to the leaders' failures to anticipate the complexities of the innovation they hoped to implement. While change leaders don't need to have all the answers at the outset, they must be prepared to deal with the ambiguity and uncertainty that they will surely encounter. They also must clearly convey to the followers the uncertain nature of change and the undeniable fact that obstacles and roadblocks will inevitably be encountered. This hails back to the leadership quality of "confident uncertainty" we discussed in previous chapters.

In his article "The Change Leader," Michael Fullan argues that all change involves uncertainty, and people will not venture into uncertainty unless they come to understand that the difficulties they will inevitably encounter are a natural part of the process. It is up to the leader to become a "critical friend" to the organization. As a critical friend, the leader again "walks the talk" by openly sharing bad news about problems, issues, and failures associated with the change effort. Effective leaders don't dwell on the doom and gloom aspects of failure, but use the situation as a starting point for analysis, learning, and collective and collaborative inquiry. They create a culture where problems are viewed as friends, not enemies, and mistakes are seen as valuable knowledge in the pursuit of the mission.

"The measure of success is not whether you have a tough problem to deal with, but whether it is the same problem you had last year."

— *John Foster Dulles*
Former U.S.
Secretary of State

This requires that the leader create strong, supportive relationships with and among the followers to prevent them from feeling threatened by bad news, new ideas, or challenges to the current way of conducting business. The effective leader encourages stakeholders to take professional risks, to honestly assess their current ways of doing things, and to commit to trying new and different ways of doing things. To do this, the leader must lead the way in discussing what's working and what's not, and in debating new ideas. The leader must remind the followers that "we are in this together," all lifelong learners who must confront obstacles, investigate and try new approaches, and share ideas to improve their skills. Without such an open and accepting culture, this type of discussion and leadership is very threatening to teachers and other stakeholders, resulting in little or no meaningful change.

A variation on the concept of the critical friend would be to invite an outside team of trusted colleagues to visit your school or district. Educators are generally familiar with the concept of a site-visit team for accreditation purposes.

With this approach, you would send the visiting team your data and action plans prior to their visit so that they come to the site visit knowledgeable about what you are trying to accomplish. You would ask them to provide written feedback. Fresh eyes looking at the continuous improvement work of the school or district can truly enrich the conversation in a useful manner.

On the other hand, if the leader refuses the role of critical friend and attempts to gloss over difficulties and failures, or sweep them under the rug, it won't be long before that leader loses credibility with the followers. Trustworthy leaders "tell it like it is," and project the belief that the problems can be overcome and the learning for all mission attained.

> *"To be persuasive we must be believable; to be believable we must be credible; to be credible we must be truthful."*
>
> — *Edward R. Murrow*
> *Journalist*

DEALING WITH OBSTACLES TO CHANGE

In his book *Taking Charge of Change: 10 Principles for Managing People and Performance*, Douglas K. Smith asserts that implementation of even the best action plan often eludes organizations when their people must learn and exhibit new behaviors and ways of working. But, he adds, few people are out-and-out resistant to change. Instead, most people can recognize and understand the need for change, but are reluctant to do so. A number of factors affect an individual's willingness to change. Most of them, if you have followed our suggested steps, will have been prevented or addressed early on in the reform effort. However, individuals embrace change at differing rates and in differing ways and you may find yourself facing either resistance or reluctance from important stakeholders. Effective leaders anticipate resistance and are ready to address it. Most of the strategies leaders use to address these issues revolve around continued and enthusiastic communication and providing the followers with the skills, knowledge, and resources they need.

Leader Assignment:

To assist you in understanding reasons for the resistance and reluctance you may encounter from individuals involved in the change process, we've created a chart in Appendix A, Exercise 15 (pg. 257) using the items identified by Doug Smith, as well as some suggested strategies you might try to address them. As you review the chart, identify which sources of resistance exist or are likely to crop up as you implement the action plans. Then use the System Check-Up for Promoting Successful Change in Appendix A, Exercise 16 (pg. 261) to ensure that you've "covered all the bases" in promoting successful implementation of the action plans.

CAPTAIN OF THE CHEERLEADING TEAM

Change requires effort. Sustainable change requires continuing effort. The level of effort required to both initiate and sustain the change must be renewed as time goes on. As the work required to implement the changes begins to become a burden, the head cheerleader needs to step up and encourage the staff to stay the course. And the head cheerleader is you, the leader.

One of the most effective strategies for inspiring the staff to stay the course is to celebrate successes, both large and small. These celebrations can offer a renewed sense of energy to those involved in the change effort, as they are able to see that their efforts are making things happen. Effective leaders have found creative ways to celebrate successes. Years ago, there was a superintendent who would personally deliver the state assessment results to the individual schools within the district. If a school had shown improvement, the results were delivered with cake and ice cream as a way of the local school board expressing its appreciation for the hard work on the part of the staff. Good leaders are very creative at finding low-cost, high-yield, and highly visible ways to celebrate successes.

"Git-R-Done!"

— *Larry the Cable Guy*
Comedian on the
Blue Collar Tour

11

LEADERSHIP AND THE ENDLESS JOURNEY

> "He who stops being better
> stops being good."
>
> — *Sir Oliver Cromwell*
> *British Military*
> *Leader & Politician*

At the outset of this book, you may have thought (or hoped) that within these pages you would find a recipe for school improvement that would yield a "finished product." Perhaps you thought that your work as the leader would be completed—at least, for the most part—when the action plans were implemented. As you have progressed through these pages, however, and if we have done our job properly, you have come to the realization that continuous school improvement—intentional change in pursuit of the "learning for all" mission—is an ongoing and never-ending process.

What does this mean in terms of your ongoing presence and engagement as the leader of the change effort?

A FOCUSING FORCE FOR DAILY ACTION

The comments of one outstanding superintendent, who had been implementing district-wide continuous improvement for five years, will offer insight on the leaders' ongoing role in the process. When asked what issues still demanded his attention, he replied that—even after five years—the primary challenge was still "the will to do it." He noted that if he didn't keep the light shining on the effort, the old system-in-place would inevitably pull the culture and the staff behaviors back to the old ways of doing things, back to the "paths of least resistance." As we discussed earlier, old, well-established paths of least resistance linger long and disappear slowly.

When it comes to sustaining change efforts, the leaders must be constantly vigilant to be sure that those old mindsets don't return and drive out the changes all have worked so hard to plan and implement.

A Focusing Force for Daily Action

Another example of the leaders' ongoing role comes from the former CEO of a large U.S. company. In a flight magazine interview, the reporter asked the retired corporate leader what he actually *did* when he went to work. While this may at first seem like a pretty dumb question, the CEO's response offers exceptional insight into the challenges leaders face and effectively characterizes the ongoing work of the educational leader. The CEO said that most of his time was taken up with reminding everyone who worked in or with the company of the company's mission and core values. Beyond that, if he had any time left, he would use it to try to build an company in which all the workers could feel both productive and satisfied in contributing to the mission.

Why do leaders need to spend so much time and effort on keeping the company and its people centered on its mission and core values?

Once again, we turn to two noted authors for some insight into the question. Tom Peters and Robert Waterman, authors of *In Search of Excellence*, stated that big organizations by virtue of their very size are always apt to "drift" away from their mission and core values. You'll find it interesting to note that their definition of a "big" organization is any organization that employees more than *four* people. By that criterion, virtually every school and every school district is subject to this problem of "mission drift."

A useful analogy to how organizations drift away from their missions is the carnival ride that spins faster and faster. The faster the ride spins, the more those riding feel the centrifugal force that pushes them away from the center of the circle. The force is so great, that when the bottom of the ride drops out, the riders "stick" to the walls. Similarly, the day-to-day activities of the organization, further complicated by daily crises and disruptions, tend to push the workers away from the organization's "center"—its mission and core values. What's needed is a countervailing *centripetal* force that draws the workers back toward to the mission and core values, and toward each other. The ongoing role of the educational leader is to be that countervailing force. The educational leader, like our CEO, must find a thousand and one ways to keep people centered on the mission and core values. Proactively, reactively, and interactively, the leader must continually champion the mission and values.

INSTITUTIONALIZING CHANGE

Organizational scholar and author, Terrence Deal, gives us two different definitions of organizational culture. His first definition of culture is, "That's the way we do things here." His second definition of culture is, "That's *not* the way we do things here." Sustainable change means that the new behaviors, policies, and practices must actually reengineer the paths of least resistance. As the leader, you may finally be able to take a break when it can be said that the changes truly constitute "the way we do things here." Until that occurs, your time, attention, and ongoing inspiration will be the best ways to neutralize the pull of the paths of least resistance. Once the changes we seek become part and parcel of the school's culture, they begin to generate their own sustaining energy.

> "To lead people, walk beside them.... When the best leader's work is done, the people say, 'We did it ourselves!'"
>
> — *Lao-tsu*
> *Chinese Philosopher*

No Two Leaders Are Alike

In the beginning of this book, we said that all leadership is contextual. Every situation is different, as is every individual who embraces the role of leader. And yet, there are similarities among effective leaders. In their groundbreaking book *In Their Time: The Greatest Business Leaders of the 20th Century*, authors Anthony Mayo and Nitin Nohria identify three prototypical leadership styles among the greatest leaders.

- **The Entrepreneurial Leader.** The genius of the entrepreneurial leader lies in combining things in a way that no one has ever seen before. In education, such leaders would be those who truly envision the learning-for-all system that takes the best of current practice and integrates it with technology to create highly engaging learning environments.

- **The Managerial Leader.** The leader-as-manager is an individual who is able to get the most out of something that already exists. They might be what one would call "value maximizers." Most school and district leaders that have proven to be outstanding effective school leaders fall in this category. Over the last 30 years, we have worked with many men and women who were able to make the changes required to advance the learning-for-all mission without the extraordinary infusion of resources beyond what the school would normally have available. Many of the recommendations offered throughout this manuscript are based on lessons learned from outstanding leaders who were hired not to lead, but to manage.

- **The Charismatic Leader.** Charismatic leaders are seen by most of us almost as a celebrity because of their flamboyant personalities and leader behaviors. Years ago, CBS's 60 Minutes aired a piece on the recognized and celebrated teacher, Marva Collins. After that program aired, both the print and electronic media called Ron Edmonds for his comment on this celebrity-teacher. Ron's response was memorable: "I've never met Marva Collins, but if she is as the media has portrayed her, she must be a truly gifted and charismatic teacher. . . . But, he went on to say, "we can't build our institutions and systems based on charisma, because we don't know where to find it or how to create it. We need to build our institutions based on the best knowledge we have at the time."

These three profiles were presented to make two points. First, leadership can take different forms and no one style has a corner on the leadership "market." Second, effective leaders, to some degree, embody a bit of all three styles. Clearly, we need to be one part entrepreneur and see new possibilities, one part manager and make the best from what we have, and one part charismatic, so we stand out for who we are and our passionate commitment for what we do.

> *"Desire is the key to motivation, but it's determination and commitment to an unrelenting pursuit of your goal—a commitment to excellence—that will enable you to attain the success you seek."*
>
> — *Mario Andretti*
> *World Champion*
> *Auto Racing Driver*

Leader Assignment:

Think about these three leadership styles: entrepreneurial, managerial, and charismatic. Which of these styles best fits your own vision of yourself as an effective leader? How could you cultivate attributes of the other leadership styles and integrate them into your personal style to make you an even better leader?

The Sustainable Leader

It is the leader's role to sustain the change effort, but who sustains the leader? Or, more to the point, how do successful leaders sustain their motivation, energy, and enthusiasm for the task at-hand? Two educational researchers, Sheryl Boris-Schacter and Susan Merrifield, sought to answer this question.

The researchers interviewed 19 principals, eight men and 11 women, who were considered "particularly good" by their peers—defined as those "who were successfully incorporating the new initiatives of reform into their schools and whose leadership could serve as a model for aspiring principals." The interviewees represented urban and suburban schools, were ethnically diverse, and had a wide range of experience; six held doctoral degrees.

Through these interviews, the researchers sought to determine what activities helped these individuals continue to be principals, where they received "professional nourishment and renewal," and how they learned to be more effective educational leaders. They discovered that these individuals shared certain characteristics that contributed to their success. These characteristics fell into three categories: professional identity, influence of the liberal arts, and personal identity.

- **Professional Identity.**
  Improvement of teaching and learning was at the heart of their professional identity. They were passionate about the importance of good teaching, about putting student needs first, and about not settling for the status quo. They were unconcerned about job security and were energized by the challenges of change. They did not view themselves as managers, but rather as facilitators and learners, rejecting the old paradigm of the autocratic principal.

  One remarkable characteristic of these principals was the degree to which they perceived themselves as lifelong learners and viewed professional development as a continuous process of improvement. Though some complained about not having enough time, or felt guilty about using time and resources for their own development, none of them worried about being viewed as a "work in progress." Many described the performance areas where they felt weak and what they were doing to improve. They recognized that it was impossible to be an expert on everything and looked to staff for assistance and expertise. The professional development activities they reported included attending conferences, reading journals, and the on-the-job training of their day-to-day activities. All agreed they could do more if they had enough time. Many viewed their mentoring of graduate interns as a professional development opportunity that reduced the isolation typical of the principalship and forced them to reflect on their own practice and decision-making.

- **Influence of the Liberal Arts.**
  Many of the principals cited involvement in creative projects as an important aspect of their professional lives. For example, one travel-loving principal shared his interest in different cultures, while another modeled personal development by taking a pottery class. A third mentored students by sharing his love of sailing and the sea. These activities typically impacted large groups and attracted the attention of colleagues. While each principal's project was different, the common denominator was a connection to the liberal arts.

- **Personal Identity.** Unlike overwhelmed principals, the professionals in the study didn't sacrifice or shut off their real lives when they entered the schoolhouse door. Instead, they were able to integrate their professional and personal lives and understand how one impacts the other. These principals drew valuable lessons from each and every experience, and used the knowledge and skills they gained to perform competently, whether as a principal, or parent and family member. They were able to foster a mutual respect and fluidity between home and school, while maintaining appropriate boundaries.

This study offers insight to current and aspiring leaders who wonder if they'll be able to face the challenges of leading the fundamental change called for by the new mission of public education. It wasn't a lack of problems that allowed these individuals to thrive and persist in their work. They faced the same difficulties of leading change and in balancing the demands of work and home as every other principal. But these "particularly good" principals were able to turn their challenges into learning opportunities to become better administrators, learners, parents, family members, and friends. The interrelationship of the principalship, personal interests, and the liberal arts was a recurring theme.

It is particularly notable that these effective principals embraced a lifelong learning orientation—for their students, their staff, and themselves. Effective leaders never stop learning. They find ways to renew themselves, both professionally and personally. They consciously work to reach out to others, to overcome the isolation inherent in their leadership positions. They attend conferences, network with peers and colleagues, and become co-learners with their staff members and students. With a learning orientation in hand, the effective leader comes to view every problem becomes an opportunity for learning and growth, and models a passion for learning that inspires everyone involved.

> *"In everyone's life, at some time, our inner fire goes out. It is then burst into flame by an encounter with another human being. We should all be thankful for those people who rekindle the inner spirit."*
>
> — *Albert Schweitzer*
> *Doctor, Missionary,*
> *& Theologian*

WHAT'S WORTH FIGHTING FOR?

In the forward of this book, we stated that the stakes are very high for our country when it comes to school reform. Our system of public education was created because our founders recognized that an educated citizenry was fundamental to a democratic way of life. Andy Hargreaves and Michael Fullan reinforce this and other reasons for improving public education in their book *What's Worth Fighting for Out There?* and advocate two basic reforms.

First, say Hargreaves and Fullan, if we are going to bring about significant improvements in teaching and learning within the schools, we must forge strong, open, and interactive connections with communities beyond them. To do this, schools must go "wider" by developing new relationships with parents, employees, universities, technology, and the broader community. Second, schools must go "deeper" into the heart of the education profession to rediscover the passion and moral purposes that make teaching and learning exciting and effective. We must infuse education with a commitment to caring, empowerment, and service, in addition to a focus on learning.

However, leaders are rarely, if ever, encouraged to explore the deeper moral purposes of education. When someone suggests that the moral issues need to be discussed, far too many educators' eyes glaze over. But to engender the kind of commitment needed to create and sustain a school community committed to learning for all, leaders must engage the faculty in the deeper issues of why they are there, and the moral dimensions of education in a democracy. "Going deeper" will stir the passion and hope that lies at the heart of good teaching and provides the leader's best recipe for avoiding staff burnout and moral martyrdom.

Likewise, far too many educators don't realize—until it's too late—that parents and the broader community want to be full partners in the reform of the public's schools; and why shouldn't they feel this way? Going wider, to use the phrase coined by the authors, is a sensible way to proceed. Asking and engaging the stakeholders from the beginning is not simply the right thing to do; it also represents smart self-interest, because if you don't involve them, your hard work may be swept away on a moment's notice.

In a democracy aiming to endure, schools must first be the world we want to see. To lead others in creating the schools that model our democratic ideals, you must also first "be" the world you want to see.

BE THE WORLD
YOU WANT TO SEE

We've used this phrase frequently throughout this book. It is perhaps the single most important advice we can give those who seek to lead others and deserves repeating. If you expect the followers to make and follow through on the commitments required by the continuous improvement process, you must—above all—have credibility with the followers. There is only one way to do this: you must model the mission, values, and behaviors that you are asking the followers to embrace and demonstrate. You cannot ask the staff to work collaboratively if you are autocratic in your own decision making. You cannot foster a culture of inquiry if you are not yourself a learner. You cannot demand that everyone maintain high expectations if you're making excuses for the poor performance of some students.

Leaders are always under the "hot lights," especially by those who would resist change. When the leader "walks the talk," it makes it far more difficult for the change resisters to muster support. But if critics can show the leader to be hypocritical to the mission, vision, and values they espouse, support for the leader and the change effort will be hard to find.

This doesn't mean that a leader must be perfect, or never make mistakes. Mistakes are part and parcel of the continuous improvement process. But the way in which leaders deal with their mistakes can either increase their trustworthiness and credibility in the eyes of the followers, or diminish them.

> *"People may doubt what you say, but they will believe what you do."*
>
> — *Lewis Cass*
> *American Statesman*

FOSTERING LEADERSHIP AMONG THE FOLLOWERS

We have made the case that there are only two kinds of schools—improving or declining; therefore, continuous school improvement is no longer optional. By mandate and moral imperative, we must create learning communities where all students learn, where "no child is left behind." Not only must schools get better at educating our youth, *they must get better at getting better*. This fact and the other realities that 21st century schools are confronting demands broad leadership from administrators, teachers, and other school stakeholders. As a result, today's leaders must recognize the need to cultivate leaders for the long term. The school improvement process provides a natural laboratory for growing leaders in all our schools. It's up to us to take advantage of the opportunities for leadership development inherent in the school improvement process and use them to increase leadership capacity in every school. The long-term survival of public education as we know it depends, in no small measure, on leadership development.

ARE YOU READY TO "STEP UP"?

With this book, we have tried to create a vision for public education that will empower you and inspire you to "step up" to the role of leader. Within these pages, we've presented lessons about effective leadership garnered from the effective schools research and decades of experience working with schools and districts throughout the U.S. and Canada. We've offered you exercises and additional resources for you to pursue that we hope will guide you in leading your school or district in the quest for excellence. But, as they say, there's no better teacher than experience, and the only way to become a great leader is to begin.

> *"There comes a moment when you have to stop revving up the car and shove it into gear."*
>
> — *David Mahoney*
> *American Business-*
> *man & Philan-*
> *thropist*

Our wish for you is this: by working shoulder-to-shoulder with those you are privileged to lead, you and your colleagues are successful in weaving the unlimited possibilities of what public education <u>can</u> be into a tapestry of "learning for all" for each and every child.

Our children and our schools deserve nothing less.

APPENDIX A

Organized Abandonment

One of the most difficult issues educational leaders face is finding time to focus on the change effort. On the following pages, you will find Jack Bowsher's list of tasks and responsibilities for which principals are typically responsible. Use the checklist to identify those responsibilities and activities you can delegate or eliminate altogether.

Remember: By delegating responsibility, you are not only streamlining your own workload, but you will be empowering others and giving them opportunities to develop their own leadership skills.

Directions:

- Review Jack Bowsher's list of 122 tasks and responsibilities grouped into 11 categories. In the first column, check those items you currently are supposed to be doing, including those things that you never or rarely get to because of time constraints.

- In column two, put a "D" in the box next to the tasks and responsibilities you can delegate and an "A" in the box next to those you can abandon altogether.

- Brainstorm ideas for how and to whom you will delegate the tasks you checked and how you will abandon the specified items. Begin to develop a plan of organized abandonment, starting with those items you can easily and quickly drop, and working up to those tasks and responsibilities that may require restructuring and staff buy-in.

Things I currently do.	Things I can delegate or abandon.	
		General Leadership
❑	❑	Develops a shared vision and mission to achieve the goals and objectives established by the state department of education, school district, federal agencies, and other related groups.
❑	❑	Develops goals and strategic plans to implement the shared vision.
❑	❑	Keeps staff moving toward the vision and stays consistent with it by saying "no" to things that do not fit within the vision and approving projects that do.
❑	❑	Maintains a clear focus on the expected outcomes.
❑	❑	Implements an organizational structure that enables classified employees and the teaching staff to have embraceable responsibilities.
❑	❑	Conducts staff meetings and provides written communication to the staff, students, and community.
❑	❑	Provides top performers with appropriate forms of recognition.
❑	❑	Designs and provides a formal system for suggestions on how to improve the school's operations and learning processes.
❑	❑	Maintains a positive working relationship with the school district and the Board of Education.
❑	❑	Attends appropriate conferences to learn "best practices" for school leadership.
❑	❑	Reads appropriate journals to learn "best practices" for school leadership.
❑	❑	Mobilizes the talents of staff members and brings out the best in each.
❑	❑	Develops a leadership capacity that is people-oriented and action-focused.

Things I currently do.	Things I can delegate or abandon.	
		Management and Operations
❏	❏	Ensures the school is open during regular and extended hours, and is properly staffed with appropriate personnel.
❏	❏	Obtains qualified substitute teachers, staff, and temporary employees, on both a short- and long-term basis as needed.
❏	❏	Ensures the school is clean, well-maintained, secured, and well supervised before and after school, during special events, and whenever visitors are on campus.
❏	❏	Inspects facilities regularly, and assures that custodial staff maintains the school grounds and buildings daily.
❏	❏	Works with general contractors and subcontractors on all building repairs, maintenance, and improvements.
❏	❏	Works with transportation supervisors to assure that bus schedules are aligned with the school's instructional needs.
❏	❏	Monitors student safety patrol programs, crossing guards, and student safety issues related to before- and after-school traffic in and around the school.
❏	❏	Assures that all hallways, bus pick-up areas, and student entrances and exits are supervised, safe, and efficient for pedestrians, bus riders, and student carpoolers.
❏	❏	Develops a Safe Schools Plan to cover any major disaster or violent act on campus.
❏	❏	Works with the local police and fire departments to assure fast responses and contingency plans for additional security if needed.
❏	❏	Conducts regular fire safety/disaster preparedness drills.
❏	❏	Meets with the local fire department officials to conduct safety inspections and compliance with fire safety regulations.

Things I currently do.	Things I can delegate or abandon.	

Management and Operations continued

| ❑ | ❑ | Supervises on-site health services staff and ensures there are adequate medical supplies in the nurse's office and in all classrooms. |
| ❑ | ❑ | Assures that all staff have up-to-date training for First Aid, CPR, and blood-borne pathogen handling. |

Human Resources

❑	❑	Reviews and understands the district policies, practices, and procedures to assure consistent and fair implementation of personnel guidelines and contract agreements.
❑	❑	Interviews and hires competent employees based on a review of documents, a thorough check of references, and an interview designed to assess knowledge and skills.
❑	❑	Provides a thorough orientation for new employees, including a manual that enables new employees to know what equipment and services are available for their use within the school.
❑	❑	Provides and reviews with all employees the performance management system that clearly outlines their job responsibilities. This review explains how employees will be evaluated, on what schedule, and what the expected performance levels will be.
❑	❑	Provides coaching to new, inexperienced, and low-performing employees to raise their performance to an "A" or "B" level. ("A" = Outstanding; "B" = Very Good; all others rated as "Needs to Improve.")
❑	❑	Provides employees who need to improve an opportunity to discuss complaints/problems and make adjustments necessary for them to become "A" or "B" performers with high morale.
❑	❑	Handles difficult or problem employees with a firm but fair approach and motivates them to become "A" or "B" performers.

Things I currently do.   **Things I can delegate or abandon.**

Human Resources continued

❑   ❑   Develops and conducts an annual morale survey to determine the level of satisfaction in place at school and then takes appropriate action to improve morale.

❑   ❑   Works with union representatives to resolve issues regarding working conditions and low-performing employees.

❑   ❑   Develops selected personnel to a performance level where they become candidates for positions of greater responsibility.

❑   ❑   Conducts exit interviews with all employees who leave the school.

❑   ❑   Handles all violations of personnel policies and practices in a firm, fair, and consistent manner.

❑   ❑   Counsels unsatisfactory employees into considering other kinds of work, and if necessary, terminates unsatisfactory employees.

❑   ❑   Handles all benefit issues based on the guidelines established by the school district (vacation, personal necessity leave, health issues, etc.).

❑   ❑   Works with the Assistant Superintendent of Human Resources on all major personnel issues and provides input to the district on how to improve personnel policies and practices.

❑   ❑   Implements a performance management system to achieve maximum productivity with the workforce.

❑   ❑   Supervises special education staff to assure compliance with timelines, assessment dates, student IEP learning goals, and staff/student ratios.

❑   ❑   Supervises counselors who assist students with academic, behavioral, social, and other school-related issues.

Things I currently do.	**Things I can delegate or abandon.**	

Human Resources continued

❑	❑	Monitors work of school cafeteria employees for quality, cleanliness, and efficiency of service.
❑	❑	Reviews and approves all extracurricular events, activities, club meetings, etc.
❑	❑	Conducts periodic meetings with classified and support staff employed at the school.

Discipline Policies and Procedures

❑	❑	Develops, publishes, and distributes the school and district policies on discipline, suspension, and expulsion.
❑	❑	Handles student discipline problems by consistently following the policies of the school and district.
❑	❑	Attends administrative hearings regarding students whose behavior warrants such hearings.
❑	❑	Works with staff to assure that preventive discipline is used throughout classrooms and on school grounds to eliminate problems before they begin.
❑	❑	Develops schoolwide strategies, together with district specialists, to eliminate the possibility of serious disciplinary issues occurring.
❑	❑	Follows all legal procedures for reporting student and other criminal activity to police and district officials.

Administrative Systems

| ❑ | ❑ | Works with the school district to implement an administrative system that minimizes work for teaching and support staff while providing adequate record-keeping. |
| ❑ | ❑ | Supervises attendance clerk and approves attendance data, procedures used for collecting attendance data, and follow-up phone calls on all absences. |

Things I currently do...	Things I can delegate or abandon...	
		Administrative Systems continued
❏	❏	Implements motivating strategies to improve student attendance, late arrivals, etc.
❏	❏	Supervises school office staff, assuring that efficient procedures are used to maintain effective and supportive school office operations.
❏	❏	Supervises and conducts weekly meetings with school secretary to plan, monitor, and modify daily office procedures, support for staff, work with parents, and effective communication systems within and outside of the school.
❏	❏	Reviews and approves all district, state, and federal reports.
❏	❏	Develops annual budgets for general school operations, special education, school improvement programs, and all other specially funded programs.
❏	❏	Reviews monthly operating reports and financial statements, takes appropriate action to assure that budgets are in alignment, and meets all district requirements for expenditures and submission of requisitions.
❏	❏	Provides all necessary and required student data for school/district/county/state/federal reports.
❏	❏	Provides necessary information to payroll department, including information about attendance, benefits, etc.
❏	❏	Attends district-required staff meetings.
❏	❏	Reads and attends seminars to become knowledgeable about laws related to school operations, student attendance, parent custody rights, etc.
❏	❏	Meets with district staff and attorneys when lawsuits, depositions, and testimonies are required.
❏	❏	Trains school staff on their roles related to avoiding lawsuits and minimizing exposure to claims made against the school/district.

Things I currently do. **Things I can delegate or abandon.**

Administrative Systems continued

❑ ❑ Answers e-mails promptly.

❑ ❑ Returns telephone messages promptly.

❑ ❑ Reads appropriate journals and publications on operating procedures used in successful schools.

❑ ❑ Implements and supervises an efficient and cost-effective system to purchase supplies, learning materials, technology, etc.

❑ ❑ Supports and assists with fundraising events.

Community and Public Relations

❑ ❑ Prepares for and speaks at appropriate community meetings, including Rotary, Lions, Kiwanis, etc.

❑ ❑ Attends community events, especially those designed to support schools and student activities.

❑ ❑ Responds to press inquiries and provides positive stories to the press regarding school activities and athletic events.

❑ ❑ Attends extracurricular and athletic events.

❑ ❑ Sponsors Open House events for parents and the community.

❑ ❑ Participates in community-wide school reform events.

❑ ❑ Supports local business organizations such as the Business Round Table and Chamber of Commerce.

❑ ❑ Attends Board of Education Meetings and, when appropriate, City Council Meetings.

Things I currently do.	Things I can delegate or abandon.	

Encouragement of Parent Involvement

❏ ❏ Conducts Back-to-School Nights and other Open House events for parents.

❏ ❏ Provides various ongoing communications to parents, including the following:
  • Expected learning at each grade level/subject area
  • Homework policy
  • Assessment systems
  • Discipline policy
  • Dress code requirements
  • Attendance requirements
  • Grading system
  • Parental support expectations
  • Extracurricular opportunities
  • Parent volunteer opportunities
  • School Site Council

❏ ❏ Participates in all PTA and School-Site Council meetings.

❏ ❏ Works with parents to develop Adult and Parent Education Programs.

❏ ❏ Encourages parents to volunteer at school and to support school programs and activities.

❏ ❏ Supervises and coordinates volunteer activities.

❏ ❏ Provides support and recognition for all volunteers.

Diversity

❏ ❏ Understands the relevant cultural issues related to the school's student/staff population.

❏ ❏ Provides for the education and language needs of students who are still learning English.

❏ ❏ Provides multicultural experiences for all students and staff, including special celebrations and events.

❏ ❏ Provides team-building activities for staff.

Things I currently do.	Things I can delegate or abandon.	

Technology and Communication Systems continued

❑	❑	Meets with district Director of Information Services to develop the school's technology and communication system to streamline required tasks and responsibilities.
❑	❑	Hires and trains appropriate school personnel to implement and maintain administrative, financial, learning, and assessment systems.
❑	❑	Ensures that equipment, software, and courseware are properly used and maintained.
❑	❑	Provides or arranges for training of classified employees and teachers to achieve maximum productivity with computerized systems.
❑	❑	Uses Student Information Systems to review student data, enter new information, and develop plans based on the data.
❑	❑	Ensures that a security system for all equipment is in place.
❑	❑	Develops a Technology Plan that includes future equipment, software, training, and staffing needs.

Leadership for Learning

❑	❑	Recruits teachers and support staff who match the school's needs and goals and who support the school's mission.
❑	❑	Implements an integrated curriculum based on the learning standards established by the district and state department of education.
❑	❑	Works with master teachers to select, modify, or develop validated lesson plans that enable the vast majority of students (at least 90%) to learn lessons included in the integrated curriculum.

Things I currently do.	Things I can delegate or abandon.	
		Leadership for Learning continued
❏	❏	Conducts weekly walk-through classroom observations throughout the school, using established criteria for teaching and learning.
❏	❏	Analyzes data collected in walk-through sessions, determining next-steps based on the observation data.
❏	❏	Establishes goals and objectives for each teacher based on student performance data and teacher requirements.
❏	❏	Reviews each teacher's progress toward goals at regular intervals throughout the year.
❏	❏	Assures that each teacher uses assessments at the end of each chapter or unit of study to measure student achievement toward grade-level expectations.
❏	❏	Provides professional development for new, inexperienced, and low-performing teachers based on validated lessons and lesson planning. (The professional development covers subject matter, teaching methods, and class management skills.)
❏	❏	Provides leadership to support preparing students for state and district assessments.
❏	❏	Develops recognition programs for staff and departments who inspire outstanding student academic performance.
❏	❏	Coaches teachers on improving performance when significant numbers of students in the class are not learning their lessons at the appropriate grade level.
❏	❏	Provides annual performance reviews for teachers using pre-established standards of teaching/learning as a guide.
❏	❏	Provides tutoring sessions for students who do not pass the assessments for end-of-chapter/end-of-unit instruction.

Things I currently do.	Things I can delegate or abandon.	
		Leadership for Learning continued
❑	❑	Provides enrichment lessons for students who complete their assessments successfully on the first effort and provides extra credit or other positive recognition for students.
		Change Management
❑	❑	Becomes a practitioner of proven change management methods and procedures.
❑	❑	Creates and manages change based on the shared vision for the school and the district.
❑	❑	Develops and uses effective motivational techniques, including collaborative decision-making, to build support for change.
❑	❑	Takes adequate time to inform and recruit support so that the vision for change is shared by the majority of the school staff.
❑	❑	Creates a sense of urgency related to needed change.
❑	❑	Provides ongoing reinforcement for progress in change implementation.
❑	❑	Creates exciting alternatives to traditional practice.
❑	❑	Identifies and removes significant obstacles to change.

RECOGNIZING LEVEL 5 LEADERSHIP

According to Jim Collins in his book *Good to Great*, there is a hierarchy of leadership behaviors. Within this hierarchy are the five levels described below. Through extensive research, Collins found that the for-profit companies that made the leap from good to great, without exception, had a Level 5 leader at the helm.

LEVEL 5 — EXECUTIVE
Builds enduring greatness through a paradoxical blend of personal humility and professional will.

LEVEL 4 — EFFECTIVE LEADER
Catalyzes commitment to and vigorous pursuit of a clear and compelling vision, stimulating higher performance standards.

LEVEL 3 — COMPETENT MANAGER
Organizes people and resources toward the effective and efficient pursuit of predetermined objectives.

LEVEL 2 — CONTRIBUTING TEAM MEMBER
Contributes individual capabilities to the achievement of group objectives and works effectively with others in a group setting.

LEVEL 1 — HIGHLY CAPABLE INDIVIDUAL
Makes productive contributions through talent, knowledge, skills, and good work habits.

Directions:

- Think about someone you know, have known, or know of, who is a Level 5 leader. Identify those characteristics that, in your opinion, make that person a Level 5 leader.

- Do you know someone who qualifies as a Level 4 leader, but doesn't quite make the leap to Level 5? What prevents this individual from being a Level 5 leader?

- Think about your own leadership style. Which level best describes you as a leader? What can you do to move up the hierarchy and eventually become a Level 5 leader?

THE PURPOSE OF SCHOOLING

John Goodlad in his book *What Schools Are For* asks just that—What should we be asking our schools to do? He suggests that to preserve our democratic society, we must revisit why we educate our children and what they must ultimately know, not only to become employable, but to become *educated*.

Directions:

- The following list of goals for schooling is taken from Goodlad's book. Circle the statements with which you agree. Cross out the ones you think are beyond the scope of the school.

- Using a highlighter, highlight the ones you think are most important. Using a different color, highlight those you consider the next highest priority. Using a third and even fourth color, group the statements into relative priorities. You may treat an entire category as one unit, or each statement individually.

- Think about your top priority group. What prompted those particular choices? If a parent or staff member asked you to justify your choices, what would you say? Do your choices truly reflect your personal beliefs? Does the curriculum and instructional program of your school or district currently reflect these priorities?

- Write a brief statement summarizing your beliefs about the purpose of schooling. Write as persuasively and passionately as you can. This will help you when you are trying to communicate your vision to others.

Goals for Schooling in the United States

1. Mastery of basic skills or fundamental processes.
    1.1   Develop the ability to acquire ideas through reading and listening.
    1.2   Develop the ability to communicate ideas through writing and speaking.
    1.3   Develop the ability to understand and utilize mathematical concepts.
    1.4   Develop the ability to utilize available sources of information.
    1.5   Develop the ability to read, write, and handle basic arithmetical operations.

2. Career education—vocational education.
    2.1   Develop the ability to select an occupation that will be personally satisfying and suitable to one's skills and interests.
    2.2   Develop salable skills and specialized knowledge that will prepare one to become economically independent.
    2.3   Develop attitudes and habits (such as pride in good workmanship) that will make the worker a productive participant in economic life.
    2.4   Develop positive attitudes toward work, including acceptance of the necessity of making a living and an appreciation of the social value and dignity of work.

3. Intellectual Development
    3.1   Develop the ability to think rationally; i.e., thinking and problem-solving skills, use of reasoning, and the application of principles of logic, and skill in using different models of inquiry.
    3.2   Develop the ability to use and evaluate knowledge; i.e., critical and independent thinking that enables one to make judgments and decisions in a wide variety of life roles (e.g., citizen, consumer, worker, etc.) as well as in intellectual activities.
    3.3   Accumulate a general fund of knowledge, including information and concepts in mathematics, literature, natural science, and social science.
    3.4   Develop the ability to make use of knowledge sources, utilizing technology to gain access to needed information.
    3.5   Develop positive attitudes toward intellectual activity, including intellectual curiosity and a desire for further learning.

4. Enculturation
    4.1 Develop insight into the values and characteristics of the civilization of which one is a member.
    4.2 Develop awareness of one's cultural and historical heritages—the literacy, aesthetic, and scientific traditions of the past—and familiarity with the ideas that have inspired and influenced mankind.
    4.3 Develop understanding of the manner in which heritages and traditions of the past are operative today and influence the direction and values of society.
    4.4 Acquire and accept the norms, values, standards, and traditions of the groups of which one is a member.
    4.5 Examine the norms, values, standards, and traditions of the groups of which one is a member.

5. Interpersonal Relations
    5.1 Develop a knowledge of opposing value systems and their influence on the individual and society.
    5.2 Develop an understanding of how members of a family function under different family patterns.
    5.3 Develop skill in communicating effectively in groups.
    5.4 Develop the ability to identify with and advance the goals and concerns of others.
    5.5 Develop the ability to form productive and satisfying relations with others based on respect, trust, cooperation, consideration, and caring.
    5.6 Develop an understanding of the factors that affect social behavior.

6. Autonomy
    6.1 Develop a positive attitude toward learning.
    6.2 Develop skill in selecting personal learning goals.
    6.3 Develop skill in coping with and accepting continuing change.
    6.4 Develop skill in making decisions with purpose.
    6.5 Develop the ability to plan and organize the environment in order to realize one's goals.
    6.6 Develop the willingness to accept responsibility for and the consequences of one's own decisions.

7.   Citizenship
    7.1   Develop a sense of historical perspective.
    7.2   Develop knowledge of the basic workings of the government.
    7.3   Develop a commitment to the values of liberty, government by consent of the governed, representational government, and responsibility for the welfare of all.
    7.4   Develop an attitude of inquiry in order to examine societal values.
    7.5   Develop the ability to think productively about the improvement of society (refer to No. 3).
    7.6   Develop skill in democratic action in large and small groups (refer to No. 5).
    7.7   Develop a willingness to participate in the political life of the nation and community.
    7.8   Develop a commitment to the fulfillment of humanitarian ideas everywhere.
    7.9   Develop a commitment to involve oneself in resolving social issues.

8.   Creative and aesthetic perception
    8.1   Develop the ability to motivate oneself, to deal with new problems in original ways.
    8.2   Develop the ability to be sensitive to problems and tolerant of new ideas.
    8.3   Develop the ability to be flexible, to redefine skills, and to see an object from different points of view.
    8.4   Develop the ability to enjoy and be willing to experience the act of creation.
    8.5   Develop the ability to understand creative contributions of others and to evaluate them.
    8.6   Develop the ability to communicate through creative work in an active way (as a creator) or a perceptive way (as a consumer).
    8.7   Develop the commitment to enrich cultural and social life.

9.   Self-concept
    9.1   Develop the ability to search for meaning in one's activity.
    9.2   Develop the self-confidence needed for confronting one's self.
    9.3   Develop the ability to live with one's limitations and strengths.
    9.4   Develop both general knowledge and interest in other human beings as a means of knowing oneself.
    9.5   Develop an internal framework by which an individual can organize his concept of "self."
    9.6   Develop a knowledge of one's own body and a positive attitude toward one's own physical appearance.

10. Emotional and physical well-being
    10.1 Develop the willingness to receive new impressions and to expand affective sensitivity.
    10.2 Develop the competence and skills for continuous adjustment and emotional stability.
    10.3 Develop the ability to control or release the emotions according to one's values.
    10.4 Develop the ability to use leisure time effectively.
    10.5 Develop positive attitudes and habits toward health and physical fitness.
    10.6 Develop physical fitness and psychomotor skills.

11. Moral and ethical character
    11.1 Develop the judgment to evaluate phenomena as good or evil.
    11.2 Develop a commitment to truth and values.
    11.3 Develop the ability to utilize values in determining choices.
    11.4 Develop moral integrity.
    11.5 Develop an understanding of the necessity for moral conduct.
    11.6 Develop a desire to strengthen the moral fabric of society.

12. Self-realization
    12.1 The ideal of self-realization is based on the idea that there is more than one way of being a human being and that efforts to develop a better self contribute to the development of a better society.

CLARIFYING YOUR VALUES ABOUT THE NATURE OF TEACHING AND LEARNING

Here is a list of fundamental value statements taken from David Purpel's book, *The Moral and Spiritual Crisis in Education*, about what schools should emphasize when teaching children to become "a good person functioning in a good world." As you review the list, note your reaction to each statement. How does it "sit" with you? Is the statement consistent with your personal values, or at odds with them?

On the next page, each pair of values has been placed on a continuum. Rate where you think schools should put their emphasis between the two values. Finally, rank them according to the importance you believe it has to your vision of a successful school.

Individuality: Schools should emphasize individual uniqueness, autonomy, independence, and a strong, well-defined ego.

Community: Schools should emphasize the interdependence of all people, and the need to develop strong relationships and a sense of belonging.

Worth: Schools should emphasize the inherent worth and dignity of each individual.

Achievement: Schools should emphasize that individual worth and dignity should be recognized through what one accomplishes.

Equality: Schools should emphasize our strong tradition of activism for social and economic equality.

Competition: Schools should emphasize that free-market models will, in the long run, overcome anomalies and inequities.

Compassion: Schools should emphasize concern for the welfare of others to the point of helping and nurturing them.

Sentimentality: Schools should emphasize personal responsibility, and that individual misfortune must be dealt with by the individual.

Responsibility: Schools should emphasize helping people to sort out their legitimate responsibilities and help them to develop the intellectual, psychological, and spiritual resources necessary to respond appropriately.

Guilt: Schools should emphasize that guilt is unproductive and feeling guilty for the misfortunes of others is to be discouraged.

Authority: Schools should emphasize that there exists a shared set of principles as to what constitutes the true, good, and beautiful.

Coercion: Schools should emphasize that what constitutes the "true, good, and beautiful" is to be imposed by those who have the power to make such impositions.

Control: Schools should emphasize and nurture democracy and serve as a laboratory of democratic experiences.

Democracy: Schools should emphasize that schools and the students in them need to be responsive and responsible to community concerns for accountability.

Ethnocentrism: Schools should emphasize the inculcation of love of, and loyalty to, our country.

Univeralism: Schools should emphasize ideas and programs such as global education and international education.

Commitment: Schools should emphasize facilitating the individual's pursuit of socioeconomic success and preserving the existing social and political frameworks.

Alienation: Schools should emphasize the search for, and the affirmation of, an overarching moral and spiritual framework that provides a center of meaning for the culture.

BELIEFS AND VALUES:
A FOUNDATION FOR ACTION

Rate where you think schools should fall on the continuum for each item.

Individual vs. Community   **Priority:** _____

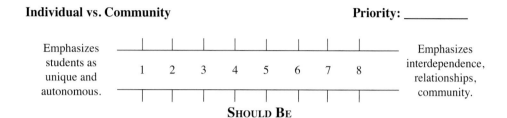

Emphasizes students as unique and autonomous.

1   2   3   4   5   6   7   8

SHOULD BE

Emphasizes interdependence, relationships, community.

Worth vs. Achievement   **Priority:** _____

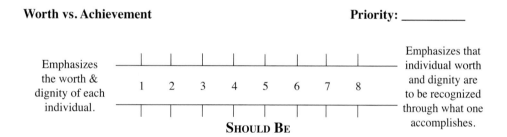

Emphasizes the worth & dignity of each individual.

1   2   3   4   5   6   7   8

SHOULD BE

Emphasizes that individual worth and dignity are to be recognized through what one accomplishes.

Equality vs. Competition   **Priority:** _____

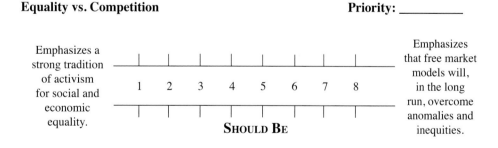

Emphasizes a strong tradition of activism for social and economic equality.

1   2   3   4   5   6   7   8

SHOULD BE

Emphasizes that free market models will, in the long run, overcome anomalies and inequities.

Compassion vs. Sentimentality   Priority: _____

Emphasizes that students should be concerned about the welfare of others to the point of helping and nurturing them.

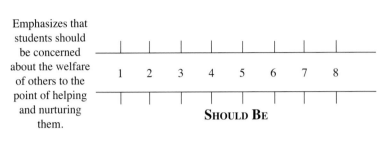

Emphasizes that individual fortune or misfortune is the individual's problem and must be dealt with by the individual.

Responsibility vs. Guilt   Priority: _____

Emphasizes helping people recognize and respond appropriately to their legitimate responsibilities.

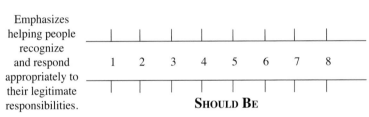

Emphasizes that guilt is unproductive and feeling guilty for the misfortunes of others is to be discouraged.

Authority vs. Coercion   Priority: _____

Emphasizes a shared set of principles as to what constitutes the true, good, and beautiful.

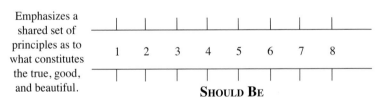

Emphasizes that the "true, good, and beautiful" is determined by those who have the power to make such impositions.

Control vs. Democracy   Priority: _____

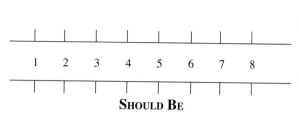

Emphasizes and nurtures democracy and serves as a laboratory of democratic experiences.

1   2   3   4   5   6   7   8

SHOULD BE

Emphasizes that schools and the students in them need to be responsive and responsible to community concerns for accountability.

Ethnocentrism vs. Universalism   Priority: _____

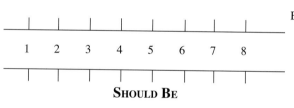

Emphasizes the inculcation of love of, and loyalty to, our country.

1   2   3   4   5   6   7   8

SHOULD BE

Emphasizes ideas and programs such as global education and international education.

Commitment vs. Alienation   Priority: _____

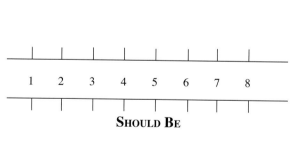

Emphasizes the search for, and the affirmation of, an overarching moral and spiritual framework that provides a center of meaning for the culture.

1   2   3   4   5   6   7   8

SHOULD BE

Emphasizes facilitating the individual's pursuit of socioeconomic success and preserving the existing social and political frameworks.

WHAT'S YOUR LEADERSHIP PARADIGM?

How we view leadership and the role it plays in our schools, by definition, affects how we lead others. The chart below outlines three leadership paradigms based on the work of Richard Axelrod in his book, *Terms of Engagement: Changing the Way We Change Organizations*.

Comparison of Three Change Paradigms			
	Top-Down Paradigm	**Change Management Paradigm**	**Engagement Paradigm**
Positive Aspects	• Clear directions • Leaders stay in charge • Decisions can be made quickly • Everyone knows what leadership wants	• Diverse participation • Reduction in bureaucracy • System orientation • Builds ownership and commitment	• High involvement speeds implementation • Whole-system involvement produces high-quality, integrated solutions • Democratic principles build trust, create commitment, and increase creativity • Increases organizational capacity to change
Negative Aspects	• Creates resistance from those not involved • Decisions lack critical information from those at lower levels	• Emphasis on only the best and brightest participating • Often increases bureaucracy rather than reducing it • Involves relatively few people, thereby creating "in groups" and "out groups"	• Is more chaotic than other paradigms • Requires leaders to let go of paradigm • Requires a higher initial investment of people and resources • Is more visible than other paradigms

Directions:

- Review each paradigm and consider which one you feel is more suitable to leading continuous improvement in your school or district. That is, which paradigm will lead to long-term, sustainable, and self-renewing change?

- Now consider your own leadership style. Is how you currently lead consistent with the paradigm you consider to be most appropriate to the ends you are trying to achieve?

- If there is a disconnect between the paradigm under which your school currently operates and the desired paradigm, consider ways that the current leadership paradigm could evolve and grow toward the desired one.

ASSESSING THE SYSTEM-IN-PLACE:
BELIEFS AND VALUES

Below are the beliefs based on David Purpel's book, *The Moral and Spiritual Crisis in Education*. Rate where you think your school currently is and where you think it should fall on the continuum for each item.

Individual vs. Community   **Priority:** _____

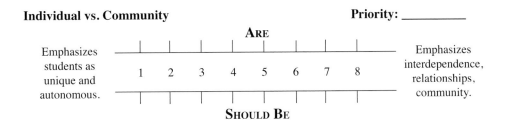

Worth vs. Achievement   **Priority:** _____

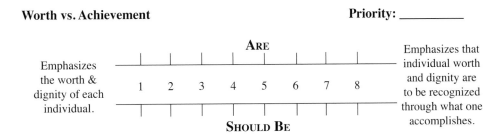

Equality vs. Competition   **Priority:** _____

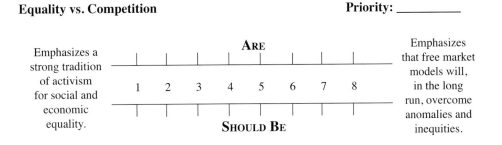

Compassion vs. Sentimentality   **Priority:** _____

Emphasizes that students should be concerned about the welfare of others to the point of helping and nurturing them.

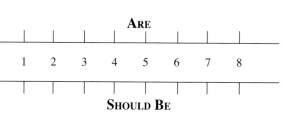

Emphasizes that individual fortune or misfortune is the individual's problem and must be dealt with by the individual.

Responsibility vs. Guilt   **Priority:** _____

Emphasizes helping people recognize and respond appropriately to their legitimate responsibilities.

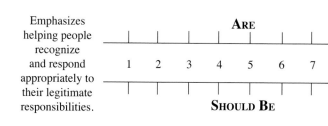

Emphasizes that guilt is unproductive and feeling guilty for the misfortunes of others is to be discouraged.

Authority vs. Coercion   **Priority:** _____

Emphasizes a shared set of principles as to what constitutes the true, good, and beautiful.

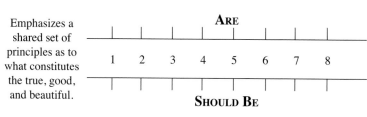

Emphasizes that the "true, good, and beautiful" is to be imposed by those who have the power to make such impositions.

Control vs. Democracy   Priority: _____

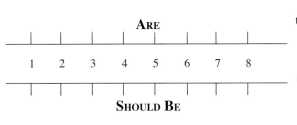

Emphasizes and nurtures democracy and serves as a laboratory of democratic experiences.

Emphasizes that schools and the students in them need to be responsive and responsible to community concerns for accountability.

Ethnocentrism vs. Universalism   Priority: _____

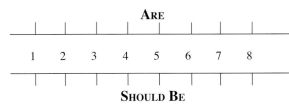

Emphasizes the inculcation of love of, and loyalty to, our country.

Emphasizes ideas and programs such as global education and international education.

Commitment vs. Alienation   Priority: _____

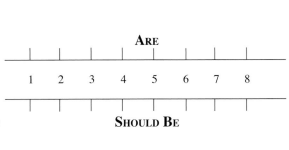

Emphasizes the search for, and the affirmation of, an overarching moral and spiritual framework that provides a center of meaning for the culture.

Emphasizes facilitating the individual's pursuit of socioeconomic success and preserving the existing social and political frameworks.

ASSESSING THE SYSTEM-IN-PLACE:
CURRENT POSITION ON THE
CONTINUOUS SCHOOL IMPROVEMENT JOURNEY

The assessments outlined on the following pages will help guide you in the continuous school improvement process and in assessing where your school currently is in relation to that process. We have listed the key components to successful, sustainable, and continuous school improvement that are applicable pretty much across the board, from school to school and district to district. We have also left space for you to add indicators specific to your school or district. Feel free to add more on another sheet of paper.

Attached to each criterion is a rating scale. For each item, honestly rate the degree to which it is occurring (or has occurred) in your school. Resist the temptation to look through "rose-colored glasses," because effective leaders "look at 'current reality' as an ally, not an enemy…are deeply inquisitive, committed to continually seeing reality more and more accurately." (Senge, 1994) Only when you honestly assess where your school currently is in terms of leading indicators, its readiness for change, and progress-to-date on continuous school improvement, will you as a leader be able to meet participants in the process "where they are" and develop the appropriate strategies to move your school toward improved student achievement resulting from continuous improvement.

CONTINUOUS SCHOOL IMPROVEMENT PROCESS
ASSESSMENT

Instructions

On a scale of 1 to 5, with 5 being high, please assess the degree to which each of the indicators below is in existence or has taken place at your school by circling the appropriate number in the appropriate column. Compute the average for each major section.

Steps in the School Improvement Process	Not at All		To a	High Degree	
Getting Ready for Continuous School Improvement					
• Initial and systematic orientation of faculty and staff to the continuous school improvement process.	1	2	3	4	5
• Faculty and staff understand the essential attributes of continuous school improvement.	1	2	3	4	5
• Faculty and staff are thoroughly knowledgeable of the Correlates of Effective Schools.	1	2	3	4	5
• Faculty and staff are knowledgeable of effective schools research, systems theory, and total quality management.	1	2	3	4	5
• Faculty and staff are prepared for systemic change.	1	2	3	4	5
• Stakeholder groups identified; representatives from each stakeholder group are engaged in the process.	1	2	3	4	5
• School improvement team has been identified, trained, and empowered.	1	2	3	4	5
• A plan for ongoing two-way communication between and among leadership and stakeholders has been developed and implemented.	1	2	3	4	5
Computed Average					
Clarifying Mission, Core Beliefs, and Core Values					
• Mission, core values, and core beliefs have been explicitly stated and discussed.	1	2	3	4	5
• Mission, core values, and core beliefs are reaffirmed regularly and systematically.	1	2	3	4	5
• All staff members are committed to the school improvement process and school goals.	1	2	3	4	5
• School stakeholder groups are aware of and committed to the school mission, core values, and beliefs.	1	2	3	4	5
Computed Average					

Steps in the School Improvement Process (continued)	Not at All		To a High Degree		
Assuring Instructional Focus					
• State grade-level standards and benchmarks are known and incorporated into the curriculum.	1	2	3	4	5
• District grade-level standards and benchmarks are known and incorporated into the curriculum.	1	2	3	4	5
• Standards are prioritized according to school/student needs (power standards).	1	2	3	4	5
• Pacing charts for each grade have been created to guide staff in what should be taught and by when.	1	2	3	4	5
• Benchmark assessments have been developed to assure curricular mastery.	1	2	3	4	5
• The intended, taught, and assessed curricula are aligned.	1	2	3	4	5
Computed Average					
Study					
• Faculty and staff understand the collection, disaggregation, analysis, and utilization of data.	1	2	3	4	5
• Leading and trailing indicators identified; data sources identified.	1	2	3	4	5
• Student achievement/performance data has been collected.	1	2	3	4	5
• Current and trend performance data has been analyzed.	1	2	3	4	5
• Internal and external scanning of stakeholder perceptions and school conditions (surveys) are complete.	1	2	3	4	5
• Gaps between expected and actual levels of performance, perceptions, and conditions calculated.	1	2	3	4	5
• Problem statements developed.	1	2	3	4	5
• Root causes have been explored and identified.	1	2	3	4	5
Computed Average					
Reflect					
• Continuous school improvement goals have been identified based upon data analysis and findings.	1	2	3	4	5
• School improvement goals and objectives address quality and equity.	1	2	3	4	5
• Leading indicator data has been linked to problem statements.	1	2	3	4	5
• Internal and external scanning for related research, best practices, and potential solutions complete.	1	2	3	4	5
Computed Average					

Steps in the School Improvement Process (continued)	Not at All				To a High Degree
Plan					
• Now/then matrix completed for each continuous school improvement goal.	1	2	3	4	5
• Subcommittees consisting of representatives of stakeholder groups formed to address each goal.	1	2	3	4	5
• Evidence of systems thinking is observable throughout the planning process.	1	2	3	4	5
• School improvement objectives have been identified and driven by data analyses and findings.	1	2	3	4	5
• School improvement objectives focus on quality and equity.	1	2	3	4	5
• Expected levels of student performance/behaviors are established across the curriculum and grade levels.	1	2	3	4	5
• Action plans include timelines, persons responsible, research-based strategies, and staff development.	1	2	3	4	5
• Action plans include systematic monitoring of implementation and assessments of results.	1	2	3	4	5
• The action plan is regularly and effectively communicated to faculty, staff, and stakeholders.	1	2	3	4	5
• Abandonment targets are included in the plan.	1	2	3	4	5
Computed Average					
Do					
• The action plan is systematically presented to the faculty and staff for implementation.	1	2	3	4	5
• Implementation of the action plan is monitored systematically.	1	2	3	4	5
• Progress on implementation is reported to stakeholders on a regular basis.	1	2	3	4	5
• Leading indicator data collected and analyzed periodically.	1	2	3	4	5
• Results from leading indicator analysis is reported to stakeholders on a regular basis.	1	2	3	4	5
• Curricular and/or instructional practices are modified based upon student performance and leading indicator data.	1	2	3	4	5
• Successes large and small are celebrated.	1	2	3	4	5
• The process is maintained and sustained through ongoing application of the study-reflect-plan-do process.	1	2	3	4	5
Computed Average					

ORIENTING THE STAKEHOLDERS

Now that you've identified the stakeholders, it's important to introduce them to the continuous school improvement model and process. This gives everyone a common language and shared understanding that will provide the basis for upcoming activities. Use the questions below to plan the orientation.

1. **Who?** Will you provide one orientation session for everyone—staff, parents, community—or will it be more effective to tailor your presentation to each group separately?

2. **When?** Keep in mind the best time for each group to participate in an orientation session; staff will prefer a session during the workday (or in-service day), parents and community members will generally prefer evenings.

3. **What?** Tailor your message to the audience, keeping your explanations and descriptions as clear and concise as possible. Here are some key points to include when describing the process; make sure to delete and add points as appropriate to your audience.

    a) Why are we doing this?
        *   To meet state and federal mandates for 100 percent student proficiency.
        *   To provide our children with the best education possible.
        *   To determine where we are now and how we can improve.
        *   To ensure that **all** our students are being adequately educated.
        *
        *
        *

    b) Why this model?
        *   Research-based: It is based on what we've learned from other successful schools over the last 3+ decades.
        *   Data-driven: It relies on information specific to your school.
        *   Results-oriented.
        *   Focused on quality and equity in learning (learning for all).
        *   Collaborative and inclusive so that all voices are heard.
        *   Ongoing and self-renewing.
        *   Not a "band-aid" approach; seeks to identify root causes and promotes meaningful change.
        *
        *

c)   How does the process work?
- Identify what we want students to know and be able to do when they leave our school/district and at each level of learning.
- STUDY: Collect and analyze appropriate data to see where we are.
- REFLECT: Through research and our own resources, develop strategies for improvement.
- PLAN: Develop a workable plan with measurable outcomes and a way to monitor completion and evaluate success.
- DO: Implement strategies and celebrate success!
-
-
-

d)   Who will be involved? In what ways will groups and individuals be involved in the process? Role of the leadership team.

e)   How long will the process take?

f)   Question and answer session.

Key to winning stakeholder commitment is clearly conveying the importance of this process and the leadership's commitment to a collaborative and inclusive process where everyone has a voice. To that end, develop and distribute an evaluation soliciting feedback about what stakeholders heard and feel about the process and their involvement.

REVIEWING THE RESEARCH #1

Review the following research summary on collective efficacy and reflect on the guiding questions.

CITATION: Goddard, Roger D., Wayne K. Hoy, and Anita Woolfolk Hoy, "Collective Efficacy Beliefs: Theoretical Developments, Empirical Evidence, and Future Directions," *Educational Researcher* 33, 3 (April 2004): 3-13.

What Did the Researchers Do?

Self-efficacy has been defined as one's belief in their capacity to organize and execute the actions required to produce a given outcome. In the case of the student, sense of efficacy could be described as the student's belief in his/her ability to successfully complete a major research paper, pass the semester examine, or effectively deliver a speech. In the case of the teacher, sense of efficacy could be described as the teacher's belief in his/her ability to effectively teach the standards in the curriculum, manage the classroom, or communicate effectively with parents. A great deal of research has been done on both student and teacher sense of efficacy and the evidence is clear: both have an influence on subsequent behaviors (e.g., level of effort exerted, persistence in the face of obstacles) and ultimately teacher and student achievement.

In this research study, the authors, using the framework of social cognitive theory, introduce us to a relatively unexplored dimension of efficacy, namely the concept of a school's sense of collective efficacy. In this context, collective efficacy can be described as the "beliefs of group members [school faculty and staff] concerning the performance capability of the [school] social system as a whole." (p. 4)

Why is the construct of collective efficacy important within our current school reform context? The standards, assessment, and accountability movement generally, and No Child Left Behind specifically, sets forth clear performance expectations for schools as a whole. The question then becomes, Does the school, as a collective of individuals, believe that they can organize and execute the actions required to produce the expected performance outcomes now and in the future? If the research shows that collective efficacy matters in explaining student achievement, then leaders of school reform must consider it in the scheme of things when it comes to school change.

Before getting into the researchers' methods and findings, two additional insights are important. First, efficacy— whether individual or collective—always pertains to the future (e.g., scoring well on an upcoming final exam, or meeting next year's Adequate Yearly Progress benchmarks). Second, efficacy—whether individual or collective—is generally context specific. That is to say, a student might feel very efficacious about his/her literature exam, but have a low sense of perceived efficacy about the calculus final. These two factors clearly make perceived efficacy different from self-esteem and other, more general, personal, or organizational qualities.

As we look at the synthesis of the research provided by the authors, we are left with two central questions. First, does the way perceived collective efficacy is measured matter in explaining the importance of this construct? Second, does perceived collective efficacy help to explain important differences in student and staff performance and, ultimately, student achievement?

What Did the Researchers Find?

In examining the existing theory and research on collective efficacy, the researchers looked at two different ways of measuring the construct. The first method involved determining the individual teacher's perceived self efficacy, adding up the scores, and calculating the mean for the school. The second method involved asking each teacher for their perceptions of the staff's capability *as a whole* to organize and execute the necessary actions to attain the goals set for the school, adding up the scores, and calculating the mean.

When they averaged the sum of teachers' individual sense of efficacy ("How I feel about my ability to do my job.") to indicate the perceived collective efficacy for the school, the result was very little variance from school to school. They attributed this to the fact that individuals will usually express confidence in their individual capabilities (high self efficacy), even if they have doubts about the capability of the others or of the group as a whole.

However, when they used an indicator *specific* to collective efficacy ("How I feel about the school's ability to accomplish the task."), perceived collective efficacy was found to vary greatly among schools and to be a strong and positive predictor of student achievement. Using the more direct measure of perceived collective capability yielded a more accurate picture of how teachers actually feel about the ability of the school to meet its goals.

What factors tend to shape or influence perceived collective efficacy? The literature suggested four different sources of influence on the efficacy variable, although not enough research has been conducted to determine the differential significance of each.

The mastery experience. The knowledge or perception that a task or performance like the one being considered has already been successfully or unsuccessfully accomplished in the past. It is the most powerful source of information that shapes the perceived collective efficacy of an individual or school.

Vicarious experience. If someone I know, trust, and have confidence in has been successful with the task in the past, I may express more confidence in my or our ability to be successful.

Social persuasion. Coaches, supervisors, and trusted colleagues, through feedback and encouragement, can influence an individual's self or collective sense of efficacy. As might be expected, the potency of persuasion depends on the credibility, trustworthiness, and expertise of the persuader.

Affective states. The level of arousal, as either anxiety or excitement, adds to an individual's perceptions of self-capability or incompetence.

As one can imagine, these four factors will positively or negatively influence on one's perceived sense of efficacy. In characterizing the perceived collective efficacy of the school staff, it would be useful to also take a reading on each of these sources of influence in the school. Knowing how these variables stack up within the school would be a good indicator of how the perceived collective efficacy might change—for the better or the worse—as the accountability "bar" gets raised.

What Are Possible Implications for School Improvement?

The long-term success of No Child Left Behind (NCLB) is, in no small measure, dependent on the extent to which educators have a shared sense of the moral imperative that is reflected in the law, i.e., "learning for all." While we can and should debate the nuances around NCLB, most teachers and administrators would feel good about themselves and their schools if they were making authentic progress toward the "learning for all" mission.

The long-term attainment of the goals of NCLB—in no small measure—depends on the perceived collective efficacy of the educators to organize and execute the actions necessary at their school. They are not likely to have a robust sense of collective efficacy in their school unless they are able to influence the instructional and curricular processes in the school.

The bold goals of NCLB and the other accountability and standards systems require that local educational leaders use all four influence factors when leading the reform effort. Principals and superintendents need to find and nurture teacher and school strengths (mastery), bring in trusted educators who have "been there, done that" (vicarious success), practice their own skills as persuaders, and finally, be willing and able to be the leading cheerleader for the improvement of student learning and student performance in the school and district.

With the focus on school improvement as measured almost exclusively by student achievement, whatever leaders and policymakers can do to have a positive influence on the factors that influence collective efficacy, the more likely a school is to have a robust sense of collective efficacy, which in turn will positively affect student achievement.

Guiding Questions:

- How would you rate your school or district's sense of collective efficacy on a scale of 1-5, 1 being nonexistent and 5 being excellent?

- Consider specific ways you as the leader can improve the collective efficacy of your staff.

Reviewing the Research #2

Review the following research summary and sketch out a preliminary plan for aligning the intended, taught, and assessed curricula.

Citation: Bradshaw, Lynn K., Marsha Craft-Tripp, and Allan Glatthorn, "Taking the Offensive," *Principal Leadership* 4, 1 (September 2003): 55-59.

What Did the Researchers Do?

With federal and state accountability systems preoccupying teachers and school administrators today, educators are scrambling for ways to enable students to do well on these high-stake tests. Typically, most efforts focus on the test (e.g., skill-and-drill sessions) rather than implementing a systemic curriculum alignment process that helps to ensure that the concepts that will be tested get taught.

"Northside High School is one of three small rural high schools in a district that serves about 7,500 students in North Carolina." (p. 55) They have a proud tradition of success in academics, athletics, and the arts. Their scores on the state tests were typically above expectations and higher than other schools in the county. However, the Northside leadership team, after looking at the data, realized that their school could become a low-performing school if they didn't make changes.

With help from a curriculum specialist at East Carolina University, Project Excellence at Northside (PEN) was created. In this program, teachers worked to align their curriculum with the North Carolina Standard Course of Study

(NCSCOS). The underlying belief of this approach was twofold: 1) If the curriculum was aligned, student performance would improve without the emphasis on practice tests; and 2) by allowing teachers to take ownership of the tested curriculum, "teachers [would] make better decisions about what to teach, students [would] recognize connections across disciplines, and student learning [would] increase." (p. 56)

Each phase of the curriculum development project was supported by professional development that helped teachers build knowledge and learn skills. Sessions were held both during the workday and after school and included large-group information sessions and small-group task work.

Milestone events for this project included:

Orienting the faculty. Each teacher received a copy of the NCSCOS for his/her respective content area. Some didn't realize this document existed and others had been working with outdated information. They "also received a variety of other resources, including a survey, planning guides, information about types of objectives, suggestions for setting priorities, and timeline information." (p. 57) Teachers found these materials to be helpful and adaptable to any curriculum area.

Forming core-area teams. Four core-area teams were formed in the spring of the first year, one for each content area that was tested: English/language arts, math, science, and social studies. Every teacher was assigned to one of the four core-area teams. Other teachers who taught nontested areas of the curriculum "were assigned to the most relevant core area that offered opportunities for curriculum integration." (p. 58)

Reviewing the state curriculum. Each of the core-area teams analyzed state standards and benchmarks and categorized them as mastery, continuing development, or enrichment. Mastery benchmarks "are important for all students, likely to be tested, and best learned when taught at a specific grade . . . . Continuing development benchmarks are important and likely to be tested...[and] are stressed at multiple grade levels. Enrichment benchmarks are 'nice to know,' but are not essential for all students." (pp. 56-57)

Developing a planning calendar. The review and analysis of state standards allowed staff to prioritize the essential standards and benchmarks that needed to be taught. Once the scope and sequence was reviewed and finalized, teachers then began blocking in units of study and producing term planning calendars. "The planning calendars show[ed] proposed unit titles, sequence, length, and the benchmarks that [they] addressed." (p. 57) To ensure that each benchmark in the NCSCOS was covered, a number of objectives and standards were blended. University faculty reviewed each team's planning calendar and provided positive and constructive feedback to each group.

Developing a unit. The teachers then needed to create study units based on the identified performance tasks and assessments. Each core-area team developed a unit listed on the planning calendar. Again, university faculty reviewed the completed units and provided feedback.

What Did the Researchers Find?

Since PEN was implemented at Northside High School, student scores on state tests have steadily improved. Even though it is difficult to pinpoint the reasons for the gain, "it is likely PEN contributed." (p. 58) There is also evidence that the curriculum development process has had a positive impact on student and teacher learning. Some of the visible results are:

"Teachers are more knowledgeable of the curriculum and are making better decisions about what to teach." (p. 58) During the early stages of PEN, teachers were skeptical about the project's value and wondered whether it would last. But once the faculty began working on the project, attitudes changed and they slowly became committed to its success as they began to see useful results. Teachers now had a better understanding of the importance of curriculum to student learning and more were interested in curriculum development.

"Teachers have recognized their interdependence." (p. 59) Teachers now recognize the connections between their content areas and the tested curriculum. Also, content-area teachers are aware of and appreciate the contributions that teachers in elective courses make to improved student learning. Teachers in nontested areas feel that they are making a contribution as well.

"The tested curriculum, the NCSCOS, is being addressed more completely." (p. 59) The curriculum became more manageable for teachers after they prioritized the NCSCOS benchmarks. As a result "students had more opportunities to learn the mandated and tested curriculum." (p. 59) Teachers now have specific objectives in mind when they plan a lesson and mark off on a grid the curriculum objectives that have been taught.

"Students are recognizing connections among courses." (p. 59) Even though students were probably not aware of PEN, teachers have noted that students are making connections between courses. History students have mentioned that they had discussed the same topic in English class. Similar observations were also noted for the other core-area subjects, as well as for the nontested courses.

What Are Possible Implications for School Improvement?

Project Excellence at Northside was successful at strengthening the alignment between the written and taught curriculum. "The process for reviewing the state curriculum, prioritizing the goals and objectives, and developing a term plan for each tested area, including units of study, worked well." (p. 59) All teachers became more familiar with the state curriculum and recognized the need to make sure that all objectives got addressed. This curriculum alignment process helped teachers prioritize what was essential and what was more supplemental. The PEN curriculum alignment process also reinforced the accountability role of all teachers, for both tested and nontested areas of the curriculum.

Through the implementation of PEN, Northside has reinforced the linkages between school improvement and professional development. While developing their skills in curriculum development, teachers have improved their teaching skills. The school has also been able to incorporate PEN into their accreditation process "by showing that they are involved in school improvement that identifies problems through analysis of student test scores and develops curriculum strategies to address those needs." (p. 59)

One thing the Northside faculty has found is that this process takes time. They have discovered that it will take two or three more years to complete all of the units for each of the core-area subjects. What began as a one-year project has evolved into a continuous process of improvement and revitalization that has resulted in higher achievement for their students.

CREATING IMPROVEMENT GOALS

When setting improvement goals, remember the acronym **SMART***:

SPECIFIC

MEASURABLE

ATTAINABLE, BUT CHALLENGING

RELEVANT

TIME-BASED

Specific: Avoid vague goals such as "Improve schoolwide literacy." A goal such as this doesn't build in accountability. A well-written improvement goal will address who will do what by when and how the results will be measured.

Measurable: The key concept here is: what gets measured, gets done. How will you know when you've accomplished your goal unless you set up, from the beginning, how you will measure its accomplishment?

Attainable, but Challenging: Goals that are unrealistic will only serve as a source of frustration for teachers, students, and administrators alike. Goals that are too easy generally won't effect the kind of change needed to make significant and sustainable improvement.

Relevant: Goals should link back to the stated educational aims and missions of the school and be derived from a careful analysis of data.

Time-based: In the current educational climate, schools are expected to improve and improve quickly. Setting a timeframe for the goal gives it urgency and helps move it to the top of the priority list of everyday activities.

On the following page, we've given you an example of an improvement goal that incorporates the SMART components. Review the example and use the SMART rubric when evaluating your school or district's improvement goals. A sample is provided on the following page.

* Source Unknown.

Sample Problem Statement

Over the past three years, girls have not mastered the essential mathematics learnings. Evidence indicates that an average of 40 percent of the girls in Grades 2 to 5 received less than a "C" grade in mathematics; in addition, an average of only 28 percent of fourth graders achieved proficiency status on the mathematics portion of the state standardized test over the past three years.

Relevant

Sample Improvement Goal

By the last week of June (insert year), at least 80 percent of the girls in Grades 2 to 5 will have mastered the essential mathematics learnings for their grade level. The evidence used will be end-of-year grades of "C" or higher in Grades 2 to 5, as well as a score of proficient on the mathematics portion of the state standardized test for fourth graders.

Specific

Q: WHO will perform?

A: 80 percent of the Grade 2 to 5 girls.

Attainable, but challenging

Q: WHAT activity will be performed?

A: Mastery of the essential mathematics learnings.

Q: WHEN will it be performed?

A: By the last week of June, (year).   *Time-based*

Q: HOW will it be measured?

A: A letter grade of "C" or higher in mathematics for girls in grades 2 to 5 and a score of "proficient" on the fourth-grade math portion of the state standardized test.

Measurable

CHALLENGING THE GRAMMAR OF SCHOOLING

What is the "grammar of schooling"?

According to Tyack and Cuban in *Tinkering Toward Utopia*, the "grammar of schooling" describes the popularized idea of what a "real school" looks like. The authors specifically identify our current grading system and the "Carnegie unit" as two prime examples of the grammar of schooling.

- What other examples of the grammar of schooling can you identify?
- Where do these institutionalized conceptions of a "real school" conflict with the new "learning for all" mission of public education?

Why is it so important to become familiar with the grammar of schooling?

Fundamental reforms that violate the stakeholder ideas of a "real school" will create opposition that makes sustainable change difficult to impossible.

How do you change the grammar of schooling?

Tyack and Cuban suggest that, "Reformers who want to change the grammar of schooling today need to enlist the support of parents, school boards, and the community more generally. Participation of the public in school decision-making can, of course, lead to conflict and seem to threaten professional autonomy. But in a democracy, fundamental reforms that seek to alter the cultural constructions of a "real school" cannot succeed without lengthy and searching public dialogue about the ends and means of schooling.

Directions:

- List the major reforms you and your school are considering or pursuing. Identify what "grammar of schooling" — i.e., long-held institutional conceptions of school and schooling — each reform may challenge and create a strategy tailored to the anticipated concerns of each stakeholder group.

A SYSTEMS APPROACH TO PLANNING

Creating an action plan isn't easy. It is far more complex than just adopting a new program. When schools adopt a program without looking at all the areas that will be affected by the change, they often find that the program failed to produce the desired results because a key related factor was overlooked.

In Chapter 9, we presented the following model to help ensure that you "cover all the bases" when you create your action plan. On the following page, we offer you an example of how you might use the model to guide the action-planning process.

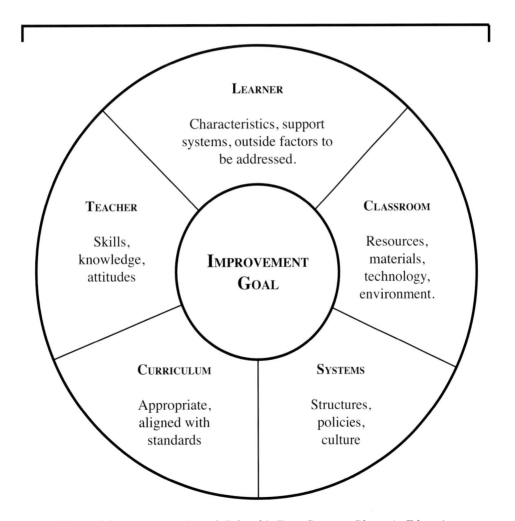

LEARNER

Characteristics, support systems, outside factors to be addressed.

TEACHER

Skills, knowledge, attitudes

IMPROVEMENT GOAL

CLASSROOM

Resources, materials, technology, environment.

CURRICULUM

Appropriate, aligned with standards

SYSTEMS

Structures, policies, culture

The model incorporates Joseph Schwab's Four Common Places in Education.

Improvement Goal

By Spring (year), 100 percent of students exiting fifth grade will meet minimum literacy standards as evidenced by scores of proficient or above on the standardized state test and cumulative grades in language arts of "C" or above.

Action Planning

Learner

What will you have to do to support the student who is struggling with literacy? Involve parents? Assess other problems and issues? Reduce absenteeism? Begin a tutoring program?

Curriculum

Is the current literacy curriculum adequate? Do you need to align the curriculum with state standards so that students learn what is being tested? How will you evaluate and choose a new curriculum for literacy? Will you make literacy a schoolwide focus in every grade across all subject areas?

Teacher

Do your teachers have the skills and knowledge they need to effectively and efficiently teach literacy skills? What training will they need? How will they get it?

Classroom

Are the materials and resources available to support the literacy effort? How will technology be incorporated into the plan? What additional financial resources will you need to provide books, support materials, training for teachers, release time for teachers to attend training, computers, etc.?

System

- **Structures.** How will you organize the school day? Will you adopt block scheduling? Increase time spent on reading and writing, etc.? What structures may obstruct progress on the reform effort? How might you deal with these issues?
- **Policies.** What school or district policies must you consider when creating your plan? Can these be changed if necessary? Who needs to be "in the loop" when addressing these issues?
- **Culture.** Do teacher, administrator, and student attitudes and behaviors support the reform effort? What needs to be done in this area so that the plan can be implemented and the goal achieved?

This model will give you a useful tool for considering the wide variety of issues related to creating an action plan objective and related strategies. Many of those issues will fall into more than one category and will be closely interrelated. This tool simply gives you a way to organize your thinking as you create an action plan.

CREATING AN ACTION PLAN

Imagine that you and your colleagues have discovered, through a thorough analysis of student achievement data, that the students in your school would benefit most broadly and immediately by improving their literacy skills. You have also discovered, through a parent survey, that parents aren't aware of the literacy initiative your school has begun, neither do they have much confidence in their ability to assist their children in becoming better readers and writers. Therefore, through a collaborative process, the school has adopted several action plan objectives for meeting the newly designated literacy improvement goal. One of those objectives is to increase communication between the school and parents concerning what literacy standards will be addressed during each marking period, and how parents can assist students at home.

On the following page is an example of an Action Plan Activity and Monitoring Matrix. Using the chart as a guide, map out three (3) strategies suited to your school's cultural demographics that will accomplish the objective outlined above. Make sure to identify the person responsible (this can be a fictional person, or if you are planning to use this in your school, a real individual), who will measure progress, and all the other items called for on the chart.

We've also provided an example of a Gantt chart. Using the chart as a guide, map out the timeline over the entire school year that reflects your three strategies.

ACTION PLAN ACTIVITY AND MONITORING MATRIX

Action Plan Objective: Increase communication between school and parents concerning what literacy standards are being addressed and how parents can assist at home.

ACTION PLAN				MONITORING COMPONENT		
Strategy	Person Responsible	Timeline	Completion Evidence	Current Status Date: 10/1	Current Status Date: 11/1	Current Status Date: 12/1

Gantt Chart

Activity	Who's Responsible	Sept.	Oct.	Nov.	Dec.	Jan.	Feb.	Mar.	Apr.	May	June
Action Plan 1 Task 1											
Action Plan 1 Task 2											
Action Plan 1 Task 3											
Action Plan 1 Task 4											

OBSTACLES TO CHANGE

The table on the following pages lists the various types of resistance and reluctance outlined by Douglas Smith in his book *Taking Charge of Change*, and steps you can take to address them. Most of the strategies revolve around continued and enthusiastic communication and providing individuals with the skills, knowledge, and resources they need. The ultimate goal is to connect performance with purpose, first cognitively and then in concrete, workable ways.

> *"When leaders work every day to connect purpose, performance, and change, most people convert anxieties and fears into positive motivation… by using performance to make change real, leaders give people the chance to take that measure of control available to them."*
>
> — *Douglas K. Smith*
> *Author, Taking*
> *Charge of Change*

Reason for Reluctance/ Resistance	Leader Strategy
The purpose of the change is not clear.	Reinforce and re-explain the vision, mission, core values and beliefs. Discuss the context of the change—increased demands for accountability, etc.
Fear of the unknown	Since most stakeholders have been involved to some extent in the planning of the reform effort, most individuals should be aware of exactly what is/should occur. The leader must also continually exhibit "confident uncertainty"—that whatever happens, we can meet the challenges ahead.
Fear of failure	Plan initial steps carefully to ensure some early successes. Stress that failure is indeed a part of change and that if failure occurs, we will learn from it and improve.
Lack of incentive	Incentives take many forms and research shows that monetary rewards, while important, are not the most important factor in teacher satisfaction. The intrinsic satisfaction of a collaborative professional learning community will become self-reinforcing over time. Early successes will build enthusiasm and incentive. Review your reward system—both monetary and nonmonetary—to encourage involvement and commitment to implementing the plan. Celebrate successes large and small.
The feeling that "this too shall pass"	Communicate to all stakeholders that "we" are working together for continuous and sustained improvement. That the external and internal factors that are requiring change are not going away—the "learning for all" mission is here to stay. Emphasize that this is not a quick fix or "Band-Aid" program, but that we are working towards systemic change, we are fundamentally changing how we do business.
Lack of needed skills	When people feel that don't have the necessary skills to make the required changes, they become anxious and reluctant to try. Use surveys, observation, and one-on-one interaction to identify the knowledge and skills stakeholders need to successfully implement the plan, and then make sure the get the training they need. This relates to staff, administrators, parents, and students alike.
Lack of needed resources	Procuring the necessary resources should have been included in the overall school improvement plan. Resources should include not only physical resources like new computers, but the training, support, and encouragement for the change efforts. Don't just assume you know what faculty and other stakeholders need...ask. Help people identify the resources they need and how they will get them. Create networks of support by matching those who are successfully implementing the desired change with those who are struggling.

Reason for Reluctance/ Resistance	Leader Strategy
An "I" versus "We" Mentality	Teaching has historically been an isolated, solitary pursuit. According to Michael Fullan, "large-scale change cannot be achieved if teachers identify only with their own classrooms, and are not similarly concerned with the success of other teachers and the whole school." Without this sense of "we" or collegiality, reform efforts will produce only short-term, piecemeal improvement followed by a return to "business as usual." Use language and action to create and reinforce a sense of community, a climate of teamwork and collegiality. Create the infrastructure necessary to allow staff to work together, including peer mentoring, ad hoc teams for special projects, gatherings to reflect on progress to date, and social gatherings to reinforce the sense of community.
Unwilling to change	These are the folks who like the way things are, are not influenced by the contextual need for change, and aren't intimidated by the new accountability, new policies, procedures, or programs. Fortunately, there are usually very few of these individuals. There's not much you can do with these individuals except move them to a position where they can do no harm or, if possible, let them go.

SYSTEM CHECK-UP FOR PROMOTING SUCCESSFUL CHANGE

Why is change so difficult in schools? While change isn't generally easy in any organization, it seems particularly difficult to implement and sustain in schools. The answer to this lies in the fact that truly successful and sustainable change will depend on everyone making fundamental changes in their behaviors, which is simply the most difficult change to achieve. Behavioral change must be nurtured, supported, and rewarded, and that's no easy task. It is, however, achievable. Below is a checklist of factors that you must consider and address when implementing change. For every "no" you check, consider what you will do to address that issue.

Prerequisite Factor	Yes	No
All stakeholders understand and have embraced the vision and mission of the school.		
All stakeholders clearly understand and accept why change is needed.		
All stakeholders clearly understand and agree on what specific outcomes we are pursuing.		
All stakeholders clearly understand the link between the specific outcomes we are pursuing and the action plan.		
All stakeholders clearly understand what new behaviors and skills they will need to learn and implement as part of the action plan.		
All stakeholders clearly understand how the manner in which they implement their portion of the action plan contributes to the achievement of the overall improvement goal.		
Current staff has the capacity and willingness to learn new ways of doing things.		
We have a system in place to provide the needed training so that staff can learn new ways of doing things.		
We have a system in place to support the implementation of new knowledge and skills.		
We have a system in place to ensure that individuals are held accountable for results.		
We have a support system in place to nurture, encourage, and reward individuals as they implement new ways of doing things.		

CONNECTING LEADERSHIP TO STUDENT LEARNING

While we've always believed that leadership influenced student learning, the actual connection has historically been somewhat fuzzy. Recent research, however, has been able to show a strong connection between the two, as well as define what aspects of leadership are most important.

LEADERSHIP MATTERS!

Research shows that some things leaders do matter more than others in affecting student achievement. Use the following exercises to explore the relationship between leadership and student learning, and compare what you do as a leader to what the research says makes the greatest impact on student achievement.

LEADERSHIP AND LEARNING:
A COMPLEX BUT CRITICAL RELATIONSHIP

Kenneth Leithwood has written widely on leadership and education. In a report titled *How Leadership Influences Student Learning: A Review of Research*, commissioned by the Wallace Foundation, Leithwood and his colleagues shed light on the complex relationship between what leaders do and how well students learn. Specifically, they sought to answer five questions: 1) What effects does successful leadership have on student learning? 2) How should the competing forms of leadership visible in the literature be reconciled? 3) Is there a common set of "basic" leadership practices used by successful leaders in most circumstances? 4) What else, beyond the basics, is required for successful leadership? and 5) How does successful leadership exercise its influence on the learning of students?

To find the answer, Leithwood and his colleagues conducted an extensive literature review of the available research, including approximately 300 sources. Their review confirmed that successful leadership plays a highly significant role in improving student learning. In fact, the researchers found that leadership is second only to classroom instruction among all the school-related factors that contribute to what students learn at school. Furthermore, the leadership effects are usually largest where and when they are needed most.

According to Leithwood, et al., leaders contribute to student learning most significantly in an indirect way. Specifically, leaders exert a positive or negative influence on the individuals who in turn directly influence student learning (teachers) and on the relevant features of their organizations (schools). The chart, based on Leithwood's work, on the following page depicts this relationship.

How Leadership Influences Student Learning

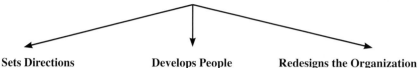

Sets Directions	Develops People	Redesigns the Organization
1. Identifies and articulates a vision.	1. Offers intellectual stimulation.	1. Stengthens district and school culture.
2. Fosters the acceptance of group goals.	2. Provides individualized support.	2. Modifies organizational structures.
3. Creates high performance expectations.	3. Provides appropriate models of best practices and beliefs.	3. Builds collaborative processes.
4. Monitors organizational performance.		
5. Promotes effective communications.		
6. Helps develop shared organizational purposes.		

Leader Assignment:

Think about the specific ways leadership impacts student learning within the context of your school or district. What would you add to the list under the various categories specific to your school? How would you rate yourself in terms of these leadership functions? How do Leithwood's findings on leadership's impact on student learning affect your perception of leadership in general, and of your own leadership priorities in specific? Does it reinforce how you currently spend your time, or does it give you pause to reevaluate your current leadership priorities?

INTENTIONAL LEADERSHIP

Reinforcing Leithwood's work, a recent McRel study by Waters, Marzano, and Mc-Nulty also found a substantial link between leadership and student achievement. The researchers found 21 specific leadership responsibilities significantly correlated with student achievement. In addition, they found some other very interesting aspects of leadership. First, the relationship between leadership and student achievement works **both ways**. Specifically, they report that "just as leaders can have a positive impact on achievement, they also can have a marginal, or worse, negative impact on achievement."

Second, the researchers found that not all change has the same magnitude. The researchers have categorized these differing magnitudes as "first order" and "second order." According to the researchers, "a change becomes second order when it is not obvious how it will make things better for people with similar interests, it requires individuals or groups of stakeholders to learn new approaches, or it conflicts with prevailing values or norms. The following chart taken from the McRel study, describes the characteristics of first and second order change.

First Order Change	Second Order Change
An extension of the past	A break with the past
Within existing paradigms	Outside existing paradigms
Consistent with prevailing values and norms	Conflicted with prevailing values and norms
Focused	Emergent
Bounded	Unbounded
Incremental	Complex
Linear	Nonlinear
Marginal	A disturbance to every element of a system
Implemented with existing knowledge & skills	Requires new knowledge and skills to implement
Problem- and solution-oriented	Neither problem- nor solution-oriented
Implemented by experts	Implemented by stakeholders

Schools are clearly faced with the need for second order change, since it requires teachers, administrators, students, and parents to learn new approaches and act in ways very different from what they are used to. This doesn't mean that first-order changes are unnecessary. In fact, first-order changes provide the foundation for second-order change. The school leader plays a critical role as the catalyst for both types of change, but second-order change is key to the long-term sustainability of continuous improvement.

Leader Assignment:

Use the following McRel chart as a self-assessment tool for your current leadership practices. The following chart shows specific practices associated with first- and second-order change. Next to each practice is a box. Check the boxes that describe your current practices. Of those you checked, think about how you'd go about instituting these practices, and highlight those areas you'd like to work on more, or improve upon. Of those you left unchecked, identify those practices you would like to institute and prioritize them. Develop a plan that identifies what new knowledge and skills you will need to institute these practices.

Leadership Responsibilities & Effect Sizes (ES)	Appropriate for First Order Change	Practices ⟶	Appropriate for Second Order Change
Situational awareness (.33)	❏ Is aware of informal groups and relationships among staff of the school		❏ Is aware of issues in the school that have not surfaced but could create discord ❏ Can predict what could go wrong from day to day
Intellectual stimulation (.32)	❏ Keeps informed about current research and theory regarding effective schooling ❏ Continuously involves staff in reading articles and books about effective practices		❏ Continually exposes staff to cutting edge ideas about how to be effective ❏ Systemically engages staff in discussions about current research and theory
Change Agent (.30)			❏ Consciously challenges the status quo ❏ Is comfortable leading change initiatives with uncertain outcomes ❏ Systemically considers new and better ways of doing things
Input (.30)	❏ Provides opportunity for input on all important decisions		❏ Provides opportunities for staff to be involved in developing school policies ❏ Uses a leadership team in decision making
Culture (.29)	❏ Promotes cooperation among staff ❏ Promotes a sense of well-being ❏ Promotes cohesion among staff		❏ Develops shared understanding of purpose ❏ Develops a shared vision of what the school could be like

Leadership Responsibilities & Effect Sizes (ES)	Appropriate for First Order Change	Practices ⟶	Appropriate for Second Order Change
Monitors/evaluates (.28)	❏ Monitors and evaluates the effectiveness of curriculum, instruction, and assessment		
Outreach (.28)	❏ Assures that the school is in compliance with district and state mandates ❏ Advocates on behalf of the school in the community ❏ Advocates for the school with parents of the students ❏ Ensures that the central office is aware of the school's accomplishments		
Order (.26)	❏ Provides and enforces clear structures, rules, and procedures for students ❏ Provides and enforces clear structures, rules, and procedures for staff ❏ Establishes routines regarding the running of the school that staff understand and follow		
Resources (.26)	❏ Ensures that teachers have necessary materials and equipment	❏ Ensures that teachers have necessary staff development opportunities that directly enhance their teaching	
Affirmation (.25)	❏ Systemically and fairly recognizes and celebrates accomplishments of teachers ❏ Systemically and fairly recognizes and celebrates accomplishments of students	❏ Systemically acknowledges failures and celebrates accomplishment of the school	
Ideals/Beliefs (.25)	❏ Shares beliefs about schooling, teachers, and learning with staff and parents ❏ Demonstrates behaviors that are consistent with beliefs	❏ Holds strong professional beliefs about schools, teaching, and learning	

Leadership Responsibilities & Effect Sizes (ES)	Appropriate for First Order Change	Practices →	Appropriate for Second Order Change
Discipline (.24)	❑ Protects instructional times from interruptions ❑ Protects/shelters teachers from distraction		
Focus (.24)	❑ Establishes concrete goals for all curriculum, instruction, and assessment ❑ Establishes concrete goals for the general functioning of the school ❑ Continually keeps attention on established goals		❑ Establishes high, concrete goals and expectations that all students meet them
Knowledge of curriculum, instruction, assessment (.24)	❑ Is knowledgeable about instructional practices ❑ Is knowledgeable about assessment practices ❑ Provides conceptual guidance for teachers regarding effective classroom practice		
Communication (.23)	❑ Is easily accessible to teachers ❑ Develops effective means for teachers to communicate with one another ❑ Maintains open and effective lines of communication with staff		
Flexibility (.22)		❑ Can be directive or nondirective as the situation warrants	❑ Is comfortable with major changes in how things are done ❑ Encourages people to express opinions contrary to those of authority ❑ Adapts leadership style to needs of specific situations

Leadership Responsibilities & Effect Sizes (ES)	Appropriate for First Order Change	Practices ——————▶	Appropriate for Second Order Change
Optimizer (.20)	❑ Inspires teachers to accomplish things that might seem beyond their grasp ❑ Portrays a positive attitude about the ability of the staff to accomplish substantial things		❑ Is a driving force behind major initiatives
Relationship (.19)	❑ Remains aware of personal needs of teachers ❑ Maintains personal relationships with teachers ❑ Is informed about significant personal issues within lives of staff ❑ Acknowledges significant events in the lives of staff		
Curriculum, instruction, assessment (.16)	❑ Ensures that teachers have necessary materials and equipment ❑ Is involved with teachers to address instructional issues in their classrooms ❑ Is involved with teachers to address assessment issues		
Visibility (.16)	❑ Makes systemic and frequent visits to classrooms ❑ Maintains high visibility around the school ❑ Has frequent contact with students		
Contingent rewards (.15)	❑ Recognizes individuals who excel		❑ Uses performance vs. seniority as the primary criterion for reward and advancement ❑ Uses hard work and results as the basis for reward and recognition

LEADER SELF-ASSESSMENT

Throughout this book, we've discussed many aspects of leadership. Here's your chance to assess your own leadership practices in light of what makes an educational leader effective using the survey on the following pages.

The attributes outlined on this survey are an amalgam of the many leadership resources used throughout this book, as well as items taken from the Instructional Leadership category of Reality Check™. More information on Reality Check is available in Appendix C.

Once you've taken the survey, go back and reflect on your answers. Highlight the areas you would like to target for improvement. Brainstorm ideas on how to improve those areas: Do you need more training? Mentoring? Logistical support?

Now highlight the areas which you think you're especially good at. It's important to recognize our strengths as well as our weaknesses. Now consider how you can nurture these skills in others.

Instructions

Use the questions below to reflect on your own leadership and practices.

SA	=	**Strongly Agree**
A	=	**Agree**
U	=	**Undecided**
D	=	**Disagree**
SD	=	**Strongly Disagree**
NA	=	**Not Applicable or No Opinion**

Achievement Focus

#	Item	SA	A	U	D	SD	NA
1	I direct most of my energies toward specific short- and long-term goals of improving student learning.	❏	❏	❏	❏	❏	❏
2	I foster a focus on achievement by ensuring that the content and procedures of faculty meetings emphasize student learning and effective instruction.	❏	❏	❏	❏	❏	❏
3	I make regular formal and informal classroom visits.	❏	❏	❏	❏	❏	❏
4	I foster an achievement focus by providing rewards for students who show outstanding progress.	❏	❏	❏	❏	❏	❏
5	I articulate clear expectations and goals for student and adult learning.	❏	❏	❏	❏	❏	❏
6	I understand and can use student achievement data to assess student learning.	❏	❏	❏	❏	❏	❏
7	I understand and can use leading indicators of learning to find root causes of poor student outcomes.	❏	❏	❏	❏	❏	❏

This survey can easily be created and analyzed using the Effective Schools Reality Check[SM] *Tool.*

#	Item	SA	A	U	D	SD	NA
8	I understand and can facilitate the process of curriculum alignment.	❏	❏	❏	❏	❏	❏
9	I actively communicate the need for teachers to monitor student performance and adjust instruction accordingly.	❏	❏	❏	❏	❏	❏
10	I actively seek to limit daily interruptions of instructional time.	❏	❏	❏	❏	❏	❏

Inspiring Followership

#	Item	SA	A	U	D	SD	NA
11	I can clearly articulate my vision of school improvement and its end product.	❏	❏	❏	❏	❏	❏
12	I actively and clearly communicate my vision, the school's mission, and its instructional goals on a daily basis to staff, students, and parents.	❏	❏	❏	❏	❏	❏
13	I demonstrate through my daily decisions and actions my beliefs about teaching and learning and my commitment to continuous improvement	❏	❏	❏	❏	❏	❏
14	I actively seek to involve all stakeholders in the decisions that affect them and in the school improvement process.	❏	❏	❏	❏	❏	❏
15	I actively solicit and listen to stakeholder concerns and suggestions.	❏	❏	❏	❏	❏	❏
16	I keep stakeholders informed of decisions and actions before they are instituted, why those decisions/actions have been adopted, and what those decisions mean to them.	❏	❏	❏	❏	❏	❏
17	I publicly recognize the efforts of staff members	❏	❏	❏	❏	❏	❏
18	I find ways to reward staff members for outstanding contributions.	❏	❏	❏	❏	❏	❏
19	Faculty, staff, and students can count on my fairness and consistency in making decisions.	❏	❏	❏	❏	❏	❏

This survey can easily be created and analyzed using the Effective Schools Reality Check[SM] Tool.

#	Item	SA	A	U	D	SD	NA
20	I am visible throughout the school on a regular basis.	❏	❏	❏	❏	❏	❏
21	I promote a sense of pride in my school by my attitudes, comments, and actions.	❏	❏	❏	❏	❏	❏

Developing the Capacity of Others

#	Item	SA	A	U	D	SD	NA
22	I provide leadership opportunities for staff.	❏	❏	❏	❏	❏	❏
23	I have identified expert teachers and have given them opportunities to share their expertise.	❏	❏	❏	❏	❏	❏
24	I provide regular opportunities for faculty to learn from one another.	❏	❏	❏	❏	❏	❏
25	I feel capable of adequately assessing a variety of classroom teaching and evaluation strategies.	❏	❏	❏	❏	❏	❏
26	I provide teachers with specific and constructive feedback on their performances based on data collected in the classroom.	❏	❏	❏	❏	❏	❏
27	I provide faculty members with supervision and development activities appropriate to their needs.	❏	❏	❏	❏	❏	❏
28	I circulate relevant research articles on effective instruction and other ways to improve student learning among the staff.	❏	❏	❏	❏	❏	❏
29	I find specific ways to foster active staff discussions on curriculum and instruction.	❏	❏	❏	❏	❏	❏
30	I assist the staff in interpreting test results.	❏	❏	❏	❏	❏	❏
31	I encourage staff to try new instructional strategies and support their professional growth.	❏	❏	❏	❏	❏	❏
32	I encourage parents to participate in the continuous improvement planning process.	❏	❏	❏	❏	❏	❏

This survey can easily be created and analyzed using the Effective Schools Reality Check^{SM} Tool.

APPENDIX B

A Leadership Perspective on the Correlates of Effective Schools

Since the Coleman report in 1966, many researchers have sought to discover why some schools were successful in teaching all children, regardless of their demographics or disadvantages. Over the decades, the accumulated research into effective schools has yielded a set of common characteristics that all effective schools share. These characteristics are so consistently prevalent among successful schools, they have come to be known as the Correlates of Effective Schools. The original correlate descriptions, which we call "The First Generation," represent what the original effective schools research found to be the minimum standards of a particular characteristic that a school must meet to be effective. "The Second Generation" of each correlate incorporates subsequent research findings into our understanding of each characteristic, and represents a developmental step beyond the first that, when successfully accomplished, will move the school even closer to the mission of *"learning for all."* It is your job as leader to not only see that the original correlate is in place, but to guide your school or district in embracing the next generation.

1. Safe and Orderly Environment

The First Generation: In the effective school, there is an orderly, purposeful, and businesslike atmosphere that is free from the threat of physical harm. The school climate is not oppressive and is conducive to teaching and learning.

The Second Generation: The second generation moves beyond the elimination of undesirable behavior and places increased emphasis on the presence of certain desirable behaviors, such as collaboration and teamwork. Since schools as workplaces are characterized by their isolation, creating more collaborative and cooperative environments for both the adults and students will require substantial commitment and change in most schools. Educational leaders must nurture the belief that collaboration, which often requires more time initially, will help schools to be more effective and satisfying in the long run. They must embrace and promote acceptance of and respect for diversity and multiculturalism, help teachers learn the "technologies" of teamwork, and create the "opportunity structures" for collaboration. Leaders must model these behaviors, as well, and "be the world we want to see."

2. Climate of High Expectations for Success

The First Generation: In the effective school, the staff believes that all students can master of the essential school skills, and that they have the capability to help all students achieve that mastery.

The Second Generation: In the second generation, the emphasis placed on high expectations for success is broadened significantly. Here, high expectations will be judged, not only by the staff's initial beliefs and behaviors, but also by the organization's—and by association, the leader's—response when some students do not learn. For example, if the teacher plans and delivers a lesson, finds that some students did not learn, but still goes on to the next lesson, then that teacher didn't expect the students to learn in the first place. If the leader, through silence, condones that teacher's behavior, then that leader apparently did not expect these students to learn either, or the teacher to teach them.

The second generation represents significant challenge to the leaders who must help their schools, as cultural organizations, transform from teaching-centered institutions to learning-centered organizations where teachers have high expectations of themselves as teachers, and have access to more "tools" to help them ensure that every child learns.

3. Instructional Leadership

The First Generation: In the effective school, the principal acts as an instructional leader and effectively and persistently communicates that mission to the staff, parents, and students. The principal understands and applies the characteristics of instructional effectiveness in the management of the instructional program.

The Second Generation: Here the concept of instructional leadership is broadened to encompass all adults, especially the teachers. The role of the principal becomes "a leader of leaders," rather than a leader of followers. The leader's greatest contribution in this generation will be to articulate a vision to which all stakeholders can commit, and create a community of shared values guided by the "magnetic north" of the mission. This broader concept of leadership recognizes that leadership is always delegated from the followership in any organization, and that expertise is generally distributed among many, not concentrated in a single person.

4. Clear and Focused Mission

The First Generation: In the effective school, there is a clearly articulated school mission, through which the staff shares an understanding of and commitment to the instructional goals, priorities, assessment procedures, and accountability. Staff accepts responsibility for student learning.

The Second Generation: The first generation prompted the rise of two issues. The first focused on the meaning of "learning for all." Did we really mean _all_ students or just those with whom the schools had a history of reasonable success? When it became clear that we really did mean _all_ students, especially the poor and disadvantaged, the second issue surfaced. It asked the question: _Learn what?_ Partially because of the accountability movement, and partially because of the belief that disadvantaged students could not learn higher-level curricula, the "what" focused primarily on low-level skills.

In the second generation, the focus shifts toward a more appropriate balance between higher-level learning and the basic skills that are prerequisite to their mastery, and from a teaching-centered orientation to one that is learning centered. Designing and delivering a curriculum that responds to the demands of accountability, and is responsive to the need for higher levels of learning will require substantial staff development. It will incumbent upon the leader to promote the "_learning_ for all" mission (as opposed to _teaching_) and to ensure that teachers have the necessary skills and tools to accomplish it.

5. Opportunity to Learn and Student Time on Task

The First Generation: In the effective school, teachers allocate a significant amount of classroom time to instruction in the essential skills. For a high percentage of this time students are engaged in whole-class or large-group, teacher-directed, planned learning activities.

The Second Generation: One of the reasons that many of the mandated approaches to school reform have failed is that, in every case, the local school was asked to do more! In this generation, a characteristic of the most effective schools is their willingness to declare that some things are more important than others; they are willing to abandon some less-important content so that the students master the critical content in the limited time available. Leaders will have to help their teachers become more skilled at interdisciplinary curriculum and at practicing "organized abandonment." They will have to ask the question, "What goes, and what stays?"

The only alternative to abandonment would be to adjust the available time that students spend in school, so that those who need more time to reach mastery would be given it. This may require us to reexamine past policies and practices, such as our notions about the length of the school day or school year. If we choose to extend learning time, it must be in a quality program that is not perceived as punitive by those in it, or as excessive by those who must fund it. These conditions will be a real challenge indeed!

6. Frequent Monitoring of Student Progress

The First Generation: In the effective school, student academic progress is measured frequently through a variety of assessment procedures. The results of these assessments are used to improve individual student performance and also to improve the instructional program.

The Second Generation: In this generation, technology will permit teachers to do a better and timelier job of monitoring their students' progress. This same technology will allow students to monitor their own learning and, where necessary, adjust their own behavior. The use of computerized practice tests, the ability to get immediate results on homework, and the ability to see correct solutions developed on the screen are a few of the available tools for assuring student learning. We will also continue to shift away from standardized norm-referenced tests toward more authentic assessments of curriculum mastery. This generally means that there will be less emphasis on the paper-pencil, multiple-choice tests, and more emphasis on assessments of products of student work, including performances and portfolios.

It will be up to the educational leader to ensure that there is tight alignment between the intended, taught, and tested curriculum. This will require that the leader engage the stakeholders in addressing two questions: "What's worth knowing?" and "How will we know when they know it?" This will demand our best thinking and plenty of patience to reach consensus. The good news is that once we reach that consensus, the schools will be able to deliver significant progress toward these agreed-upon outcomes.

7. Home-School Relations

The First Generation: In the effective school, parents understand and support the school's mission and are given the opportunity to play an important role in helping the school to achieve this mission.

The Second Generation: During the first generation, the role of parents in the education of their children was always somewhat unclear. While schools often gave "lip service" to having parents more involved in the schooling of their children, many educators really did not know how to effectively handle increased parent involvement. In this generation, the relationship between parents and the school must be an authentic partnership. However, it has become clear to both teachers and parents that the parent involvement issue is not simple. The leader must help teachers and parents confront this issue—and not each other—in a way that builds trust and the understanding that both teachers and parents have the same goal—a quality education and a successful future for all children!

APPENDIX C

LEARNING FOR ALL...
RESOURCES FOR MAKING IT HAPPEN

As we've advocated throughout this book, the *"learning for all"* mission requires a broader approach to improving student learning, one that incorporates three key components:

- **Effective leaders** who can share the vision and lead the process;
- **A blueprint for action** that is grounded in data and research, one that includes all those who will be affected by its results in its development; and
- **The right tools to support the process,** which will provide critical information for decision-making in a timely and efficient manner.

This book was written to help schools and school districts create, develop, and nurture effective leaders. Effective Schools Products offers other resources to support the continuous school improvement process as well. On the following pages, we've listed the resources referred to in *Stepping Up*.

For a complete list of Effective Schools resources, plus pricing and ordering information, please visit our website:

www.effectiveschools.com
— or —
call 1-800-827-8041

Assembly Required: A Continuous School Improvement System
&
Implementation Guide for Assembly Required

Annual yearly progress is just a synonym for continuous improvement. Together, these two books offer **a step-by-step action plan** for a creating a continuous improvement system that will ultimately lead to sustained improvement in student learning. *Assembly Required* offers the skills and knowledge you need to create an inclusive, data-driven, research-based, and collaborative process; the *Implementation Guide*, with its hands-on activities and exercises, and useful forms and worksheets, allows you to immediately apply what you've learned to your school. While nothing can make school reform *easy*, these two comprehensive publications, ***Assembly Required: A Continuous School Improvement System*** and its companion ***Implementation Guide*** can simplify the complicated task of improving student achievement.

Reality Check
Online Survey Tool

Surveying stakeholders builds commitment to your improvement efforts, and helps identify key issues and problems. To streamline this often time-consuming and complicated task, we've developed **Reality Check**. With Reality Check, you can easily develop and administer a survey online or on paper, in English or in Spanish, or both. You can create your own questions or draw from a bank of over 2,000 carefully crafted questions in the Reality Check database, all organized around the Correlates of Effective Schools. Compiling and displaying response data is a snap as well:

- Online responses are instantly tabulated and graphed as they are submitted.
- Paper-and-pencil responses are instantly tabulated and graphed as you easily enter the data.
- Results can be easily and quickly downloaded into a spreadsheet program for further analysis, including disaggregation of the data.

Now developing and processing a survey will take less time than ever, for far less than hiring an outside consultant.

Research LiNK
Online Research Tool

There is much to be learned from the experiences of other schools and districts and their efforts to improve student learning. Furthermore, "based on proven practices" and "research-based" have become the standard criteria by which school improvement strategies are measured. The **Research LiNK** offers you a rich online resource of the best and most relevant education research published in the last two decades. The **LiNK** is:

- **Comprehensive.** This extensive, searchable database offers you more than 1,500 research abstracts on topics ranging from strategies that work in the classroom to what works at the district level, and everything in between. We add another 72 summaries each year, keeping the Research LiNK relevant and up-to-date.

- **Clear and Concise.** Our cadre of professional educators summarize the key findings and implications of the study so that you can quickly determine if it's relevant to your needs. The full citation is included so you can access the original research if you wish.

- **Easy to Use.** The LiNK is organized around the correlates of effective schools. You can search by topic, title, author, or keyword, then simply print what you need without retyping or reformatting.

Research LiNK offers you an indispensable resource and an exceptional value. Your one-year membership entitles you and anyone you designate—members of your staff, school improvement team, or administrative team—access to this impressive body of research at your school for an entire year for one low price.

The Effective Schools League
Online Networking Tool

The old saw, "None of us is as smart as all of us!" is especially true for those of us seeking to improve student learning. There is a wealth of knowledge "out there" on ways to improve our schools and raise student achievement. But connecting with colleagues and finding the appropriate research can be difficult and time consuming. The **Effective Schools League** was created to help busy educators make those connections by offering you:

- *Easy Access to Research & Best Practices.* The League gives you access to an array of school improvement resources you won't find anywhere else, including a vast online database of school improvement research and a wealth of information on Effective Schools and school improvement, including the Correlates of Effective Schools and original papers by Ron Edmonds and Larry Lezotte, plus useful education links and other resources.

- *Opportunities to Network with Colleagues.* Perhaps most importantly, you will have the ability to talk and network with colleagues, both locally and across the U.S. and Canada.

Once you become familiar with this exceptional tool, you'll find it will provide you with the research and collegial support you've been looking for as you work to improve student learning.

Consulting & Speaking Services by Dr. Larry Lezotte

Dr. Lezotte, nationally renowned educational consultant and speaker, has taught thousands of educators across the U.S. how to create systems that lead to the *ongoing improvement* of student learning. In recognition of his efforts, Dr. Lezotte received the *2003 Council of Chief State School Officers' Distinguished Service Award*, presented each year to outstanding Americans who have made a difference in education.

Dr. Lezotte conducts a variety of leadership institutes for current and aspiring administrators and school leadership teams, as well as training on continuous school improvement for educators at all levels. He is also a sought-after speaker for conferences and institutes, as a keynote speaker, on panels, and at break-out sessions. To inquire about Dr. Lezotte's consulting and speaking availability and costs, please visit our web site to download and fill out the *Request for Information* (the link at the top of the Professional Development page) and fax it to (517) 349-8852. The information you provide will help us to better respond to your request.

REFERENCES

REFERENCES

Ackoff, Russell, *Creating the Corporate Future*. John Wiley & Sons, Inc., New York, NY, 1981.

Alexander, Karl L., Doris R. Entwisle, and Linda S. Olsen, "Schools, Achievement and Inequality: A Seasonal Perspective," *Educational Evaluation and Policy Analysis* 23, 2 (Summer 2001): 171-191.

Allen, Lew, "From Plaques to Practice: How Schools Can Breathe Life Into Their Guiding Beliefs," *Phi Delta Kappan* 83, 4 (December 2001): 289-293.

Anderson, Kirk D., "The Nature of Teacher Leadership in Schools as Reciprocal Influences Between Teacher Leaders and Principals," *School Effectiveness and School Improvement* 15, 1 (March 2004): 97-113.

Archer, Jeff, "Tackling an Impossible Job," *Education Week* 24, 3 (September 15, 2004): S3-S6.

Axelrod, Richard, *Terms of Engagement: Changing the Way We Change Organizations*. Berrett-Koehler Publishers, Inc., San Francisco, CA, 2002.

Bennis, Warren, *On Becoming a Leader*. Perseus Books Group, New York, NY, 1994.

Bennis, Warren, *Why Leaders Can't Lead: The Unconscious Conspiracy Continues*. Jossey-Bass Publishers, San Francisco, CA, 1989.

Bennis, Warren and Burt Nanus, *Leaders: The Strategies for Taking Charge*. Harper & Row Publishers, New York, NY, 1985.

Block, Peter, *The Empowered Manager: Positive Political Skills at Work*. Jossey-Bass Publishers, San Francisco, CA, 1987.

Booher-Jennings, Jennifer, "Below the Bubble: 'Educational Triage' and the Texas Accountability System," *American Educational Research Journal* 42, 2 (Summer 2005): 231-268.

Boris-Schacter, Sheryl and Susan Merrifield, "Why 'Particularly Good' Principals Don't Quit," *Journal of School Leadership* 10, 1 (January 2000): 84-98.

Bossidy, Larry and Ram Charan, *Execution: The Discipline of Getting Things Done*. Crown Business, New York, NY, 2002.

Boulding, Kenneth E., *Three Faces of Power*. Sage Publications, Newbury Park, CA, 1989.

Bowsher, Jack E., *Successful Administrators Leading Successful Schools*. Jack E.
    Bowsher, San Diego, CA, 2003.

Briggs, Kerri L. and Pricilla Wohlstetter, "Key Elements of a Successful School-Based
    Management Strategy," *School Effectiveness and School Improvement* 14, 3
    (September 2003): 351-372.

Bush, Tony and Derek Glover, *School Leadership: Concepts and Evidence*. National
    College for School Leadership, Nottingham, England, 2003.

Calhoun, Emily F., "Action Research for School Improvement," *Educational Leadership*
    59, 6 (March 2002): 18-24.

Childs-Bowen, Deborah, Gayle Moller, and Jennifer Scriver, "Principals: Leaders of
    Leaders," *NASSP Bulletin* 84, 616 (May 2000): 27-34.

Collins, Jim, *Good to Great: Why Some Companies Make the Leap... and Others Don't*.
    HarperCollins Publisher Inc., New York, NY, 2002.

Covey, Stephen R., *The 7 Habits of Highly Effective People*. Simon & Schuster, New
    York, NY, 1989.

Covey, Stephen R., *The 8th Habit: From Effectiveness to Greatness*. Free Press, New
    York, NY, 2004.

Creighton, Theodore B., "Data Analysis and the Principalship," *Principal Leadership
    (High School Edition)* 1, 9 (May/June 2001): 52-57.

Deal, Terrence E. and Kent D. Peterson, *The Leadership Paradox: Balancing Logic and
    Artistry in Schools*. Jossey-Bass Publishers, San Francisco, CA, 1994.

Deal, Terrence E. and Kent D. Peterson, *The Principal's Role in Shaping School Culture*.
    Office of Educational Research and Improvement, U.S. Department of Education,
    Washington, D.C., 1990.

Deal, Terrence E. and Kent D. Peterson, *Shaping School Culture: The Heart of
    Leadership*. Jossey-Bass Publishers, San Francisco, CA, 1999.

Deming, W. Edwards, *The New Economics: For Industry, Government, Education*.
    Massachusetts Institute of Technology, Cambridge, MA, 1993.

Dolan, W. Patrick, *Restructuring Our Schools: A Primer on Systemic Change*. Systems &
    Organization, Kansas City, MO, 1994.

Drucker, Peter, *Management Challenges for the 21st Century*. HarperCollins Publisher Inc., New York, NY, 1999.

Fritz, Robert, *The Path of Least Resistance: Learning to Become the Creative Force in Your Own Life*. Fawcett Columbine, New York, NY, 1989.

Fullan, Michael, "Coordinating Top-Down and Bottom-Up Strategies for School Reform." In *The Governance of Curriculum: 1994 ASCD Yearbook*, edited by Richard F. Elmore and Susan H. Fuhrman. Association for Supervision and Curriculum Development, Alexandria, VA, 1994.

Fullan, Michael, *Leading in a Culture of Change*. Jossey-Bass Publishers, San Francisco, CA, 2001.

Fullan, Michael, "The Change Leader," *Educational Leadership* 59, 8 (May 2002): 16-21.

Fullan, Michael, *The New Meaning of Educational Change*. Teachers College Press, Columbia University, New York, 1991.

Goddard, Roger D., Wayne K. Hoy, and Anita Woolfolk Hoy, "Collective Teacher Efficacy: Its Meaning, Measure, and Impact on Student Achievement," *American Educational Research Journal* 37, 2 (Summer 2000): 479-507.

Goodlad, John I., *What Schools Are For*. Phi Delta Kappa Educational Foundation, Bloomington, IN, 1979.

Goodlad, John I. and Timothy J. McMannon, eds., *The Public Purpose of Education and Schooling*. Jossey-Bass Publishers, San Francisco, CA, 1997.

Hargreaves, Andy and Michael Fullan, *What's Worth Fighting for Out There?* Teachers College Press, Columbia University, New York, NY, 1998.

Heritage, Margaret and Raymond Yeagley, "Data Use and School Improvement: Challenges and Prospects." In *Uses and Misuses of Data for Educational Accountability and Improvement, 104th Yearbook of the National Society for the Study of Education, Part 2*, edited by Joan L. Herman and Edward H. Haertel. Blackwell Publishing, Malden, MA, 2005.

Introduction to Data Analysis Web Site, developed by Albert Goodman, School of Information Technology at Deakin University, Melbourne, Australia. http://www.deakin.edu.au/~agoodman/sci101/index.php

Investigating the Influence of Standards: A Framework for Research in Mathematics, Science, and Technology Education. Committee on Understanding the Influence of Standards in K-12 Science, Mathematics, and Technology Education, edited by Iris R.Weiss, Michael S. Knapp, Karen S. Hollweg, and Gail Burrill. Center for Education, Division of Behavioral and Social Sciences and Education, National Research Council, National Academy Press, Washington, DC, 2001.

Junger, Sebastian, *The Perfect Storm: A True Story of Men Against the Sea.* W. W. Norton & Company, New York, NY, 1997.

Kim, W. Chan and Renee Mauborgne, "Fair Process: Managing in the Knowledge Economy," *Harvard Business Review* (January 2003): 3-11.

Kouzes, James M. and Barry Z. Posner, *The Leadership Challenge: How to Get Extraordinary Things Done in Organizations.* Jossey-Bass Inc., Publishers, San Francisco, CA, 1987.

Learner-Centered Psychological Principles: A Framework for School Redesign and Reform. American Psychological Association, Washington, DC, 1997.

Leithwood, Kenneth, "School Leadership in the Context of Accountability Policies," *International Journal of Leadership in Education* 4, 3 (July-Sept. 2001): 217-235.

Leithwood, Kenneth and Carolyn Riehl, *What We Know About Successful School Leadership.* A Report for the American Educational Research Association, Laboratory for Student Success, Temple University, Philadelphia, PA, 2003.

Leithwood, Kenneth and Nona Pristine, "Unpacking the Challenges of Leadership at the School and District Level," *The Educational Leadership Challenge: Redefining Leadership for the 21st Century.* National Society for the Study of Education, Chicago, IL, 2002.

Leithwood, Kenneth, Karen Seashore Louis, Stephen Anderson, and Kyle Wahlstrom, *How Leadership Influences Student Learning: A Review of Research.* Center for Applied Research and Educational Improvement, Minneapolis, MN, and Ontario Institute for Studies in Education, Toronto, Ontario, Canada, 2004.

Marks, Helen M. and Susan M. Printy, "Principal Leadership and School Performance: An Integration of Transformational and Instructional Leadership," *Education Administration Quarterly* 30, 3 (August 2003): 370-397.

Marzano, Robert, Debra Pickering, and Jane E. Pollock, *Classroom Instruction That Works.* Association for Supervision & Curriculum Development, Alexandria, VA, 2001.

Maxwell, John C., *21 Indispensable Qualities of a Leader*. Thomas Nelson, Inc., Nashville, TN, 1999.

Mayo, Anthony and Nitin Nohria, *In Their Time: The Greatest Business Leaders of the 20th Century*. Harvard Business School Press, Watertown, MA, 2005.

NAESP Standards for What Principals Should Know and Be Able to Do. National Association of Elementary School Principals, Alexandria, VA, 2001.

Peters, Thomas J. and Robert H. Waterman, *In Search of Excellence*. Harper & Row, New York, NY, 1982.

Purpel, David E., *The Moral and Spiritual Crisis in Education*. Bergin & Garvey, New York, NY, 1989.

Reeves, Douglas B., "Standards are Not Enough: Essential Transformations for School Success," *NASSP Bulletin* 84, 620 (December 2000): 5-19.

Ross, John A., Carol Rolheiser, and Anne Hogaboam-Gray, "Effects of Collaborative Action Research on the Knowledge of Five Canadian Teacher-Researchers," *The Elementary School Journal* 99, 3 (January 1999): 255-275.

Schlecty, Phillip, *Working on the Work: An Action Plan for Teachers, Principals, and Superintendents*. Jossey-Bass Publishers, San Francisco, CA, 2002.

Senge, Peter M., *The Fifth Discipline: The Art & Practice of the Learning Organization*. Doubleday/Currency, New York, NY, 1990.

Sergiovanni, Thomas, "The Leadership Needed for Quality Schools," In *Schooling for Tomorrow*, edited by Thomas Sergiovanni and John H. Moore. Allyn & Bacon, 1989.

Shewhart, Walter A., *Statistical Method from the Viewpoint of Quality Control*. The Graduate School, Department of Agriculture, Washington, DC, 1939. (Reprinted by Dover Publications, Mineola, NY, in 1986)

Smith, Douglas K., *Taking Charge of Change: 10 Principles for Managing People and Performance*. Perseus Books Group, New York, NY, 1997.

Stoll, Louise, and Dean Fink, "School Effectiveness and School Improvement: Voices from the Field," *School Effectiveness and School Improvement* 5, 2 (June 1994): 149-177.

Strahan, David, "Promoting a Collaborative Professional Culture in Three Elementary Schools That Have Beaten the Odds," *The Elementary School Journal* 104, 2 (November 2003): 127-146.

Tyack, David and Larry Cuban, *Tinkering Toward Utopia: A Century of Public School Reform.* Harvard University Press, Cambridge, MA, 1996.

Using Data for School Improvement: A report on the 2nd Practioners' Conference for Annenberg Challenge Sites. Annenberg Institute for School Reform at Brown University, Providence, RI, 1998.

Walton, Mark S., *Generating Buy-In.* AMACOM, New York, NY, 2004.

Waters, Tim and Sally Grubb, *Leading Schools: Distinguishing the Essential from the Important.* A McRel Report, Aurora, CO, 2004.

Waters, Tim, Robert J. Marzano, and Brian McNulty, *Balanced Leadership: What 30 Years of Research Tells Us About the Effect of Leadership on Student Achievement.* McRel, Aurora, CA, 2003.

Quotes throughout taken from the following web sites:

- The Quotations Page (www.quotationspage.com)
- BrainyQuote (www.brainyquote.com)
- Wisdom Quotes (www.wisdomquotes.com)
- Quote.com (www.quote.com)
- The Motivational and Inspirational Corner (www.motivational-inspiration-corner.com)
- LeadershipNow.com (www.leadershipnow.com/quotes.html)
- Quotations (http://quotations.about.com)
- Think Exist (www.thinkexist.com)

ABOUT THE AUTHORS

About the Authors

Dr. Lawrence W. Lezotte

Dr. Lezotte earned his doctorate from Michigan State University in 1969, joining the faculty there that same year. During his 18-year tenure at MSU, he served in various capacities, including Chair of the Department of Educational Administration; Associate Director, with Ron Edmonds, of the Center for School Improvement in the College of Education; and Chair of Urban and Metropolitan Studies in the College of Urban Affairs. Dr. Lezotte was a member of the original team of Effective Schools researchers who identified the characteristics of successful schools that have come to be known as the Correlates of Effective Schools.

Since that time, Dr. Lezotte has been at the forefront of the Effective Schools movement. He has written widely on the new mission of public education and has identified the components of a learner-centered system, as well as the theories and tools necessary for successful and continuous school improvement.

As a nationally renowned education consultant and speaker, Dr. Lezotte has devoted his career to assisting schools in their efforts to assure that all students learn. He touches the lives of thousands of educators and tens of thousands of students each year through workshops and conferences across the U.S. and Canada. Dr. Lezotte's training programs not only inspire schools and districts to adopt the "learning for all" mission, but give them the information and tools they need to plan and implement continuous school improvement and raise student achievement. In recognition of his efforts, Dr. Lezotte received the 2003 Council of Chief State School Officers' Distinguished Service Award presented each year to outstanding Americans who have made a difference in education.

Kathleen M. McKee

Ms. McKee earned her master's degree in 1980 from Michigan State University in Community and Regional Development within the College of Agriculture and Natural Resources. The primary focus of her work there was in the area of community and organizational change, and the role of leadership in creating stakeholder buy-in and consensus. This was augmented by a minor in marketing, and led to her research into the interrelationship between leadership strategies, marketing techniques, and the success of nonprofit organizations. During her time at Michigan State, she was the coordinator of the Lansing Community Network, a diverse group of citizens who, under the auspices of the College of Urban Affairs, worked together to bring about positive changes in their community. She also consulted with various communities and *(continued)* nonprofit organizations in conducting surveys of their stakeholder groups and assisting them in obtaining buy-in to their various improvement efforts.

In 1987, Ms. McKee became the executive director of an environmental education center in mid-Michigan, where she became well-acquainted with public education. Working closely with local school districts, Ms. McKee facilitated the alignment of the center's K-8 education programs with state learning objectives in core areas, and during her 10 years at the center, instituted several hands-on programs that would augment the curricula of local schools. She also has first-hand experience with education through her experiences as a substitute teacher in elementary and middle schools, and her involvement as a parent of three children. Her varied experiences with public education, combined with her knowledge of the change process and leadership, has allowed Ms. McKee to bring a unique perspective to her work at Effective Schools.

She joined Effective Schools Products in 2000 as editor of the *Effective Schools Research Abstracts*. She has coauthored two other books with Dr. Lezotte: *Assembly Required: A Continuous School Improvement System* and its companion *Implementation Guide*.